GET SMART WITH YOUR HEART

GET
SMART
WITH
YOUR
HEART

The Intelligent Woman's Guide to
Love, Lust, and Lasting Relationships

Suzanne Lopez, M.S., MFCC

G. P. PUTNAM'S SONS · NEW YORK

Grateful acknowledgment is made to the following
for material that appears on pages 139, 145–46, and 152–53.
From *The Alchemy of Love and Lust,* by Theresa L. Crenshaw.
Copyright ©1996 by The Crenshaw Writing Company, Inc.
Used by permission of G. P. Putnam's Sons,
a division of Penguin Putnam Inc.

G. P. Putnam's Sons
Publishers Since 1838
a member of
Penguin Putnam Inc.
375 Hudson Street
New York, NY 10014

Library of Congress Cataloging-in-Publication Data

Lopez, Suzanne, date.
Get smart with your heart : the intelligent woman's guide to love,
lust, and lasting relationships / Suzanne Lopez.
p.   cm.
Includes bibliographical references and index.
ISBN 0-399-14462-5 (alk. paper)
1. Love. 2. Man-woman relationships. 3. Intimacy (Psychology)
I. Title.
BF575.L8L665 1999
306.7—dc21   98-33358 CIP

Printed in the United States of America
1   3   5   7   9   10   8   6   4   2

This book is printed on acid-free paper. ∞

Book design by Tanya Maiboroda

In loving memory of my mother,

Suzanne Eileen, who gave me my heart;

John Wright, my friend and lover, who,

when he died, broke my heart;

and

Angelica Shiavani Lopez,

my daughter, who, when God brought her to me,

healed my heart and gave it back to me

Acknowledgments

Everyone whom the universe puts in our lives contributes his or her unique energy and life force to the sum total of who we are and what we will become. To all those individuals who have crossed my path and left their indelible mark, I give my thanks.

Particular thanks and gratitude go to my dear friend and sister from a different mother, Virginia Moreno, for her loving eyes, ongoing belief in who I might become, and unwavering support of who I am now. To my sister Anita whose love and nurturing has helped carry me through hard times; to my father, Rudy Lopez, his new wife, Isabel, and the rest of my nine siblings, for loving me; to my teachers Dr. John C. Pierrakos and Dr. Siegmar Gerken, who help me tap into my own energy and taught me how to take my own personal impulse out into the world in more creative and loving ways; to Don Risso, Mona Coates, and Ed Jacobs for their generosity and Enneagram expertise; to Natalie Leis and Laura Crossley for helping care for my daughter while I was working on this project; to Ms. Cole Persley for her generous hospitality in creating a safe haven in Florida to write; to David Rudinsky and David Harder; to B. J. Hatley, Meryl David, and John Randolph for their initial support and belief in the project; to John Duff of Perigee Books and Sheila Curry, senior editor, for judicious editing and support; to Eileen Cope, who sent me to Ms. Julie Merberg, the best agent in the whole world. Julie's grace, tenacity, hard work, patience, and support have been invaluable; to my assistants, Ms. Amy Landers, a bright and delicious light, who kept the flame burning by retyping and helping with the initial stages of the project, and Ms. Donna Walker, who has continued to fuel the fire with her patience, fortitude, good humor, vocabulary, and grammar; to my attorney, Mr. Scott Schwimer, who knows what the bottom line is and goes for it with gusto and humor; to Ms. Sherri (Rockin') Rifkin, whose hard work and capacity to work under a deadline with humor and diligence pulled the project out of the drink and saved it from drowning, and whose Gen-X point of view helped add another dimension and perspective.

To all the men in my life who have shown me what love is and guided me to the necessity for a deeper understanding and awareness of clear and conscious relationship choices.

To all my clients, couples, individuals, and students who have shared themselves so deeply and fully, daring to risk being who they are while expanding their capacity to be greater than they ever thought they could be. The list is too long to mention everyone by name, but you know who you are. I lovingly express my heartfelt thanks and gratitude to each of you.

Contents

Part 2 Detours, Dangers, and Disasters

Part 3 Putting the Smart Heart Partnering Process to Work

Preface

A Love Letter to Women

Webster's dictionary defines a woman as an adult female human being. My experience, however, is that we are so much more. In my almost twenty years as a psychotherapist, I have been given the great gift of assisting and coaching hundreds of women. They come in all sizes and shapes, and from every conceivable background. The one thing they all have in common is men: men they love; men they wish they didn't love; men they wish loved them; men they wish didn't love them; men who couldn't love them enough; men who loved them too much; men who were breaking their hearts; men who were breaking their bones; and men who were breaking up their families. Why were such smart, successful, beautiful women having so much trouble with men? Why were they making such poor relationship choices over and over again and consequently suffering so much that they needed to seek my support and assistance?

What I came to discover is that an intense, erotic chemistry short-circuited their capacity to think clearly. They had no frame of reference or formula for accessing simultaneous use of their heads and hearts to systematically and consciously evaluate men to whom they were attracted, thus rendering themselves incapable of clearly determining if they would be good partner choices. How could I help these women? What could be done to prevent the heartbreak yet proactively support healthy, happy, and successful partnering?

It was both out of their need and my concern for this seemingly unwarranted suffering that the Smart Heart Partnering Process was born. Over many years, the Smart Heart Partnering Process has been manifested as I have studied the latest research psychology and technology in order to create an effective, efficient, step-by-step formula that could help all women—no matter what their age or the type of relationship they were seeking—have a comprehensive checklist that could increase their odds of success, happiness, and longevity in relationship and partnering choices.

Although there are no guarantees in life, or in relationships, there is now a way that you can ensure a greater degree of success in your relationship choices as you continue to dare (as we must), to risk loving again and again. The Smart Heart Partnering Process will assist you in this endeavor. It can guide, support, and facilitate an expansion of your awareness and improve your ability to choose men more wisely and appropriately. Whether we like it or not, whether we accept it or not, whether we want to admit it or not, we are the keepers of the relationship flame. We are the bearers of the children and the makers of the home. When we look at current statistics (and I have assisted hundreds of women who comprised these statistics), it is painfully clear that women need help and more effective tools to deal with their relationships. If you use this process and lay the groundwork, the Smart Heart Partnering Process will help you stop making the same mistakes and start again (or for the first time) with a whole new way of thinking before, during, and after you fall in love.

This process is given to you with great love. Please use it. Be responsible and proactive in consciously making the most important decision of your life—to whom you choose to give yourself, your time, and your body, and with whom you choose to have children and share your life. Remember, 90 percent of your happiness in life depends on using your choice wisely. God bless you and good luck!

Introduction

Today, there is a new relationship game being played, and it's time for a new game plan that is formulated through careful design, not by careless default.

During almost two decades of private practice in Los Angeles, the land of fantasies, illusion, and delusion, it became clear to me that the women I was seeing needed specialized help with relationships. One of my first clients was a beautiful CEO of a record company who had broken through the glass ceiling of a male-dominated industry but somehow couldn't create the same success in her personal life. I became committed to developing a program that could assist intelligent, successful women in using their heads in conjunction with their hearts, to demystify romance in order to make wiser choices in relationships. The Smart Heart Partnering Process has been used successfully by hundreds of women in my psychotherapy practice to create fulfilling, long-lasting relationships.

As a result of this success, I wanted to share these tools and techniques with a wider audience than I could personally coach in my private practice. Many women have neither sufficient knowledge nor support to use their power of choice wisely. Living in a fast-paced, confusing world facing problems unknown to their mothers and grandmothers, dealing with outmoded concepts and dysfunctional family images, these women are seeking satisfying relationships but not finding them. The Smart Heart Process for achieving long-lasting love is based on the premise that the goal is not simply to find a man to marry but to find the right man, one who can provide intimate love, companionship, and growth.

Although we are all eager to have romance in our lives, the idea that using inane throwbacks to the past can entrap a man into a relationship is ludicrous. We can't look to an oversimplified past for guidelines that don't reflect our needs today. You could learn archaic rules by heart, play the game skillfully, and still lose. For women of the nineties, facing the millennium, the demands of contemporary life are complex. You might succeed in bringing a man to his knees, but will you still want him when he's crippled with arthritis? You need a strategy that will satisfy your present needs while ensuring your future happiness.

Pursuing romantic love without using our heads creates heart dis-ease, which results in a broken heart and a failed relationship. We create this malady by unconsciously forgetting who we are and what we want.

Get Smart with Your Heart is a systematic approach, much like a cookbook, that gives you the ingredients necessary in specific recipes for creating open, healthy, happy relationships. It provides you with a new outlook on dating and mating. It has already helped hundreds of women, and it can help you too! You will learn why it's important to know what you want before you even step out the door on a date; why it's important to know in which stage of life development a prospective partner is; how to know when it's time (and with whom) to safely be sexually intimate; how personality profiles can help your relationship; how to determine if he's bad news at the outset; what questions need to be asked and what topics addressed to realistically determine if a match is a stairway to heaven or a roller-coaster ride to hell.

The Smart Heart Partnering Process was refined over the course of several years, incorporating the failures and successes of hundreds of women in my private practice: CEOs, Ph.D.s, entrepreneurs, movie producers, business owners, and homemakers whose lives were successful in so many ways but who still operated under the assumption that their love alone was enough to transform the most committed bachelor into an ardent husband, a workaholic into a relaxed, attentive partner, or a substance abuser into a saint. They avoided looking at lifestyle or personal compatibility in assessing their prospects and were swayed instead by the thought of a diamond ring or dancing with Prince Charming.

We need not go far to see where this kind of thinking has brought us. The consequences of poor partnering are evident not only in divorce statistics and broken families but also in the depression, cynicism, and despair that claim each broken heart. Our children have few positive role models from whom to learn good partnering as they are shuttled from one parent to the other, playing video games and watching sitcom after sitcom. Community property divides our assets, and women's incomes plummet. We struggle to keep the household going, along with our careers, and we end up feeling frazzled and frustrated. The breakdown of the family unit correlates with an escalation in violent crime, abuse, and poverty. The solidarity and security of the nuclear family are almost nonexistent in today's world. Our sense of community is tenuous, at best.

Certainly, women have made great strides in discovering power and effectiveness in the marketplace, but we also need to learn to have purposeful, satisfying personal lives. As much as we deeply long for emotional and romantic fulfillment, we need to be willing to get smart with our hearts in order to obtain it. A fatalist may prefer that romantic roller-coaster ride to hell rather than being responsible for creating her own relationships. Nevertheless, if you view responsibility as the ability to respond appropriately, you might not have to endure a battered ego or the broken heart that goes along with a rough ride. If you opt to consider loving someone who is capable of returning your love and approach your relationships with at least as much thoughtfulness as you give to your career, financial portfolio, or even purchasing a car, you can create a more stable and pleasure-filled future.

This journey will entail changes. You may need to leave behind a poor relationship for a seemingly uncertain future; you may need to risk opening a previously closed heart; you may need to dare to love a little more deeply. Having used this process personally after I was divorced, again after I was widowed, and presently while I'm dating, I know that taking the steps toward what's right in a relationship just makes the choices better and better. Integrating your thoughts and feelings to evaluate, design, create, and maintain a long-lasting relationship is the first step toward finding fulfillment in love. *Get Smart with Your Heart* works. It has worked for me and hundreds of other women, and it can work for you. Get going, have fun, and don't quit until you get what you want.

PART 1

Getting from "Me" to "We"

There's Nothing More Romantic Than a Relationship That Works: A Systematic New Process for Designing and Creating a Relationship

hen a smart woman wants to learn about history, the arts, literature, or science, she goes to school or reads books. When a smart woman wants to learn how to conduct business, she finds a mentor and/or goes to business school. When a smart woman wants to buy a car, she visits several dealerships and comparison-shops for the car that best suits her budget needs and preferences. Yet when it comes to learning about relationships, even the smartest of women leave the choice up to chance, romance, and intuition, allowing themselves to be guided by their hearts alone. Is this smart? Statistics and time have shown that the answer is a resounding "NO!"

In addition to her professional career and lifelong spiritual path, intimate relationships are among the most important components of a woman's life, yet most women don't put as much conscious time, energy, effort, and careful planning into creating and forming relationships as they do into other areas of their lives. When it comes to matters of the heart and romance, smart women must learn to use their heads (bolstered by a heightened sense of conscious awareness) in conjunction with their hearts when they are evaluating and choosing romantic partners.

Over the past two decades in my psychotherapy practice, I have counseled hundreds of women who were not finding happiness and satisfaction in their relationships and love lives. I regularly counsel women who are CEOs of major corporations, entrepreneurs and business owners, Ph.D.s, and movie producers. They are very successful in their respective fields. They are attractive, bright, desirable, lovable, and interesting women who consistently make bad relationship choices. In their businesses and careers, they would never dream of basing their decisions on anything other than logic and sound reasoning. The way they handle their love lives, however, is a different story. Over and over again, I have seen these women become involved with louts, losers, and con artists, getting their hearts broken, their bank accounts emptied, and, in some cases, their lives shattered. I decided to investigate why.

What became painfully clear was that the majority of my patients had no clear idea of what they were looking for in a relationship and had very little information or support regarding what good choices for them might be. Although many of them would never rely on fate or the passage of time to make their business problems disappear, they were waiting for a magic "something" to occur in their romantic lives. Why would a thirty-five-year-old woman who was a wealthy, charming, and attractive movie producer choose to be with a writer who never made a dime from his craft, slept all day, wrote all night, and was unwilling to marry her and start a family even though they had been together for seven years? Why would a forty-year-old woman who ran a small company and had a large group of interesting, eclectic friends date a man for five years who hated being social and refused to spend time with her friends? Why would she stay with him when he never spent an entire night at her house and stole away at two or three o'clock in the morning? Why would a beautiful, vibrant woman of twenty-eight who was working her way up in the record business have a parade of men come in and out of her life, each of whom was more than happy to sleep with her on the first or second date, then be repeatedly surprised when they would never call her for a third or fourth date? It was evident that no one had shown these women how to use their heads, as well as their hearts, in making their relationship choices.

I saw so many smart women in my practice who were repeatedly experiencing this type of romantic blackout—who, despite all their education and professional savvy, did not know how to shake off bad relationships. It became clear to me that they needed to become conscious and aware and start making choices based on the reality of their situations. They needed to start finding men who were appropriate for them. To help these women,

4

I developed the Smart Heart Partnering Process to dispel pervasive romantic myths and delusional fears about relationships, to teach women how to look at relationships in a new way, and to demystify the process of partner selection. The Smart Heart Partnering Process gives women practical tools for making systematic, conscious choices that support their lifestyles, their goals and values, and who they are. By using the Smart Heart Partnering Process, you too can become more aware, more successful, and more satisfied with your choice of dates and mates.

Every woman, no matter what her background, financial status, level of education, or profession, needs to become aware of and willing to be responsible for designing her own relationship objectives. Whether you are eighteen or eighty, if you are a woman who is looking for high-quality relationships and conscious pairing and partnership, then this book can help you reach your objectives, whether you have been single your entire life or married for twenty years. Whether you've been in a long-term relationship or you've just graduated from college and are starting to date seriously for the first time, you will benefit and grow from using and understanding this process.

The Smart Heart Partnering Process will allow you to design and define your own unique relationship objectives and help you to answer the following questions about yourself and your prospective partner:

1 What kind of life do I envision for myself, and of what does it consist?

2 Does this man really fit in with what I am looking for in my life?

3 Is this man compatible with my relationship objectives and dreams?

4 Am I compatible with him and his life?

Before you walk out the door to go on a date, you need to understand why you are going and what you hope to get for yourself out of that time. By being conscious about what you want, you won't be swept up into an unconscious fugue of romantic myths and images, only to land in a trap of your own making with someone who is not right for you. The good news is that you can return to this flexible process over and over again as you move in and out of different phases of your life.

Being clear about their relationship objectives and continually using their heads in conjunction with their hearts to evaluate whether or not the men they are involved with support their objectives is something that women today, at every stage of their romantic lives, must make a commitment to do. It may seem easier to let yourself be carried along by the gods of love, trusting in the Fates that long-term happiness awaits you just around the corner. Divorce statistics confirm, however, that relationships aren't working. I have seen evidence of the extent of problematic relationships in the number of unhappy, dissatisfied women who come to me for help. The lack of understanding of the true nature of relationships is evident in the many men who get a bad rap for simply being themselves. It's clear that if you are not a proactive player in your own romantic life, you cannot have a successful and satisfying relationship.

We Can't Look to the Past for a Map of the Future

Women today are in the fortunate position of being able to choose their romantic partners for themselves. This was not the case even as recently as one or two generations ago. Our mothers, grandmothers, and great-grandmothers needed to be married to survive and procreate. Society provided few other options for women, other than to marry and bear children. In order to succeed and survive, women needed men to protect them and provide for them and their children. Women seldom married with the expectation that their husbands would be soul mates who would give them love, friendship, or companionship.

In the past, most marriages were arranged. A prospective husband was chosen based upon his ability to provide money, security, social standing, and healthy offspring. A prospective bride was initially chosen for her looks and her ability to bear children. Intelligence, creativity, and vitality were seldom considered valuable assets in a woman.

Your mother and, depending on your age, your grandmother didn't have to accept such arrangements, however. Rather, they were allowed to choose men for themselves based on their own criteria. Nevertheless, a woman was reliant on her husband's ability to earn a living and support the family, and a man's earning power was high on the list of attributes they and their families were looking for in a husband and provider. Some women might have married for love, but many others wed with low expectations of ever experiencing love and fulfillment in their marriages.

It wasn't until World War II that it became more fashionable to marry "for love." The war and its impending threat of danger filled American culture with romantic ideas. For the first time, women were able to go against traditional social and familial constraints and choose men because they "loved" them. Thousands of young couples fell in love and married quickly before the men were shipped overseas for duty. By the 1950s, women were beginning to question unhappy and unequal marriages because, although they might have chosen their husbands out of love, they still didn't enjoy other types of freedoms. In the fifties, divorce was still considered taboo, abortion was illegal, and women were generally not in charge of their reproductive rights. The sexual revolution of the 1960s was a time for women to freely explore their own sexuality and act on physical attraction, while shirking romance or other ideas they considered constraining.

During the liberating 1970s, millions of women declared their emancipation from outmoded ideas about marriage, partnership, and sexuality. Women attended colleges and universities in record numbers. Moving the issue of equal rights to the forefront of politics, they had more freedom over their bodies and reproductive rights than ever before. On the whole, women could be more independent, not only financially but professionally, psychologically, and emotionally as well. Having seen many of their own mothers suffer in emotionless, unhappy marriages, even if the couples didn't divorce, women became determined to marry on their own terms, if they were going to marry at all. Because millions of women were now attending college and graduate school and thus were able to work in higher-paying jobs than ever before, they no longer needed to look to a husband for financial security. This is still true today. Women don't necessarily need men to purchase homes, eat in elegant restaurants, take extravagant vacations, or buy nice clothes and furniture. Even more liberating are the advances in reproductive technology, not only in relation to birth control but also in the fact that today women don't need husbands in order to bear children.

Because divorce is so prevalent, the social construct of marriage that was originally designed to protect women and children no longer successfully serves that purpose. Most women have adapted to this shift, and many are capable of providing for themselves and their children, as necessary. Over time, especially in American society, marriage and long-term partnership have become universally accepted ways of formalizing love between two people, rather than a function of survival.

Women have found that marrying or partnering solely for romantic love is not the answer. In pursuit of passion and love, women have overlooked rational thought as an important component in mate selection. Many

7

women surmise that men with whom they have great times, great sex, and great dates would be men with whom they could be more committed and intimate over the long term.

Unfortunately, a colossal number of marriages in the last twenty years have ended in divorce, with the rate now hovering around 50 percent; for every two women who get married, one ends up divorced. (In California, the rate is even higher.) Our thought processes, or lack thereof, in the matter of partner selection have shown that during the last forty years something is obviously missing. My psychotherapy practice is filled with heartbroken women who can't figure out how something that began so hopefully could have ended so dismally.

The consequences of poor partner selection go beyond broken hearts. Too many children are being raised by parents who have divorced. It is the exception, rather than the norm, to find a child whose family is still intact. The psychological effects of divorce on children, who often blame themselves for the breakup and may feel that neither parent really wants them, are illustrated abundantly in studies and literature on the topic. My therapy practice mirrors what teachers say they observe at school. More kids are "acting out," becoming violent, or behaving as if they don't care about anything, including themselves. It's no coincidence that cynicism and apathy have risen in tandem with the divorce rate. According to studies, children of divorce have been found to have higher rates of dropping out of school and mental problems. Most children of divorce will also have problems later in life. The angry and stressful environment of a troubled, splintered household has undoubtedly contributed to children being abused.

A higher divorce rate has also created a new class of poor, i.e., divorced, women and their children. Statistics show that a man's income rises dramatically when he leaves his wife and children, whereas a woman's plunges. One report found that an astonishing 38 percent of women with children live in poverty. While many women might have advanced degrees along with solid credentials, if they are alone with small children to raise, most can barely stay afloat financially.

Obviously, these results were not what women intended when they declared an end to pragmatic pairings in favor of partnerships based on romance and love. Many women have found that they can find a man fairly easily, but the difficulty is in finding the **right** man. Women have let themselves be too easily swayed by a man's charisma, sensuality, money, or prestige. Consequently, they lose their heads as they follow their hearts down the aisle or into long-term commitments with disastrous results.

Many women feel that if they have had one relationship failure, they should give up on ever finding another relationship that might work. Over forty years ago, Margaret Mead said that a woman will have had a series of monogamous relationships over the course of her lifetime. The first one would be for sex and experimentation; the second, for creating families; the third, for career and vocational exploration; and the fourth, for spiritual union and intimacy. When we look at statistics, what Mead predicted is happening today. We could even say that today the second and third stages often occur in reverse order, because many women are pursuing careers and working before they marry and have children. The guys we wanted to fool around with in high school are not the kind of men with whom we would want to build a family, and we might not want to share a spiritual union with the men we married and with whom we are raising children. Because women live well into their seventies and eighties now, most can count on having several serially monogamous relationships over the course of their lifetimes.

Having more than one relationship in your life doesn't make you a failure. Some people may be blessed to be with the same person for their whole lives, but this is exceptional. The rest of us will be blessed by experiencing several monogamous relationships over the course of our lifetimes.

Many women still believe that they are somehow flawed if they have been in several different long-term relationships, or have been married and divorced more than once, but the problem is not that they are failures in relationships; it is rather that they are holding themselves up to an outdated model of **one lifetime, one true love.** Instead, women need to appreciate the opportunity they have had to experience different men while continuing to learn more about themselves in their growth process. Just because a relationship is over doesn't mean that you have failed. It may simply mean that you have finished that particular relationship and what it had to teach you. You have learned what you needed to learn; you have grown as much as you could during that particular situation, and now it is time to let go and move on. This is hardly indicative of failure.

Now is the time to demystify relationships and create a balance between romance and reality. Women must learn to integrate their heads and their hearts to learn how to choose a man consciously, not chemically or reactively. I am not saying that love has nothing to do with the process of choosing a long-term partner, mate, or husband. Still, I believe that it is time for women to admit that love isn't the only, or even the most important, part of creating a mutually satisfying, healthy, intimate relationship. Women need to become **smart** with their **hearts** by adding conscious and careful evaluation of the **facts** with their **feelings.**

The Smart Heart Partnering Process

The Smart Heart Partnering Process will help you make careful systematic evaluations before getting into a relationship. If you want to become a Smart Heart woman, you must put your current or future boyfriends, partners, and mates through a series of assessments if you are to do all you can to ensure a lasting and satisfying partnership. The question is not simply "Can he provide for me?" as your grandmothers asked. The question isn't "Am I in love with him?" as your mothers or sisters may have asked. The questions you must ask both yourself and a potential partner are more complicated and diverse, such as:

10

- ▶ Am I seeing this guy clearly as who he really is, or am I letting hope and hormones disguise someone who is really a bad bet?

- ▶ Am I settling for the wrong man out of misplaced feelings or fears?

- ▶ Am I hooked on this guy simply because I have had great sex with him?

- ▶ Do this man and I have compatible personalities?

- ▶ Are we in the same developmental stages in life?

- ▶ Do we share the same goals and values?

- ▶ Do we even enjoy many of the same things?

Even a decade ago, such pragmatic assessments may have seemed unromantic, but we need to wake up to the fact that **nothing is more unromantic than divorce.** Adding your head to your heart when you assess a potential life partner isn't being unromantic; it is just plain being smart.

I started counseling women about relationships in the early 1980s, and I have been struggling with my own issues about relationships since I was an adolescent. I am the oldest of ten children, and my mother never worked outside the home. My father was a dominant, critical, repressive, Hispanic father. How could I learn how to make choices that would serve and support me and my needs coming from this family system? Because other areas of my life were so different from my mother's, it was clear I could not look to her for answers. The scary thing was that there was nowhere else to look. Out of the struggles of my personal life and throughout my many years of professional practice, I was inspired to create a process that supports women in being able to combine romance with intelligence so that they could make wiser choices.

After almost two decades of looking at this issue from a professional, as well as personal, point of view, I created this process not only to support my clients but also to support myself. I found that I was able to use it quite successfully in a personal relationship with a man I met at my twentieth high-school reunion. Our relationship lasted for several years, and we were planning to be married. We had just purchased a house when he unexpectedly died, leaving me alone. Although it took me over a year to recover from that loss, I am actively back on the dating scene today, and I employ the Smart Heart Partnering Process with the men I become involved with.

Whether you like it or not, whether you are a feminist or not, whether you are a die-hard romantic or a complete pragmatist, you must be willing to understand that women are the ones who maintain, nurture, create, and manifest relationships. Men want to be with us, but we are the ones who must be conscious about whom we choose and what we want because we create the relationship and cause it to flourish or flounder.

Women must be willing to journey inward to discover what their own internal terrain looks like, where they want to go, and how they want to get there. As a woman, you need to have the courage to step into a new frontier of your own design. The tools in the Smart Heart Partnering Process will help you determine how and what you can do that is right for you relative to the current circumstances of your life, in accordance with your own personality, style, beliefs, values, and ideas.

Because each woman is unique, her choices will be unique. Using the Smart Heart Partnering Process will help you no matter who you are or what your current situation is. The process worked for Janine, a thirty-seven-year-old client of mine who was a successful producer and director of commercials. Janine lived with a man named Rob who was a successful writer. They lived together for eight years in a house they bought jointly. Although she didn't want to be married when they were first together, eventually she decided that getting married and starting a family were important to her.

Every time she broached the subject with him, Rob would say that he wasn't ready or that marriage wasn't what he wanted. By their eighth year together, she was so resentful of him that she left him.

Shortly after Janine and Rob broke up, he began to date another woman, Melissa. After nine months, Melissa said to Rob, "If you want to be with me, we need to be married. If you aren't willing, then I am not going to see you anymore." After six weeks, he proposed and they got married a few months later.

When Janine heard the news, she was completely flabbergasted. She had been too afraid to give Rob such a clear, honest, respectful ultimatum, a fear that cost her the relationship. If Janine had given Rob the clear-cut choice of marrying her or not being with her, it is likely that he would have chosen her. Unlike Janine, Melissa was confident and valued herself enough to say exactly what she wanted. Whenever Janine spoke to Rob about getting married, she gave him resentful, manipulative, attitude-filled complaints. Rob could only respond by being defensive and withdrawing. What would have been more appropriate for her to say is "This is what I want. The experience that I am looking for is this. This is what I need. If you can't give me those things, that's fine, but there is no point in my being in this with you if we are not on the same path." This is clearly what Melissa did.

With my support, and by using the Smart Heart Partnering Process, Janine started dating a lovely man who had been married before for fourteen years. Tim didn't have any children from his previous marriage. His wife had left him, and he was devastated for a long time. The break-up wasn't something he had wanted. Tim and his ex-wife remained friends, however. She moved to San Francisco for a new job, but she sometimes came back to Los Angeles on business or to see friends, and she often stayed with him at the house they had formerly shared. She still had the keys to the house and the code to the answering machine. The emotional part of the marriage was definitely over, but Tim did not completely close off all relations with his ex-wife or limit her involvement in his life.

Though Janine really liked Tim, she was very uncomfortable that his ex-wife still had total freedom to move in and out of his life without regard for her. In this situation, Janine had the Smart Heart Partnering Process as a resource. She had learned how to be clear and direct about her relationship objectives, so she spoke to Tim about her discomfort and made her request, saying "Having your ex-wife come and go as she pleases was fine before, but now you are seeing me and it makes me really uncomfortable. It doesn't work for me or seem appropriate considering you and I are intimate and need some privacy. I need you to reconsider your boundaries with this woman. I am not telling you that you are not allowed to have her in your life, as a friend, but that level of intimacy isn't appropriate any longer." He responded positively and took steps to set more appropriate boundaries with his ex-spouse. Once Tim did that, he opened up a larger space for Janine in his life and they were able to progress in their relationship. They eventually were married.

Any woman can use the Smart Heart Partnering Process to improve herself and her relationships. I call it the Smart Heart Partnering Process because it is a process that allows you to use both your head and your heart in a systematic approach to evaluate yourself and your relationship partners.

You are going to make mistakes. So what! You won't learn anything or gain very much unless you allow yourself the opportunity to take risks. This is true not only in relationships but also in all aspects of life. Welcome your mistakes. You will learn as much, if not more, from your errors as you will from doing everything "correctly." Your mistakes reveal where you need to grow and what more you need to learn. There is no such thing as failure— just a delay in the end result you are seeking. You may have made errors in judgment. You may have been with an abusive guy. You may have created obstacles for yourself this time around. Next time, you won't. It *is* possible to change the course of your relationships, provided you are *willing* to do the work and to be aware.

Here are some suggestions before you get started. Keep a pad or a notebook with you as you go through each chapter of each stage of the Smart Heart Partnering Process. Whenever an idea, a question, or a statement strikes you, write down your thoughts, reactions, responses, and comments. Writing down these thoughts will assist you in:

▶ Creating and designing your relationship objectives

▶ Assessing the qualities that you are looking for in a man and a long-term, committed relationship

▶ Deconstructing destructive personal feelings and fears

▶ Assessing your personality, as well as that of your current or future partner

▶ Delineating your values, beliefs, lifestyle, needs, and goals

13

Although I guide you throughout the process—making suggestions and providing scenarios, exercises, questions, and advice—feel free to personalize and make it your own. If you flip through it and want to start in the middle because the Personal/Partner Profiler first catches your attention, I encourage you to do that. Start where you are. The only thing I recommend is that wherever you choose to start in the process, make sure you work through all the stages, even if you do them out of order. All the various components are included because they are important parts of the overall process of self-discovery, evolution, and expansion. This is not a quick fix or instantaneous solution to all your relationship problems. I don't believe one exists. I do promise, however, that you will benefit from taking the time and energy to do the work that the Smart Heart Partnering Process suggests.

Know What You Want
Before You Start

Before you even go out the door on a date, you need to figure out what your relationship objective is. If you don't know what you want—and that applies to all areas of life, not just your love life—you will never get it. You'll won't know if you have found the man you want, even if he is sitting next to you.

When it comes to defining relationships, every woman has individual wants, needs, and her own specific criteria for a relationship partner. Today, more than ever before, each woman has to make her own choices about what she is looking for in a partner, mate, and relationship.

In the past, a young woman could view only her mother as a life-model for what she could grow up to be; but priorities, lifestyles, social mores, and ambitions have changed radically during each passing decade. Women in their twenties, thirties, and forties are not usually interested in following the same relationship paths their moms did.

With different lifestyle choices available to women, it is each woman's responsibility to determine what will work for her regarding relationships. Women must learn to look within for answers for their own lives. Past guidelines won't help. This book will help you set your own guidelines so that you can chart a personalized road map based on your own unique preferences and needs. To start getting smart about your intimate relationship choices, you first need to know what you want and why.

· ·

Exercise: What Am I Looking For, and Why?

Which of the following statements most describes how you feel now?

❶ I love/like the adventure and excitement of dating several different men and being exposed to a variety of experiences.

❷ I feel that I have been on my own long enough to accomplish what I wanted to do as a single person and am now more interested in moving on to a long-term relationship/marriage/partnership.

❸ I believe that emotionally, spiritually, and mentally I am ready to get married and perhaps even start a family, if the man I am with wants the same thing.

❹ I date men who seem interesting at first, but I never really get off the ground with any of them. I am tired of putting myself out there and circulating on the dating scene, but I don't want to be alone either.

Whatever your answers are—whether you identify with one description or are drawn to two or more of them—you can get a start on what you're looking for at this particular stage in your life and why. There is no "right" answer—just the answer that best suits you at this moment. Take a deep breath and keep reading with an open mind. When something resonates with you, you'll know it.

· ·

If You Don't Know What You Want . . .

. . . you need to stop dating until you figure it out. If you don't yet know what your relationship objectives are, keep reading and discover what your choices and alternatives are. The worst thing you can do is to allow yourself to drift through life unconsciously without direction.

As you mature and evolve, your relationship objectives will change as well. You might be dating now; however, you might meet someone who's marriage material next month or next year. This man may change your heart, as well as your mind. By using the Smart Heart Partnering Process, you may decide that marriage to him is right for you. I have known women in my practice who thought they wanted to be married but subsequently realized that marriage was what they thought they were *supposed* to want.

One of the keys to this process of self-assessment and discovery is to be flexible and open. Understand and accept that your objectives will change as you move through the different stages of your life, have diverse growth experiences, and experience different men moving in and out of your life. You may be happy and content being single and suddenly meet someone who meets your criteria for a satisfying, successful long-term relationship. You can then decide if you want to leap into this new experience not only because it feels right but also because your conscious relationship requirements are being fulfilled. Although the circumstances of your life are constantly in flux, you will be better prepared to make wise choices concerning your relationships if you have guidance in your decision-making process.

Read over the following questions. If you answer "Yes" to seven out of nine of them, you will find the Smart Heart Partnering Process valuable. It will help you systematically to determine and design your relationship objectives, in addition to increasing your personal sense of worth and value

17

Exercise: Are You Dating Consciously or Unconsciously?

❶ Do you go out on every date when you are asked because you are terrified of being home alone on a weekend night?

❷ Do you go out with men who are inappropriate for you?

❸ Do you continue to date a man even after you have decided he doesn't satisfy many of your needs or share your interests?

❹ Do you feel thrilled and excited if any man asks you out?

❺ Do you go anywhere a man chooses even if you are not interested in that activity? For example, if you like movies and the opera, do you go to rodeos and beer bars just to be out with someone?

❻ Do you come home from dates feeling exhausted and depressed because it was drudgery spending time with a new man?

❼ Do you date just so your mother will stay off your back?

❽ Do you worry that if you don't go out with whoever asks you will never get asked out again?

❾ Do you feel compelled to accept any date because your biological clock is ticking out of control?

This exercise has probably raised even more questions for you. Don't worry. Working with this process entails digging deeper than your automatic responses in order to determine what you truly think, feel, and believe. As you continue on this journey, you'll learn important distinctions between dating and mating for long-term partnership and/or marriage.

Why Are You Dating?

Webster's dictionary defines *date* as "(verb) to make an appointment, especially with a person of the opposite sex, or (noun) a person of the opposite sex with whom an appointment is made to date." Dating is much more than making an appointment. Women should begin thinking of dating as a conscious proactive choice. Stop dating passively. If you value yourself, you need to value your time as well. You are not going to make appointments with any random person who asks you out. Once you determine what you want, the Smart Heart Partnering Process can help you quickly assess, according to your objectives, whether or not the person you are dating is leading you down an undesirable path or if he is worth your time and effort.

Women's dating objectives have changed over the years. Fewer than forty years ago, the reason many women went to college wasn't to prepare themselves for entering the workforce; they went to college for what was jokingly called an "MRS" degree. Most women no longer attend college or university solely for that purpose. When I was growing up, my father believed that a woman should go to college to get a degree so that if anything happened to her husband, she could take care of her children. A college education was a life raft if a husband's ship started to sink. The goal was not for women to learn something stimulating and intellectually challenging in order to satisfy their creative needs or propel them toward a fulfilling life. Today, women attend college for a variety of reasons, and although there aren't many courses on how to find and maintain a relationship, the dating scene on college campuses can be very educational.

As you become a Smart Heart woman, you will begin to use dating as a form of research. There is nothing wrong with dating many men, regardless of your age, with no greater motivation than enjoying their company, discovering their different personality styles, sharing common interests, and receiving sexual pleasure. During this period, you need to pay attention to your own desires and needs, as well as a possible mate's. You will feel more satisfied and confident not only that you have had many enriching and enjoyable experiences but also that you have filled your data bank with information for making a conscious choice for a future long-term partnership, based on what is appropriate for you.

Because dating is a form of investigation, it should not have a negative stigma attached to it. Women date men for a variety of reasons and motivations, perhaps as many reasons and motivations as there are men and women. You can choose to date for pure pleasure just to meet men who might expand your life and support your creativity. Dating for pleasure and fun is one avenue to take, but it is not necessarily a step toward marriage or long-term partnership. Even if you are dating solely for discovery and personal awareness, you still need to do it in a conscious manner, not merely as a weekend pastime. Learn to use dating as a tool to enhance your life and to grow personally, emotionally, and spiritually. As you experience a variety of men with different tastes, interests, backgrounds, and pursuits, you can bring more pleasure, stimulation, and creativity into your life.

As a woman evolves, she goes through many life passages. There are three distinct times in a woman's life when she should be dating either for research or pure pleasure. In high school and college, it is important that a girl learn how to date because she needs to discover men in general and decipher what kind of man she may want to be with. Learning how to date is an essential part of a young woman's development because this is a time when she begins to learn about herself and what might pleasure her— physically, emotionally, intellectually, and spiritually. The more men a woman is willing to experience when she is younger, the more conscious and capable she will become at defining and designing her relationship needs and deciding what kind of man she may be compatible with in the future.

The second time in a woman's life when dating is an important aspect of her evolution is when she is establishing her career. Many high-powered women, as well as men, know that the time needed to develop a long-term, committed relationship is not generally available while they are building their careers. Careers demand tremendous energy and commitment, as do relationships. For most people, building a career and building a relationship might be mutually exclusive. A woman pursuing a career, however, doesn't cease being a woman. She still has a need for companionship, sexual pleasure, and emotional contact. Dating will help meet emotional and personal needs while she is simultaneously devoting the time necessary to establish her career.

The third time a woman will need to date is if she is divorced, widowed, or emerging from a long-term relationship. Generally, women in any of these situations should remain single for a period of time in order to cope with the pain and grief of their loss and understand the lessons of the previous relationships.

If you were married young, perhaps right out of high school or college, and were later divorced or widowed in your early thirties or forties, your life and outlook will have markedly changed over the course of time. The men you dated in high school and college will not be the same type of men you want to be with now. For a woman who has been absent from the dating scene for quite some time, dating at this stage of life becomes a highly significant period of self-discovery and personal development.

No matter what phase of life you are in, you may have your own reasons for wanting to date without long-term objectives. If you have made a commitment to years of graduate study or apprentice work, you may not want to be distracted by the demands of a serious relationship. You may feel that you have to be dedicated to your job and remain flexible about the possibility of having to relocate geographically, and you know that it's unrealistic to build a relationship you will have to leave behind.

Perhaps you have already "made it" and you are happy with the prestige, money, travel opportunities, and autonomy your life affords you. You don't want or need to change your lifestyle for another person. You've already "done it." You've had a long-term relationship or marriage with all the accoutrements and you don't want to do it again. Women who may have given up their own personal or professional ambitions or their personal freedom for a long-term relationship or marriage are less likely to do it the same way a second time. If you are this type of woman, it is a good idea to date for companionship and common interest rather than to seek involvement in another long-term relationship.

Becky is a client of mine in her late forties who recently divorced. She married, raised her family, and put her career in order. Now that she is single again, she prefers to date a variety of men who serve different interests and needs. There is one man with whom she goes to the opera, another with whom she goes on weekend jaunts, and another who cooks her dinner at home, with whom she maintains a sexual relationship. This arrangement works perfectly well for her. She owns her own house, is financially secure, and is not interested in giving up time and energy for a full-time, committed relationship. "I don't think I could ever give up my personal freedom to accommodate another husband," Becky recently admitted to me. "I have been very successful in work in such a short period of time and I love being able to do what I want with my money and time, without having to be accountable to anyone else."

If, like Becky, being on your own fulfills you, there's no reason not to stay on an autonomous path forever, or until your objectives change. You should know that you can create a lifestyle that suits your needs, with or without a relationship. You are no longer trapped in the past stigma of being an "old maid." A woman can be attractive and successful, and live on her own. **It doesn't mean that she is unfulfilled or undesirable simply because a man isn't living in her house or giving her his name.**

You also may not be seeking marriage or a serious, committed relationship if you feel it may distract you from your personal growth. In the seventies, women who left unhappy marriages stated, most commonly, that the reason they left wasn't another man but another woman: themselves. Personal growth is an important life goal, and one that some people feel can best be accomplished on their own. The most extreme examples are those who pursue inner enlightenment at monk cloisters or Hindu ashrams, leaving the distractions of other people and the rest of the world behind. Others choose to focus on self-improvement using the solitude of their homes as personal havens or retreats. There is no question that a husband and children detract from quiet, personal introspection. If you are on a spiritual path in an ashram, for example, you might want to date someone in your group in order to communicate more deeply about spiritual issues.

If you are happy being single, don't make excuses. Don't apologize for finding great pleasure and autonomy in being single, or dating simply for pleasure and companionship. Sampling every chocolate in the box gives you an idea of which ones you most prefer. As long as you don't indiscriminately eat box after box, sampling is a fine objective; just don't overindulge and make yourself sick.

While it is their choice and responsibility to determine and design their relationship objectives, it is still not easy for many women firmly to declare that remaining single and dating are their sole objectives. Many women in their twenties, thirties, and forties who choose to remain single may receive constant pressure from their mothers, who fear that their daughters are going to be "old maids" who will never give them grandchildren.

Whether you are single or in a long-term relationship, if you're comfortable with that status, be willing to stand your ground. If your mother or someone else pressures you to get married, settle down, and have a family, and if moving on to the next level of commitment and intimacy is not what you want, trust that decision. If you rush hastily into a marriage that isn't right for you, your lovingly pushy parents won't be pleased if it ends in divorce. Neither will you.

Perhaps you agree with your mother that you should be married, but you haven't yet found the right man. Perhaps you are fearful that you won't ever find the right man. Don't let your mother's pressure cause you to be filled with anxiety and self-doubt. There is nothing wrong with you simply because you are cautious or discriminating. If this describes your situation, the Smart Heart Partnering Process can help you to be self-assured in designing your personal relationship objectives.

Dating for the pure enjoyment of getting acquainted with diverse men of varying tastes, goals, and interests, or for the pleasure you may find in an uncommitted relationship, is a worthwhile goal. You have consciously chosen what you want; you are acknowledging it, trusting it, and valuing your own decision.

Dating to Mate, Marry, or for Long-term Partnership

In its definition of *mating,* the dictionary makes the distinction between pairing with someone specifically for breeding and procreation and being with someone for companionship and/or copulation **without** the purpose of breeding.

Women must also learn how to make these two distinctions themselves. Dating with the objective of meeting a long-term partner with whom you might want to start a family is different from dating only for companionship, sex, and common interests. Referring to Margaret Mead's outline of the four stages of a woman's life, mating fits into two of the stages: (1) those people in long-term, committed relationships who want companionship and partnership and (2) those who want those things in conjunction with having children and a family. Neither one of these choices is better than the other; they are just different.

A woman who is looking for a long-term committed relationship should approach her dating experience differently than a woman who is just seeking fun and companionship. It is pointless for you to continue dating a man if you realize that: (a) you are not on the same life path in terms of goals and objectives, and (b) you do not share the same lifestyle, values, interests, and beliefs that contribute to the success of serious, committed long-term relationships.

Mating doesn't just mean getting married. Mating can also mean living with someone in a monogamous, long-term relationship. A mate, partner, or husband is a serious life choice affecting not only you but also your children, if you have them or are planning to have them. If you want to become a Smart Heart woman, you must utilize the entire Smart Heart Partnering Process in order to consciously choose a mate or longtime companion wisely.

Who dates to mate? The answer is: any woman who is ready to share her life with a partner, create a family, or make a long-term commitment to the same person to live in day-to-day intimacy. What does this kind of relationship entail? Usually, mating and/or partnering means sharing your life with someone to whom you are monogamously committed sexually, spiritually, and emotionally. It also means combining your energies, finances, goals, values, future projects, and lifestyles.

Many women are ready to mate or find a regular partner after they have dated for some time. Some women may make the decision to mate in response to their biological clocks telling them that they are physically ready to be monogamous and have children. Other women decide to look for a mate or partner after they have been on their own for a few years (or many years) and want the companionship that a long-term committed relationship offers.

Long-term partnership has many positive attributes. One of the most positive aspects of a long-term, committed relationship is found in the concept of continuum. Continuum—i.e., the span of time you spend with one person—automatically creates a certain kind of intimacy. The longer you are with one man in a conscious and committed way, the closer you become to him. For example, if you go on a ski trip with a group of friends and have a wonderful time, after the trip, the only time you can relive the happy moments is when you see or talk to those friends who went with you. That could be several weeks later or never. When you go away on a trip with a long-term partner, however, you will enjoy recalling that experience over and over again because you not only have shared that time together but you also continue to share many experiences. Your long-term partner, by virtue of being in a conscious relationship continuum with you, becomes a reflection of your own journey. You can look across the dinner table to see the person you've shared time with and whom you've seen grow. He has also witnessed your growth, and together you become mirrors for each other. The relationship continuum cannot be created if you are seeing several different people simultaneously, however. It emerges from the commitment of being with a single individual—good, bad, or indifferent—and sharing time over the long run.

Exercise: Are You Dating to Mate?

Stop, think, and consider the following. If these statements ring true for you, you may be ready to move to the next level of commitment:

1. I feel satisfied and fulfilled in my career and would now like to take the next step and think about someone else, too.

2. I'm ready to "nest" with someone I love.

3. I know whom I want to be with for the foreseeable future and would like to be in an exclusive, committed relationship with him.

4. I am ready to be with a man with whom I can build and share a home.

5. I have evolved and expanded my life on my own and feel ready to combine my energy and resources with a man and build a life together.

6. I've really enjoyed spending time with my friends and not being accountable to anyone other than myself, but now I'm ready to be intimately involved with a man, to be vulnerable and open, to share my innermost thoughts and private self.

7. I want to have a child but would very much like to share that experience with a man who is as excited about kids as I am.

Perhaps reading these statements and the different descriptions of mating has helped you decide that you are interested in beginning the search for a long-term committed relationship and/or partner to experience the sweetness of a relationship continuum with deep, committed intimacy. If that is the case, let me offer a word of caution: Don't make this decision due to any internal pressure from the loud ticking of the biological clock or external pressure from mothers, families, well-meaning friends, or society. For women who feel any of these pressures, the desire to mate or become attached can feel so intense that they desperately pursue a prospective partner on the first date. One reason for becoming a Smart Heart woman is learning that holding out for the right man is more important than settling for just any man. In several of the next chapters, I debunk and demystify many fears, feelings, societal messages, and myths that may be distorting your ability to choose and design your relationship objective consciously.

If you still are not sure if what you want is authentically your own desire or if the decision is influenced by external pressures that are clouding your choice, take a deep breath and keep reading. The process of determining what you want, like the building of relationships, takes time and is best done in a relaxed yet conscious way.

Marriage Is Not a Dirty Word

Today, young but mature women may feel that they are ready for the commitment of marriage and family, but they often find that they are under another kind of pressure from family, friends, and a society that tells them that they shouldn't even think about marriage until they are older. In the past, marriage was something that all women were under pressure to pursue at a very early age. One young twenty-something even wrote an editorial in *Newsweek* defending her decision to marry. Discouraged by friends and family, she felt as if she were trying to push a rock uphill.

If you are a woman who wants to marry, don't let anyone convince you that *marriage* is a dirty word. Women who consider themselves liberated feminists might have the sneaking feeling that marriage is an institution created by men, for the benefit of men at the expense of women. *The Feminine Mystique,* by Betty Friedan, and other women's liberation philosophies may have helped women understand their isolation and unhappiness, but they didn't help the reputation of marriage. The truth is that isolation and unhappiness were not a result of the institution of marriage. Rather, they were due to the way women were marrying unconsciously and often out of desperation or due to external pressure. Even college textbooks continue to cast marriage in a negative light. One sociologist doing a study of twenty college textbooks on family life was shocked to discover that marriage was presented negatively in nearly all of them. He concluded that if women read

25

these books, they could come away with the belief that marriage is physically and psychologically debilitating for them.

If you believe that getting married is the right thing for you, pursue that objective clearly and consciously. Marriage hasn't lasted as a social institution for centuries without having provided great benefits for both sexes. You can be comforted by the fact that a large and growing body of research is finding that married women, on average, are happier, more sexually satisfied, healthier physically and emotionally, and living longer than their single counterparts.

If you are becoming a Smart Heart woman and have decided that marriage is what you want, you must not only be able to know and accept that personal truth; **you must also date men with that objective firmly in mind.**

No matter what you are looking for, don't let a man's desires or other people's agendas stand in the way of your reaching your own relationship objectives.

Are You Waiting? Don't!

Not being proactive in turning your fantasies and dreams into reality is as destructive as being unclear about what your relationship objectives are. First, you must *take an active role in deciding what you want; then, you have to go out and get it.* If you are a woman who is waiting for your white knight to come and rescue you or for "someone to watch over you," or if you believe that "someday your prince will come," stop the magical thinking. (Magical thinking is the belief that without doing anything or being responsible for making something happen, somehow your life will change.) Stop waiting. You can't sit at home watching television or reading romance novels and think that, somehow, some man will reach you and sweep you off your feet and into his life.

Why do some women wait for a relationship to find them and do nothing to make it happen?

▶ Fear

▶ Magical thinking

▶ Past pain and hurt (You don't want to take another risk or can't get over old pain.)

- Feelings of low self-esteem and inadequacy
- Not knowing how to approach men and dating

I have found that fear and magical thinking are the two most dangerous deterrents to designing your life and cause major paralysis. This paralysis causes grave side effects. Women who are frozen and waiting for their lives to start when HE comes have fallen into a cycle in which they feel helpless and hopeless. This belief makes it difficult for them to become proactive and take risks in their love lives. For instance, many women who are waiting think that they don't have to maintain their health, keep in good physical shape, or dress nicely, because they believe that magically the right man will see through their forty pounds of extra weight, their disheveled clothes, and their slovenly apartment to discover the great woman that they are inside. If you are caught in this trap, I want to help you get out.

Whatever your fear or reluctance is about meeting men, you must move forward if you want to meet someone with whom you can share common interests or a more lasting, committed relationship. Sitting at home and waiting will only get you more nights of sitting at home and waiting. Coming to terms with this fact can be difficult, especially if you dated for a while, didn't meet anyone you were interested in, and subsequently stopped going out on dates. It is easy to get sucked into believing that you never will meet someone great, or that if you're of a certain age, you have better odds of being killed by a terrorist (a misinterpreted survey that was never meant to reflect any one woman's particular odds of marriage). Don't let yourself fall victim to negative thinking. You must get back into the dating game, swing into action, and take risks to open yourself up—not only to men but also to the world.

Decide, Design, Declare, Act, and Risk: The Smart Heart Woman's Fail-proof Formula

Whether you want to date for pleasure and companionship, as a way of looking for a long-term, committed relationship, or with the objective of getting married and/or having a family, you need to follow these steps to create your conscious relationship objective:

❶ Decide what you want (whatever is right for you—there is no right or wrong).

27

2 Design your plan, keeping your objective in mind at all times.

3 Declare your plan to your friends, family, and, most important, the people whom you are dating, as well as to yourself, perhaps by writing it down.

4 Take action. **Action, action, action.** Move your feet! Move out the door. Do everything you can to meet new people.

5 Take risks, over and over again, each time being *open* to the outcome, *not attached to it.*

Only you can be the creator and designer of your life and your relationships. Utilizing the Smart Heart Partnering Process, you will be able to look at yourself and your conscious and unconscious motivations, as well as your prospective partner's, to determine if you are moving toward the kind of relationship you want. Obviously, you can't create something if you don't know what it is, but it's important to realize that the power and energy that exist within us and the universe are available to help you and can be garnered for your personal use, even when it comes to creating a specific relationship. When you firmly hold a conscious intention in your mind and heart, you will be able to draw a companion into your life with common interests or, if your commitment is to find a mate, draw that person in, as well. Taking action, i.e., diligently going through the exercises in this book, being specific about how you feel, what you think, and what you want (both internally and externally), draws more energy from the universe and helps this intention manifest itself as reality.

By using the Smart Heart Process, you will be able to focus the creative energy of your own consciousness in a specific direction designed and determined by you to support the life, relationships, love, and partnerships that you are seeking. This process allows you systematically to look within to determine where you are going, what you want and need, and who might fulfill your needs as a loving, desirable companion on your journey through life.

If you are making a concerted effort to meet men, you must be open to the outcome but not attached to it. The universe often has ways of surprising you and bringing men to you in an unexpected manner. For example, if you pay a lot of money to go to a singles' resort, you just might meet someone at your gym where you are putting in extra time exercising so you can look great in your bathing suit when you are on your vacation. When you are open to all possibilities, not only do numerous opportunities become available to you; you will also be able to recognize them more quickly and be less afraid to act on them.

Marci, thirty-one, was a single, extremely successful, bright, and funny woman who was a client of mine. After spending her twenties getting her new media business off the ground, she decided to change her relationship objective. She no longer wanted to date simply for the pleasure of being with a man on dinner dates and hiking day trips. She felt ready to meet someone with whom she could build a long-term relationship and share her life more intimately. To meet someone, she paid $500 to join a dating service. By taking this action, Marci opened herself up to the possibility of meeting someone by laying out money as well as declaring her intention to create a new reality.

Women can actually cause their energy fields to shift in such a way that they become much more open and available in *every* area of their lives, which is what happened to Marci. Instead of meeting someone special through the dating service, Marci became aware of a great guy in her office building elevator. He had been on that elevator almost every morning for the last two years. Of course, he had noticed her, but he never got the sense that she was interested in meeting him. Because she was concentrating on her business, she wasn't open to letting a man into her life. She never made eye contact with him or smiled at him, and so she never met him. One day, she noticed him. They met for lunch, which led to many dinner dates, which led to hiking in the hills on the weekends and long Sunday brunches reading the newspaper together. Eventually, they committed to each other to share a long-term relationship and last year were married. Marci is currently pregnant with their first child.

There is something that actually happens in the physical world when you

1 Clarify your internal intention

2 Declare it—speak it out loud to somebody else

3 Take a proactive action to manifest your intention

This process shifts your energy field, and this shift creates an opportunity for new things and/or people to enter into your life.

Although you may think that you know what will make you happy, if you have never taken the time to evaluate your want, need, and desire in a systematic and conscious way, you might not be aware that many of your ideas are based on false assumptions, reactionary responses, or other people's ideas for you. Working through the Smart Heart Partnering Process will allow you to become more knowledgeable about yourself. This opportunity to consciously investigate who you are will help you uncover, and perhaps rediscover, aspects of the truth about yourself, help you make distinctions among what your mother may want, what your father, sister, or friends want, to come to a clear, conscious determination of what is actually right for you.

After you have read this chapter and taken some significant time to think about what your relationship objective may be, you may think you now know what you want and what will make you happy. As you continue using the Smart Heart Partnering Process, however, you may discover that many of your existing beliefs, images, and ideas about relationships are generated by fear, low self-esteem, or past pain, or that they come from *other* people or outmoded ideas and images. The willingness to be open and to uncover the source of these deterrents to finding healthy, fulfilling, and satisfying relationships will create an opportunity for you to generate and manifest new ideas and beliefs that are really more in alignment with what you want and who you are today.

How to Identify Negative Feelings and Fears That Will Keep You from Getting It Right

A ll human beings have difficulty making distinctions among their *feelings, fears,* and the *facts.* Thus we tend to make unwise choices, not only in our relationships but in life as well. Because women and men often allow feelings and/or fears to cloud reality, they are inhibited from deciding and acting in their own best interests, particularly when pursuing relationship objectives. If you intend to become a Smart Heart woman, you must first learn to identify clearly what the facts are, to look at them in an objective manner, and to choose wisely in spite of negative feelings or irrational fears.

For example, Beth was a young woman who at age twenty-eight had a great fear that she was undesirable and unattractive to men. She was tall, didn't like to wear makeup, let her hair hang naturally around her shoulders, and preferred wearing jeans and T-shirts rather than dresses or skirts. Her fear was exacerbated by her family. According to her mother and aunts—who maintained their old school beliefs that, in order to be feminine and attractive, women needed to wear dresses, high heels, makeup, and have their hair styled in a particular fashion—no man would ever be attracted to Beth.

For many years, Beth thought that all that stuff about being feminine was ridiculous. She lived her life the way she wanted to and created a successful career for herself. By twenty-eight, however, she was still single and wondering if her mother and aunts were right after all. Maybe she wasn't attractive enough. Maybe she would never get married but would be alone for the rest of her life. The facts of Beth's situation were that she was dating four men who were all interested in her in varying degrees, but because of her busy schedule, which was filled with work and friends, she was unable to give any of these men the time and attention needed to create a committed, long-term relationship. Wherever she went, she was frequently asked out because, invariably, she was participating in interesting activities, such as snowboarding on the weekends or boxing class at the gym. Clearly, the facts of her life disproved her fears.

. . . .

Exercise: Personal Reality Check

A way to start determining whether or not your reality is distorted by fears and feelings is to create three columns listing whatever is applicable under the headings "Fears," "Feelings," and "Facts." Beth's three columns might look like this:

FEARS	FEELINGS	FACTS
I'm not feminine enough.	I'm too thin.	I'm dating four guys; two of them want to get serious.
I'll never be chosen by a great guy.	I'm unattractive/ masculine.	I have an easy time meeting men who like the same things I do.
My mother and my aunts are right; I am unattractive.	I'm out of it.	I am comfortable with myself; I like the way I dress and who I am.
I'll be an old maid forever.	I'm not feminine.	Complimented often and people like me.

The following are common fears and feelings that cause women to make unwise choices and derail their relationships. You might identify with some or several of these as you read through them. You might have variations that are completely your own. Whatever they are, write them down in columns like the ones above and spend some time figuring out what the **facts** really are. By doing so, you will be able to make decisions based on facts and eliminate needless anxieties and fears to feel more confident in your capacity to distinguish a reality that reflects the facts.

Fears

Fear

My biological clock is ticking so loudly I can't hear anything else, and I fear that if I don't grab someone now, I will never have the opportunity to have children.

Fact

As we approach the year 2000, the options for creating families have expanded in ways that were not available to our mothers. It is now true that having children and a spouse are no longer inextricably entwined. Today you can choose to have one without compromising the other. You can have a child on your own, whenever you are ready, by adopting, or you can use medical technology to help you conceive at a later age, rather than sleeping with someone in order to get pregnant or entering into a long-term relationship with someone who may not be a good father for your children and/or may not be a good partner for you.

Most women stay fertile into their forties, even fifties. If you are that age or younger, the odds might still be good that you will meet someone with whom you can get involved in a deep, committed relationship while you can still physically have a child together. By using the Smart Heart Partnering Process and not wasting time with men who aren't right for you or who don't want the same things you do, you will increase your prospects of meeting the ones who are and do.

Also, there are many possibilities for becoming a parent, in addition to giving birth. Take my situation, for example. I began going into early menopause when I was thirty-seven years old. I was involved in a long-term relationship, and we were planning to have children together. Unexpectedly, my partner died before we got the chance to act on that wish. While I was grieving over his death, my window of opportunity to conceive and bear a child closed, yet I still wanted to be a parent to a child. Later, even though I wasn't with anyone in a long-term relationship, I pursued adoption so that I could have a child and the experience of being a mother. The fear of not having your own child or of not being with someone with whom you want to have children needn't prevent you from experiencing motherhood.

Of course, having a child on your own is not easy, and the decision to do so should be made with great care. Remember that having a child even with a partner is not easy, and having a child with a partner you later divorce isn't an optimal situation either. If you have the resources and support, you'll be a wonderful mother to your child and can bring enough other men into his or her life—friends, brothers, cousins—so your child won't be lacking male companionship. Having a child never excludes the possibility of having the right man in your life who can be a good father and join your family down the line.

There are many women who find deep fulfillment, not necessarily from having their own children, but by stepping into a relationship with a man who has children from a previous relationship and becoming a parent in a blended family.

Fear

Maybe my mother and/or my partner is right. If I don't marry this guy, I won't ever find another man who will marry me.

Fact

This is your life, and only you should decide whom and when you want to marry.

One of the reasons that women choose to marry the wrong men is that they capitulate when it comes to what they want for themselves, giving in to the seduction and desire of their companions. If a man is insistent about getting married, then the woman figures he must know something she doesn't about the rightness of such a union. She trusts the man's judgment over her own.

Another variation on this theme is pressure from a woman's mother, grandmother, and other relatives. Maybe all her mother's friends' children have gotten married and she wants to be the mother of the bride. Furthermore, Mom wants grandchildren, as a growing number of her friends already do, or maybe she thinks you risk becoming an old maid.

Taking a stand for yourself and what you want is difficult. Giving in and being with the wrong person, though, is actually more difficult. When her mother was diagnosed with inoperable brain cancer, my client Jacqueline faced incredible pressure from her entire family to get married to her boyfriend. "It would make her so happy to see her youngest daughter taken care of," Jacqueline's father urged. "Waiting for a wedding would give her something to live for," her aunt advised. Jacqueline was certainly tempted to go ring shopping, but her uncertainty about whether or not Henry was the right guy held her back. After her mother passed on and some clarity returned to Jacqueline's life, she knew for sure that, for all his sweetness, Henry wasn't the guy for her. She was grateful she hadn't married him because she would have done it strictly for her dead mother, who wouldn't have been around to live with the consequences. Marrying someone to satisfy a dying person's wish is clearly not a good idea, especially if you plan to live for a long, long time. If you don't think that either the man or the time is right, then honor your opinion and don't commit until you are sure.

Fear

Dating is drudgery. It will never get better and I will never meet the right guy, so I might as well settle for the guy I am currently with.

Fact

In order to become a Smart Heart woman, you need to approach dating with a sense of fun and challenge. When you are tired of dating, or if it stops being fun, either stop dating or try a new tack, rather than jumping into the wrong relationship.

If it feels as if dating has become harder work than your day job, or you are constantly trying to figure out what to say to someone with whom you have not yet discovered common ground, or you find yourself listening to stories that bore you or going to restaurants you don't like or baseball games you've always hated simply to be agreeable, then you need a new game plan.

If dating has become unpleasant, recognize that you're burned out and take a well-deserved sabbatical. Don't check your brain at the door and grab a husband in the misguided notion that he'll save you from an endless string of boring dates or boorish men. Remember that choosing Mr. Right Now rather than Mr. Right will only lead to a failed long-term relationship or marriage, ultimately putting you back in the dating scene anyway.

Instead of dating halfheartedly, declare a moratorium for a certain period of time—one month, three months, or even longer. Decide that no

35

matter whom you meet, you're going to take a dating sabbatical and will not go out on any dates until after the time that you've agreed upon for yourself has passed. Keep renewing the contract until your dread of dating has diminished. Even if you meet a guy who seems perfect, allow yourself the faith and freedom to take care of yourself, realizing that if he is the perfect guy, he will still be around in two or three months. Devote this time to yourself. Spend the time, energy, or money you would have spent on preparing for your dates by doing something that will enhance your life—for example, buying new clothes and makeup and getting your hair done. Take a yoga class, volunteer at the local shelter, or spend more time with your best girlfriends. After you start to date again, you can continue your new activities so that your life retains more balance, allowing you to fulfill your needs with pleasurable and rewarding activities and leaving you open to new possibilities and to men who can discover who you are as you are discovering who they are in the process of dating.

You'll know you are ready to get back into the dating scene when you are able to experience meeting someone as a refreshing, exciting challenge and a change from your routine. Allow yourself to remember what dates were like the first few times you went out. Think back to high school or college, when a Saturday-night date brought on the jitters and anxious anticipation. When you first started going out with men, dates were exciting. They can be again, as long as you're willing to change your mind and attitudes. As you become a Smart Heart woman, you will learn to think about a new date as an artist thinks about a blank canvas, not knowing yet what work of art will emerge but awaiting the discovery. Your date paints a portrait of who he is, and you perceive and appreciate that expression. Dating is a natural process. As the picture fills in, over the course of several evenings together, you may realize that he's a Rembrandt, whereas you prefer a Renoir. That still doesn't take away from the fascination and fun of watching an artist in action, as you discover the man sitting across the table from you and allow him to discover you.

Fear

I fear my children will never have a father, so I'll have to settle for someone I would not normally choose for the well-being of my children.

Fact

Your children deserve not only to have a good man around but also to have you be happy, because that affects them.

Compromising your goal of finding a life mate in order to find a father for your children is seductive. You talk yourself into believing that you are doing it for your children's best interests. *You* need to be at the top of the list, however, because your children will grow up and move away and you will be left with that partner choice.

If you do choose a partner for your children and not for yourself, you could possibly grow to resent your kids for causing you to miss out on one of life's greatest joys: an intimate pairing with a man who touches your heart and soul. You can deny yourself a new coat or a better house or job because of your child, but you should not give up something as important as a soul mate. Ultimately, the man who will treat your child the best is the one who, because your union with him is so strong, begins to see the child as his own.

Fear

I am afraid to be alone.

Fact

We all were born alone, and we all die alone. Smart women know that there is a difference between being alone and being lonely. Loneliness is a result of not being capable of enjoying yourself and your time by yourself. Smart Heart women learn to enjoy their time alone and pleasurably spend it on themselves.

There are many proactive things women can do to overcome loneliness and enjoy being alone. To use a man to avoid loneliness disrespects the man and dishonors you because you are making a choice out of fear and desperation, rather than out of conscious choosing. You need to learn how to be alone, to seek out and enjoy solitary time. Not only nuns and monks seek solitude. Many ordinary people go on wilderness adventures or spiritual retreats, not purposely to set themselves apart from society but to delve more deeply into their own internal beings. Learn from what they know: it's only when you're not distracted by others that you have the opportunity truly to be at one with yourself.

For instance, you can make your home an inviting, comfortable retreat for yourself by making it smell, look, and feel nice. Stock your kitchen with healthful, good-tasting food, such as farm-fresh fruits and vegetables, soups, and salads. Buy fresh flowers for your kitchen table whenever you shop for groceries. Decorate your home in a way that makes you want to be there. Don't wait until you're married to get that homey rug for the floor or the altar candles you've always dreamed of. Read books on Feng Shui, or get help from a practitioner, to arrange your things in a way that gives off positive energy. Consider splurging on a massaging showerhead, spalike minerals, or other special bath products.

If you're not currently in a relationship, use the time at home alone not only to unwind and relax but also to really get to know yourself. What do you like to spend your time doing, thinking, and feeling? If you really want company, consider getting a pet, move closer to friends, or take in a roommate. These options can provide the companionship you are looking for without the risk of the heartache you'd have by choosing the wrong partner. You might also want to consider joining a twelve-step program, such as Co-Dependents Anonymous, which can help you learn more about how to have a healthy relationship with yourself.

If you find yourself falling victim to the belief that you'd rather be with a bad bet or a loser than nobody, remind yourself that you are not a nobody. In order to become a Smart Heart woman, you need to believe and know that you are a wonderful somebody. Even when you are alone, you are energetically connected to the family of humanity and the greater vitality of life. That's much more empowering than being with a man whose negative energy keeps your positive power from finding its expression. Think how much more honored the man you ultimately choose to be with is going to feel knowing that you have selected him because of who he is, not simply because his presence keeps you from feeling lonely and anxious.

Fear

If I tell him how I feel and am honest about what I want, he will leave me.

Fact

If you can't tell the truth to your intimate partner, then he is not the right person for you. It is better if he leaves. The willingness to be who you are and tell the truth saves you time—months, possibly years—and allows you the chance to find the man who will truly love you for yourself: a man who wants the same things from the relationship as you do.

The truth, in this case, is something different than confessing to your mom that you took a cookie when she wasn't looking. The truth is an accurate reflection of what you want and where you may be at a certain point in your life. When you are in your early twenties, you may be content to

38

meet new men and share common interests. In your late twenties and early thirties, you may decide that you would like something more long-term so you can share many experiences with one person. Later still, you may want to be with someone with whom you can start a family and share resources. You will have different needs at different times in your life.

No man can read your mind to find out where you are developmentally and what you want out of a relationship unless you tell him. You need to be clear about your relationship objectives and state them. It's as important a part of who you are as your interests, like skiing or cooking. Why would you want to hide any aspect of yourself?

For example, Sandy is a twenty-nine-year-old woman who has felt ready to be married and start a family for the past four years. She always believed it was unseemly to tell her dates that she was looking for a relationship that held long-term commitment, yet she couldn't understand why she kept getting into relationships with men who wanted only a good time. Despairing, she began to believe that she would never become involved in a relationship with a man who would love her and want to settle down.

After much coaching from me, she was finally able to be honest with the men she dated. "It was hard at first," Sandy admitted, "but ultimately it became very liberating, because I was telling the men what I really felt in my heart." While some of those "good time" guys did go walking after Sandy came clean, the right guys for her—i.e., those who were also looking for a marriage partner—were actually thrilled to hear her speak her mind. The person who was most happy to hear how Sandy felt was Billy. He also wanted to get married. He had created a successful stockbrokerage and was interested in having her come into his life and share it with him. They are now married and have two young children.

Fear

I fear that the guy I'm with is probably as good as I can get.

Fact

All women bring many wonderful qualities to their relationships. Just because the man a woman is with does not fully love, value, and appreciate her for all that she is does not mean that someone else won't.

"Sure, I'd love to marry a man who's smarter, richer, and even taller," says twenty-eight-year-old Krista. "But I'm no brain surgeon or beauty myself, so Nat is probably the best guy I can get." Not many women are as honest as Krista, but too many women are equally lacking in self-esteem. Many women erroneously think that they are not great catches, that they're not pretty enough, smart enough, or sexy enough. When men like them enough to want to marry them, these women are thrilled that anyone likes them, so they agree.

No one is perfect. You may not look like a supermodel, but then again, neither does she. Magazines set up perfect lighting to make their models look unrealistically striking. They reject hundreds of average shots and choose the one standout. They often alter the picture to make thighs appear thinner and eliminate eye wrinkles. If you care about your appearance enough not to look slovenly or sluggish, you'll be sure to attract plenty of men. Although physical appearance is important to men, energy level, personality, and a woman's sense of herself equally affect her looks.

Don't sell yourself short. If you aren't convinced that you have much to offer, sit down and make yourself a list. Write down your positive personality traits, including the great things you've done for the men in your previous relationships, as well as the reasons a man should be happy to have you. If you are honest and really take your time to do this, your list could comprise several pages.

Sometimes, women fall into the trap of thinking they can't do better if the man they consider marrying has breathtaking looks, a powerful job, or lots of money. Smart women know that, although such attributes may be seductive, they are not the only qualities they must consider when judging a life mate. If you follow the Smart Heart Partnering Process, you will learn that it is much more fulfilling to spend your life with someone with whom you share love, honor, admiration, respect, and attraction—no matter what kind of car he drives.

Fear

On a first or second date, if I tell a man that I'm looking for a husband or a long-term relationship, he might think I'm saying that he is the one.

Fact

He may or may not be, but if you don't tell him, you will never know if he's on the same page as you. You could both be wasting a lot of time and energy because you are on different pages.

You can avoid making your date feel that you have him pegged as your future husband simply by the way you state your objective. By not putting him in a position where he feels that he is interviewing for the role of your spouse, you can get your point across, learn what he wants for his own life, and still have a great date in the process. You can do this by using "I" language—i.e., starting your sentences with "I"; for example, "I would eventually like to be married, have a lifelong partnership with someone, and have a family . . ." or whatever your personal objectives may be. It is important to state your own desires, hopes, and dreams. Then, **wait and listen** so that he can tell you what his may be. More often than not, he'll volunteer the information on his own, without your asking. If he doesn't, ask him! Remember to listen to what he says, rather than for what you want to hear.

Feelings

Feeling

It is not womanly to have clear relationship objectives.

Fact

You need to know where you are going and what you want, so you can get there. If you can't articulate that to your partner, how do you know he wants to go there with you?

41

To become a Smart Heart woman, you must carefully design your relationship objectives, not just let one happen randomly or by default. This is another reason why knowing what you want and being able to communicate that to potential partners is so important to this process. Being proactive in your romantic life is as important as being proactive in all your other affairs. There is nothing unwomanly about being a responsible adult who creates the reality that she wants to live.

Feeling

I feel I'm so lucky to have this guy. I'll just hope and wait and see what happens.

Fact

Guys are lucky to have you. Hoping and waiting will never produce your relationship objective.

Many women think they are the only ones longing for that "special" connection with the opposite sex. Contrary to how you might feel, many men are just as eager to be in relationships as you are. It depends on what developmental stage a man is in; he may not be interested in forming long-term relationships in his twenties but would be very gung ho about doing so in his thirties. Being clear about whether or not this man meets your criteria will allow you to determine if it is wise to proceed with him.

Mary is a twenty-eight-year-old who has been dating Steven for the past three years. In many ways, Steven seems to really like Mary. He sends her flowers, leaves sweet messages on her answering machine, and calls every day at her office to say hello. Mary would like to get married in the near future, but she is not entirely sure Steven is the man. For now, she likes the attention Steven gives her. This would be fine if: (1) Mary were sure she loved Steven; (2) if she were only dating for the fun of sharing common interests (she is not); and (3) if Steven wanted to be in a committed, monogamous relationship with Mary (he doesn't, despite how he feels for her).

"I'm worried," Mary admitted to me in psychotherapy one day, "that if I break up with Steven, there will be no one better to take his place. It breaks my heart to hear about him dating other women, but he is so nice to me in other ways."

If Mary wants to become a Smart Heart woman, she needs to trust that there are plenty of great guys out there who will send her flowers, leave her nice messages, and call her every day if she takes the proactive risk to find them. Staying home when Steven is out on various dates is unacceptable to Mary and is getting her nowhere fast. Continuing to date Steven without taking some action to meet other men is not something a Smart Heart woman would do. The only way to make her relationship move forward with Steven is to request that the two of them begin a monogamous relationship so they can decide whether or not they should take the next step. Mary needs either to start seeing other guys, to give Steven the ultimatum that he needs to commit to her, or to release him lovingly and move on. If he does commit to her and they spend more time together, she needs to decide if she wants to take the next step by getting married or if she should just let him go. Doing nothing will get you nothing, and accepting the unacceptable is unacceptable.

Feeling

I should be married by the time I'm [fill in the blank age]. I feel that if I'm not, then there is something wrong with me and I will never get married.

Fact

There is no age that is "right" for getting married or being in a long-term partnership. The "right" age is whatever age you are when you and the man who is right for you decide that you want to be with each other. There are some timetables over which you have no control.

It is important to know that getting married or finding a long-term relationship is based on a conscious desire and decision, not the fear that if you don't get married by X age, life is going to pass you by and you will never have that "special" connection or relationship with someone.

Many women enter therapy declaring themselves ready to find a husband. This would be great if this meant that they were open to the possibility of marriage and were working consciously toward that objective. Unfortunately, that's not what they are doing. It means that they are closing in on age twenty-five, thirty, thirty-five, forty, or whatever age they have in their minds, as the right age to hook up with a lifelong partner, and they want to be married *now*.

The problem with this approach is that marriage isn't like going to college, which you can do the year after you finish high school. It isn't like buying a new stereo, which you can do as soon as you have saved up the money. *There are some timetables in life over which you have no control, and the timing for long-term partnership and marriage is one of them.* You meet the right man when you meet the right man, not when you magically enter a certain age or life stage. By utilizing the Smart Heart Partnering Process, however, you can focus your intentions and allow the process to emerge in a more direct and energetic manner. You can't force something to happen, but you can be prepared by having a clear intention and saying "Yes" when it arrives. Romantic idealism supports the illusion that, at some magical moment in time, your life will open up, someone will instantly appear, and you will marry, living happily ever after. Although you don't have total control over life's timetables, you still have to "suit up and show up ready to play." The results are in God's hands. A perfect relationship doesn't just conveniently happen because you've now turned twenty-one and are graduating from college, or because you've turned thirty and have accomplished certain career goals and are ready to move on to the next level. It happens because you are in the process of evolving and becoming the kind of woman that the man you're seeking would choose. Even if the right man comes into your life at a moment you hadn't planned on, if you're honest and clear about the kind

43

of man you want, you will have the willingness and perception to identify him when he does show up.

More dangerous still are women who have a marriage age fixated in their minds and mistakenly feel that their adult life doesn't begin until they are part of a couple. Your adult life begins the day you become an adult, however that might be signaled: graduating from high school or college, supporting yourself financially, or moving out of the house you grew up in. Married life may be different from single life in many ways, but both are simply aspects of life. Being single is not a life-in-waiting. Don't use waiting for a husband or an intimate partner as an excuse not to buy furniture, china, or a king-sized bed, to purchase your dream house, or to travel to Tibet.

Times have changed, but even some of the most progressive feminists have not yet adjusted their attitudes. Gloria Steinem, the quintessential feminist of the sixties and seventies women's movement, was caught in this trap of old thinking. In her book *Revolution from Within: A Book of Self-Esteem,* she admits that she was unconsciously abiding by the outmoded tradition of waiting for a special man and marriage before owning nice things for her home—because that is what women did. When she turned forty, she threw out all her old, cracked, mismatched dishes, torn linens and towels, and shabby furniture and bought herself all new, beautiful things. Some women even throw themselves an apartment shower when they get their first place, so that friends and relatives can buy them the appliances, towels, and knickknacks usually reserved for brides-to-be.

Live by fully breathing in and out each day, instead of waiting to exhale until he comes along. Be consciously committed in the interim to a life that is full, so that when the right man does appear, he will genuinely appreciate that you are a woman with a complete adult life of your own.

Feeling

If I don't have a dream wedding and big reception with hundreds of friends and family, a formal bridal party, a huge diamond, and a beautiful white dress, life won't be complete.

Fact

A Smart Heart woman doesn't focus on having a big party on one special day. She focuses on the quality of a life that will last the thousands of days after her wedding day.

44

Big, fancy weddings are a commercial attempt at creating a modern-day fairy tale that seduces women and their families into spending tens of thousands of dollars to christen a relationship. Magazines, books, and wedding consultants exist to make the day a larger-than-life, once-in-a-lifetime event, when what really matters is everything that happens *after* the wedding day. I'm not against a joyous celebration or a memorable day, with friends and family there to witness the transition from one chapter of your life to the next, but don't allow yourself to be swept up by the commercialism. This can keep you from thinking clearly and prevent you from considering the long-term ramifications of choosing a person to marry because you are too caught up in fantasies and plans for a one-day event.

Today, one or both partners have often already been married, have had a big, traditional ceremony and reception, and don't want another one. Jim and Patricia, both clients of mine, had been married previously. Patricia did not have a big first wedding. She and her former husband got married by a justice of the peace in Lake Tahoe. She did not have a white dress or any of the traditional trimmings. Jim, on the other hand, had been forced to participate in a huge wedding production by his first wife and her family, who didn't give him any say whatsoever. When Jim and Patricia married each other ten years ago, they too got married by a justice of the peace, even though Patricia wanted to have a party to celebrate. Over time, Patricia became angrier and angrier because she wanted the two of them to exchange vows publicly among friends and family who would celebrate their love with them. She almost considered breaking up with Jim because he resisted doing this. Jim would not bend on this issue because he felt that he had chosen Patricia and her son in a very conscious, committed way and didn't see the importance of making a public statement about that choice. He didn't want to repeat the negative experience he had had at his first wedding.

With my help, Jim was able to recognize how important it was for Patricia to be chosen by him in the presence of other people. For their tenth wedding anniversary, she is going to wear a white wedding dress and they are going to say their vows in front of a few friends and family. This story illustrates the importance of commemorating a special day: a wedding should be a personal expression of your and your fiancé's needs and special love.

We live in a time when a two-income family is the norm and families often set aside funds for a large, elaborate wedding. Rather than spending all that money on one single day during which the frazzled couple-of-honor usually doesn't even enjoy the event, why not put the funds to a different use? The money could be used for a down payment on a house, devoted to future child-care needs, or even to take an extended honeymoon that you and your partner can share and remember for the rest of your lives.

Feeling

If only I were married or in a committed relationship, I'd live happily ever after; all my problems would disappear, and my life would be so much better.

Fact

Only you have the ability to make yourself happy or solve your own problems. Any problems you have before you are married or involved with someone are still going to be with you in your marriage or long-term relationship.

Before you are married or involved with someone, if you are unhappy, on Prozac, or have an unrewarding job and an old, run-down jalopy, you will still be unhappy, on Prozac, with a rotten job and a broken car after you're married or involved with someone—you'll just be married or in a relationship, too. The desire to be rescued has its appeal, especially if you're struggling financially or emotionally, but marriage or long-term relationships aren't capable of rectifying a bad situation. As cult comic book hero Buckaroo Bonzai says, "Wherever you go, there you are."

Katie was on Prozac before she got married and was prone to bouts of feelings of such low self-worth that she contemplated suicide on several occasions. Although Dan was a terrific man and an excellent match for Katie, it should have come as no surprise that Katie still needed Prozac during her marriage and continued to think about hastening her demise. Dan tried to be supportive of her, but Katie's inner demons haven't been banished simply by his entering her life and marrying her.

Consider the things that are making you unhappy and deal with them yourself. Switch jobs. Seek therapy. Join a support group. Begin pursuing a spiritual path. Then, when you do get married, "there you are" will be a peaceful, joyful, more integrated and less troubled place to be.

Feeling

It's not romantic to be clear about wanting marriage or long-term partnership. It's supposed to just magically happen.

Fact

Leaving one of life's most important decisions, for example, a long-term relationship or marriage, to chance and romance is just plain ignorant—even if it is an understandable error given society's pervasive message that "romance is king."

No other decision about life should command half as much clarity and planning as the choice of marriage or a long-term partner. Wishful thinking is counterproductive. Clarity and intent are the elements that manifest your romantic vision.

These romantic fantasies will be addressed at length later, but suffice it to say that the world does not function like a Disney movie. A real woman who spends her entire life locked in an evil witch's tower is likely to die there without having met a single man, rather than being rescued by a prince and chosen to be his princess. Your odds might be slightly better if you are Snow White. You might meet some really cute single doctors at the hospital emergency room after you eat the poison apple. Even then, the chances are slim that any doctor is going to find you sexy while you are having your stomach pumped.

If you have identified some of the preceding feelings and fears, both conscious or unconscious, as your own, you will be better able to determine your actual situation, rather than what you wish, hope, and pray for. These are only a few of the prevalent fears and feelings that deter us from reaching our relationship objectives. You may want to add your own fears and feelings to the list of ones noted here. As you were reading them, perhaps some other thoughts, feelings, and fears were triggered by your life experience, such as "I could never surrender myself to any man because I come from an abusive family in which my father screamed at and hit my mother. I don't want to be open or vulnerable to that kind of situation ever again."

Over the course of utilizing the Smart Heart Partnering Process, you will be able to gather more factual information to determine whether someone is the appropriate partner for you and you for him. **In the end, however, if the answers point to "no," let him go, now!** (More on this in the next two chapters.)

47

Rotten Reruns, Repeat Performances, and Media Distortions

D espite their best intentions, women often get themselves into relationships which either are reminiscent of previous ones that caused unhappiness or didn't meet their objectives. If you are repeatedly attracting the same type of undesirable man, these repeat performances require examination to discover the unconscious influences motivating your destructive actions. We all are subject to operating from unconscious influences until we examine our patterns and bring them into conscious awareness.

Historically, these unconscious images can be traced back to your family of origin. Your image of yourself as a woman and how relationships work is connected to the images that you received from your mother and your father, both consciously and unconsciously. You have absorbed the beliefs, fears, and feelings that your mother and father had in their marriage or partnerships. These images stay freeze-framed in your unconscious mind, and your images of men mirror the qualities of your father, uncles, brothers, and grandfather.

How can you determine if you are being held hostage by your own unconscious distorted images? First you have to look into your life and acknowledge whether or not you keep attracting the kind of men and relationships that don't work. For example, you might find yourself leaving one man who has a drinking problem only to enter a relationship with another who is addicted to drugs. Even if you resolve no longer to tolerate a relationship partner with an addiction, men with these problems somehow keep appearing in your life. If marriage is your aim but you keep attracting married men, or you hate confrontation but keep having relationships with men who constantly argue with you, you need to realize that you are creating a destructive pattern in your life.

In order to avoid these damaging repeat performances in the future, women need to look beyond the superficial details of their relationship histories to unearth their unconscious motivation and figure out exactly how these patterns relate to a current relationship in order to change their present course and design new relationships. Unconscious images and the need continually to attract men who are not right for you originate in family conditioning that affects you whether you are aware of it or not. This chapter will help you investigate, quantify, and articulate the images that might be holding you hostage and creating painful repetition that prevents you from reaching your relationship objectives.

If these frozen ideas and images remain unexamined, you will be doomed to repeat the errors of the past over and over. It's like trying to accelerate the car while your unconscious mind has slipped you into reverse. When our beliefs and fears remain unexamined beneath the surface, they prevent us from controlling our destiny.

Rotten Reruns: The Unconscious Map of Defeat

Without realizing it, you learned lessons about men from the time you bounced on your mother's knee. Clearly, though, all the troubles that you may have with men and relationships are not your mother's fault. As an adult, you need to take responsibility for your life, your own images, and your ideas about men. Still, it is important to be aware of what imprints, both conscious and unconscious, have been made by your family of origin. These images and beliefs may be distorting the picture of your relationships today and interfering with your progress toward your objectives. The Smart Heart Partnering Process is not about shame, blame, or guilt. Rather, it is about becoming consciously aware of what conditions and patterns you need to change, modify, or invent in order to support your present needs and desires better.

When you are very young, you are influenced on two levels by what you experience in your family of origin. The influence could have been explicit or implicit; either kind has a major impact on a young child. For instance, you can receive the message that all men are bad if your father left your mother and not a day went by when she didn't rant and rave about how no man can be trusted (explicit). Alternatively, she may never have said a word about your father's departure but never again had a relationship with another man (implicit). The end result is the same, because your mother transmitted a negative message that men couldn't be trusted and would always leave.

An unconscious map of defeat steming from your parents' unsuccessful and negative relationship choices becomes an unconscious blueprint for defeat in your own adult partnerships. This unconscious blueprint determines how you run your life in a number of ways. It may override your conscious design for a relationship by attracting you to men who are similar to the men your mother selected. It may color your view of what men want, how you react to them, whom you can trust, and what is acceptable from them. It could cause you unknowingly to attempt to mold a man into someone like your father, who is therefore familiar. It may simply cause you to avoid intimate relationships completely.

To see how this unconscious map of defeat operates, consider the experience of one of my clients. Tina was a successful thirty-three-year-old advertising account executive. When she turned twenty-one, she made a conscious decision that her relationships would not turn out like her mother's who, before dying of cancer, had spent her life subjugating her needs to those of her husband. Even though Tina's mother was on her deathbed, all her father could think about was himself. He never once focused on what his dying wife needed. "My mother is better off dead than spending more years as an unappreciated maid, cook, chauffeur, and call girl to a man who isn't interested in her," Tina thought to herself.

Tina was an adorable woman who found herself the center of men's attention at whatever party or business event she attended. Yet she didn't find herself interested in the many guys she met through her friends or work. Instead, it was the tall, dark, and handsome foreigners who set her pulse racing. She hoped one of them would someday become her husband.

Rafael was typical of the men she dated. With his jet-black hair and dark eyes, he made Tina melt whenever he looked her way or whispered words in his native Italian to her. After six months of dating, Tina enjoyed being with Rafael so much that she invited him to move in with her, even though she knew that his student visa would expire in a few months and he would be returning to Sicily. When those months flew by, Tina knew she had two choices: either marry Rafael so he could stay in this country with her or let him return home. She didn't feel ready to make a marriage commitment to someone she had known for less than a year, so she sadly took him to the airport and said good-bye.

When Tina felt ready to date again some months later, she went to a party at the International House dormitory at the nearby university. This was where she had met Rafael, and she hoped she would meet another exotic foreigner. Her wish came true. Through mutual friends, she met a man who was from South America. Carlos was also dark and handsome. Tina was smitten from the moment he opened his mouth and spoke in heavily accented, halting English. An intense, passionate affair ensued. Carlos, however, was nearing the end of the exchange program that had brought him to the university. Thus, it wasn't long before he, too, boarded a plane for home, leaving Tina behind at the airport with a broken heart.

Although Tina believed that she was genuinely attracted to exotic, foreign men, together we discovered, using the Smart Heart Partnering Process, that her true, unconscious motivation for falling for geographically undesirable men was that she knew they were unavailable. They could never meet any of her needs in the long run and therefore would not be able to hurt her. Although, on the surface, this motivation looked different from her mother's choice, after much work, Tina finally recognized the similarity. The men she found herself interested in were as unavailable to meet her needs as her father had been to meet her mother's. Until now, Tina had been able to rationalize that men like Rafael couldn't meet her needs because they lived so far away, not because they were uncaring. In reality, her choice was the same as her mother's. It was simply wrapped in a different package.

Because Tina's images from her childhood were that men cause heartbreak and loss and are never there for a woman, it was not surprising that she unconsciously chose partners who brought out the same dynamic in her own relationships. Only by bringing these images into her conscious mind and examining them could she finally choose to be with men who were actually available to support and love her in the way that she deserved.

51

Getting Off the Unconscious Treadmill: What's Running Your Relationship?

Each family is unique, with its own distinct personality, relationship dynamic, and positive and negative attributes. Whatever kind of family we grew up in, we assume that all families were like ours. When we get older, we realize that each family is quite different. We are emotionally invested in our primary family because, as children, we loved and looked up to the parents who brought us into the world and were charged with our care. Our views of our parents are shaped during the vulnerable time of childhood when we need them for support. Without them, we wouldn't have had food, clothing, or shelter and, even more important, love and affection. When we grow to adulthood, we can still find it difficult to view our parents' choices in a more mature light and let go of the images we developed in childhood.

Like Tina, you did not actually learn unconscious "lessons" by sitting behind a desk and listening to your parents' instructions like a student in a classroom. You learned the way a toddler does—by observing and listening to those around you. What makes these images and beliefs so insidious is that you aren't aware that you have them or what alternatives exist.

Holding unconscious images means unknowingly choosing men like the one your mother selected because that is the kind of man around whom you are most comfortable—not necessarily because he's the right man for you. If your father enjoyed watching sports on TV but your mother was always in another room reading, you may choose a guy who is glued to the tube every weekend. If your father was compulsive, you may be similarly attracted to men who alphabetize their books and CD collection. If your father beat your mother, you might consciously avoid guys who actually hit (at first, anyway), but someone who responds to situations with rage and anger may insinuate himself into your comfort zone.

You might make choices in reaction to your parents by choosing men who are the *opposite* of your father, ensuring that your situation is not like your mother's. On close examination, however, your partners may resemble your father in less obvious ways. If your father was an alcoholic, your partner may not be falling down drunk but may still need a few nips of booze to get him through the day.

If you are adopted, additional circumstances come into play. Not only will you be affected by your adoptive parents' patterns and behaviors; you may also have genetically inherited traits of which you are unaware. For example, I had a client who struggled with obesity. Both of her parents were thin, energetic, and never had weight problems. After her adoptive father passed away, she pursued finding her birth mother. At the age of thirty-seven, she was finally able to establish contact and discovered that her birth mother suffered from obesity. Proclivities toward certain kinds of illness, addictions, or violence could be based within your biological family. If you are adopted, many of these issues will remain hidden if you do not pursue information about your birth parents in addition to the information relative to your adoptive family. This information can influence you and be reflected in your life choices and patterns.

The only way to get off the unconscious treadmill is by bringing unconscious images and beliefs into the light of awareness. By stepping back and trying objectively to see how your parents treated each other, and you as a child, you can learn to apply that knowledge to your own relationships. You do not have to repeat your parents' patterns. It is possible to choose to bring this unconscious material into your conscious awareness to change your pattern.

In order to do this, you need to:

❶ Review your past

❷ Identify your patterns

❸ Free your future

Review Your Past

The following examples are guides for more in-depth analysis and identification of your patterns. Review these carefully to see if they reflect situations similar to your own family and how they might contribute to unconscious beliefs you hold about yourself, men, and relationships. The goal is to become more aware of these beliefs in order to discover which ones, to varying degrees, may be running or ruining your relationships. If you are not aware of these deeply held images, you are not in a position to make a conscious choice. You need to assess your actual beliefs and let the involuntary images go so that you can design and create your life.

The purpose of looking at these scenarios is neither to place blame nor to judge your parents. You need to love your parents and know that they did the best they could, but also, as an adult, you need to look honestly at the ways in which their choices may not be the right ones for you. Reading the following may be painful and reveal things that you don't want to see. Your willingness to address and examine the roots of these unconscious images offers you an opportunity to have the freedom to make your own choices.

Even if there isn't a sample situation that mirrors that of your family, these scenarios should at least spark thought about other circumstances that might be adversely affecting your relationship patterns. You may find that these statements and stories trigger images or feelings. Keep a pad of paper and a pencil nearby to note what might be relevant to review in a more in-depth way with family, friends, advisor, or therapist.

Be aware that the first three situations described are extreme. If you are the product of such a family, you may need a psychotherapist or other outsider to help you get past the tremendous negative imprint such traumas create for a child. The next three situations are more moderate examples, with the final ones representing seemingly innocuous environments that nonetheless leave a hidden destructive impression.

Dangerous Family Situations

Family Situation #1: Your father/mother was an alcoholic, addict, or rage-oholic.

Unconscious Messages You Might Have Learned
Men are:
- Unreliable
- Unpredictable
- Violent
- Mean
- Angry
- Dangerous

Caution: Women who grew up in households with alcoholic- or drug-addicted parents often become alcoholic or drug addicted themselves and/or choose men who are also alcoholics or drug addicts.

If you grew up in this situation, you need to:

▶ Confront your past (best done in psychotherapy).

▶ Seek professional assistance to process the pain that comes from numbing yourself to terror and violence.

▶ Seek help from twelve-step groups such as Alanon, Adult Children of Alcoholics, and Co-Dependents Anonymous to accelerate your process of recovery and further your personal growth.

The reality is that growing up in the unpredictable and often violent environment of an addict/alcoholic/rage-oholic's world leaves many women searching for love in all the wrong places. The statistics show that a child who grew up in such a household has a 99 percent chance of marrying an addict, alcoholic, or abuser, or becoming one herself. If you grew up in such a situation, you are at high risk and need to seek counseling or get more information on how healthy relationships function. Professional help offers a different perspective to help you create a more spontaneous, fuller, more productive life.

Sabrina grew up in a home where the words *Dad* and *loving* were never uttered in the same sentence. An obnoxious drunk, her father, Allen, was an embarrassment to Sabrina. Like many children of alcoholics, she grew up in a household where rage, chaos, and unreliability were as familiar as family dinners and bedtime prayers were in her neighbors' homes. Fortunately, Sabrina was spared a direct hit from her dad's violent outbursts. Most of those were aimed at her mother and older brother. She couldn't be sheltered from the emotional pain, though. Sabrina left the house the day she turned eighteen and never looked back.

Sabrina may have thought she had finally escaped the clutches of her alcoholic father, but she didn't realize, until entering psychotherapy, that her dad was still living in her head rent-free. This manifested as low self-esteem and poor partner choices. Sabrina did not believe that she deserved to be with men who were reliable, responsible, and generous, the opposite of her father. When she went on a date with a man who showed up when he said he would, brought her to expensive restaurants, and treated her like someone special, Sabrina had the uncomfortable sense that something was wrong. "I'm not worthy of such treatment," she would say to me. "Even though I know this is how normal men are supposed to act, I feel out of place, unnerved, and anxiety ridden with a man who behaves this way." Because of her past conditioning, the one man she let into her life for more than a few dates was Tyler, who came over whenever he felt like it, stood her up, and secretly had his own drinking problem, although he drank so discreetly his colleagues would never have guessed.

As a child, you are powerless to prevent your parents from destroying themselves and the family. As an adult, however, you have the power to make conscious decisions not to destroy yourself or your life. If you grew up in an abusive situation, you can look to hundreds of self-help books that address these issues as well as twelve-step programs to help support and expand your maturation and personal growth. You might also want to consider psychotherapy as a supportive avenue for confronting your past. You are responsible for dealing with the past in order to prevent it from destroying your future. If you do this work, you will move into a healthier life and find partners who are able to support you and your well-being.

Family Situation #2: Your father abandoned your mother, or your mother abandoned your father.

Unconscious Messages You Might Have Learned
Men:

- Always leave
- Are unreliable
- Are untrustworthy
- Are hurtful and abandon you when you love them
- Are unavailable

If you grew up in this situation, you will have difficulty:

- Staying in a relationship and will want to leave it before you are rejected
- Maintaining long-term relationships
- Believing a man would commit to you
- Believing a man would care and choose to stay
- Feeling worthy of love and kindness

Christina was raised on the edge of a tidy suburb outside a charming Canadian city in a quaint house by a loving mother. Mom was as supportive as any girl could hope for, and she worked hard to ensure that her day job as a nurse didn't take away from quality time with Christina. Dad lived only about forty-five minutes away, in an apartment downtown. Neither Christina nor her mother ever went to see him. To them, Dad was the low-down scum who had abandoned a woman with a one-year-old infant to attend to his own infantile gratification. The father's few, admittedly halfhearted, attempts to provide for his daughter by sending birthday presents or occasional checks in the mail were all sent back unopened. Christina decided as a very young girl that her father had abandoned her and she would abandon him right back.

As an adult, she had trouble staying in a long-term relationship. Somewhere in the back of her mind, she always believed that her current partner was going to leave her, that, to quote her mother's mantra, "all men eventually run away from responsibility." To prevent this from happening, Christina's unconscious directed her to leave her boyfriends first, before they had a chance to abandon her. On the rare occasion when a man exited the relationship before she had a chance to leave, Christina used that to confirm her belief that men never stay around. Furthermore, because she felt abandoned by her father, and therefore believed herself to be unworthy of his love, she felt unworthy of the love of the men she dated and unable comfortably to accept their kindness, love, and generosity.

Adult life is always more complicated than we see it as a child. Christina's father's reasons for his departure were never explained to her. If they had been, perhaps she would have seen him as a troubled human being rather than a monster. She might also have come to see that her mother chose to take on the role of lifelong martyr. During all those years, Mom never opted to give up the sad story of loss and loneliness by going out with other men.

When young girls have been abandoned by their fathers, they often believe or fear that men can't be trusted, that they themselves are not worthy of someone's commitment to them, and they want to leave before they are left. Without more objectively seeing how she devalues and distrusts men's intentions, a woman with this background might meet the best bachelor in town but won't give herself the chance to find happiness with him. She needs to learn that some men can be trusted and that others can't and to know that she is capable of making better decisions than her mother did.

Family Situation #3: Your mother chose to stay in a relationship with a man who was in it only for sex and convenience; she chose to live in a loveless marriage for her own security and that of her children.

Unconscious Messages You Might Have Learned

Men are:

▶ Interested in women only for selfish purposes, i.e., sex and house-keeping

▶ Able to provide security, and women should accept the unacceptable to get it

▶ Incapable of respecting women

▶ Incapable of loving women

▶ Important only for what they can do for you or give to you

▶ Self-absorbed

If you grew up in this situation:

▶ The message is that it doesn't matter who you are or how you feel.

▶ You use men to get what you want by providing sex, meals, a clean house, and children.

▶ You need to know that you deserve to be seen and acknowledged as a distinct human being, in addition to being valued for the things you can do for a man.

▶ You need to know you are capable of creating your own sense of security within yourself and can be self-reliant.

▶ You need to know you are capable of being loved and cherished by a man by simply being you.

The belief that men will only love you if you give them something—e.g., sex, money, a place to live—pervades the unconscious of many women who were raised in dysfunctional families. A daughter would have clearly seen that her father didn't love and cherish her mother but stayed in the marriage only because he got a tangible benefit. In exchange for what she gave him, the mother kept her husband, while perhaps receiving financial support or security.

Seen in this light, marriage becomes little more than long-term prostitution without any spiritual or emotional connection or exchange. A woman who comes from this type of home often has little respect for women in general, including herself, because she has virtually no expectation that a man might want to be with her simply because he enjoys her company. Her unconscious mind believes that she needs to "put out" in some way to snare a man and that, when she does, he will only want to stay as long as her legs, and the front door, stay open.

Every adult woman faces choices in her relationships. You need to learn that although your mother did not have the self-esteem to get rid of a man who didn't respect or love her, you have the freedom to make different choices. If you are struggling financially, you don't have to take in a man simply because he can pay the bills. Know that you can pay your own bills and wait until a mate comes along who is more than merely a provider. You deserve someone who will love and respect you, as well.

Family Situation #4: Your mother chose men who were emotionally uninvolved and distant.

Unconscious Messages You Might Have Learned
Men:
- Are superficial and incapable of deep emotions or feelings, except anger or indifference
- Are incapable of affection and the expression of sensitive feelings
- Believe showing emotion is a sign of weakness and vulnerability
- Are not capable of giving emotional support
- Believe that it is a sign of strength and manliness to bottle up feelings

If you grew up in this situation:
- You need to know that you'll be initially uncomfortable when a man expresses his feelings, in spite of the fact that you desire him to do so.
- You have difficulty expressing your own deep emotions and feelings.
- You need to learn that emotional warmth and physical affection (non-sexual touching) are necessary parts of personal growth.
- You need to know you deserve to be with a man who is generous, not only financially but also emotionally and physically.

Marge dearly loved her dad, who showered his wife and two children with treats each day when he returned from the office. To him, love meant giving, and Marge eagerly accepted his many treasures. Emotionally, however, Dad was unavailable, never sharing his true inner feelings. Marge deduced from her mother and father that men may be great providers, but it is your girlfriends to whom you go for your emotional satisfaction and sharing.

As an adult, however, Marge decided that she wanted a different kind of husband, one with whom she could share intimacy, including sharing how she was feeling about all aspects of her life. She sought out sensitive, emotionally extravagant men who splattered their emotions on the table like a Jackson Pollack painting, eagerly asking her to reciprocate. Rather than feeling grateful that she was attracting men unlike her father, Marge was terrified at the thought of opening up to them. She belittled these emotional men as wimpy and weak, quickly cutting her ties to them while trying to manage her own anxiety.

Despite a desire to marry a man unlike her father, Marge unconsciously felt too much discomfort with the open expression of emotions. Until she took time in therapy to understand her motivations, she was unable to integrate her desire with her discomfort. If you are not comfortable being with men who show their emotions because you have never experienced the open and direct expression of emotions from your father, you need: (1) to discover your own emotional inner life and 2) to practice managing your anxiety when others share theirs with you. After working through her discomfort during her next few relationships, she was able to be more at ease with an emotionally expressive and available man, as well as with her own deep feelings.

Another variation on this situation appears in many Latino households, in which the man appears to be the dominant one, but the mother really controls the family. The father may be the strong one in terms of supporting the family financially, but the mother is involved with the emotional concerns of all family members. The father is completely out of that loop. The motto in such families is "Don't tell Dad anything emotionally upsetting because he can't handle it." Children who grow up in this kind of family situation believe that men can't be trusted with deeper feelings because they will make them angry or physically ill, or the men just cannot handle them.

I grew up in a family with an emotionally distant father who provided well for us but didn't share with his ten children any of his deep feelings or much of his time. I thought I was being clever in college when I chose blond, blue-eyed men who looked very different from my dark-haired, Latino father in the misguided belief that if they looked different, they would behave differently. I later realized that the men I chose were just like my father, stingy with their time and unable to share their feelings. I unwittingly felt comfortable with men like my dad. Thankfully, as I learned more about my psyche, I was able to trade these distant, emotionally stingy men for ones who were more emotionally accessible and generous with the expression of their feelings and their time.

Family Situation #5: Your mother was a doormat.

Unconscious Messages You Might Have Learned
Men are:
- Tyrants
- Controlling/repressive
- Only using women
- Sometimes emotionally and/or physically abusive

If you grew up in this situation:
- You feel you exist only to serve a man's needs and wants.
- You believe you must give up yourself in order to have a man.
- You allow men to use you for their own purposes while you feel you have no right to express your own opinions, desires, and needs.
- You disowned and distrusted the feminine part of yourself, overcompensating by cultivating your masculine energy, making it very difficult for you to be receiving and caring. You fear that if you reveal your softer qualities, you will be used and abused by a man.
- You see women as weak and pathetic.
- You need to learn that you can stand up for yourself.
- You need to learn that there are no victims, only volunteers—stop being a doormat.
- You need to attend a twelve-step group like CODA or Alanon.
- You need to practice ways to build your self-esteem.
- You need to reclaim your feminine self and integrate it with your male energy.

Donna's large family, which included eleven kids, saw her mother acquiescing in her domineering father's every wish. Dad got to choose the food

61

they would eat for dinner, their activities when he was off work, and the friends with whom the family would socialize. Mom may have been strong when only the kids were around, but when Dad came home, Donna observed, her mother's once-proud voice became meek and childlike. Donna's mother didn't appear to mind, but Donna was outraged.

Women raised in this type of household sometimes react by deciding that they will never be like their mothers. They overdevelop their masculine attributes and qualities while disowning their feminine side. They either end up with men who have an overly developed feminine side whom they treat like doormats, acting out their fathers' roles, or they will attract domineering, repressive men similar to their fathers, with whom they will fight constantly in order not be treated like doormats themselves. It is important as a woman on a path of conscious awareness to be able to integrate both masculine and feminine energies. By maintaining balance within yourself, you can allow the man in your relationship to be the man he truly is. There is room for only one person with strong male energy in a relationship. If that is your situation, you need to develop your masculine *in conjunction with your feminine side* so that when you come home to your partner, your feminine side is available to create a more balanced energy between you and him. Otherwise, you will keep drawing in either weak men or strong ones whom you will attempt to emasculate so that they can't walk all over you. You need to be careful that you don't reenact your father's role on some poor, unsuspecting guy.

In order to become a Smart Heart woman, you need to find your own happy balance of feminine and masculine energies and stop unconsciously reacting based on what your parents chose for themselves.

Family Situation #6: Your mother chose weak men whom she then didn't respect.

Unconscious Messages You Might Have Learned
Men are:
- Pathetic
- Unworthy of respect
- Unworthy of trust
- Weak, ineffectual, or impotent
- Incapable, unreliable, and undependable

If you grew up in this situation:

▶ You need to learn to be less controlling and see men's capabilities and positive qualities.

▶ You need to learn that a healthy partnership entails loving, mutual respect.

▶ You need to learn to let men contribute to you with their time, energy, and expertise.

▶ You need to focus on developing your feminine energy and allow yourself to be receptive and cooperative, permitting others to do things their way rather than insisting on your own way all the time.

Tess grew up in a house where her mom wore the pants—both literally and figuratively. Her mother, Emma, managed the family business, ran the household, and controlled the kids. When Tess and her siblings had questions or problems, they bypassed Dad entirely, viewing him as impotent and ineffectual in their lives.

As an adult, Tess vowed that her husband would be worthy of her admiration because of his strength, involvement, and actions. No meek men for her. The men she attracted as boyfriends wanted to run things, often having their own businesses and a take-charge view of household affairs. Tess would unknowingly begin to tear down their manhood. Her carping would start innocently enough, criticizing the way her partner did one thing, and then another, until she was picking apart his every action. After a while, men stopped wanting to be with her. Although Tess was hurt and angry, she always felt a strange relief. Her unconscious mind was actually more comfortable because she could now dive in and run the show herself. This was the role she grew up with and the one in which she felt more secure.

By consciously trying not to be like her domineering mother, Tess attempted to turn every man into a ninety-pound weakling, no matter how strong he was. Even the most self-assured man can be emasculated by a woman's constant criticism until he reaches the point where, instead of using his power to please her, he reacts by withholding that power, becoming passive and weak. **You need to look at yourself to see if you have become the man you want to marry.** If so, you need to expand your capacity for tenderness and be more receptive, accepting, and trusting of the man you are with.

Family Situation #7: Your parents fell in "love at first sight" and married a week after meeting.

Unconscious Messages You Might Have Learned
Men:

▶ Must inspire love from the moment you meet them, or they are not the right ones for you

▶ Must be enchanting; love hits you both like a bolt of lightning, and you know instantaneously "This is it!" Otherwise there is no possibility of a good and strong relationship developing

If you grew up in this situation:

▶ You need to separate the myth of your family history from the reality of how most relationships develop.

▶ You need to understand that the odds of a lasting, meaningful, successful marriage/long-term partnership resulting from "love at first sight" are not in your favor.

▶ You need to learn that most relationships take time to develop and are a lot of hard work, even if your parents were among the "lucky ones."

▶ You need to be aware that there's a lot your parents haven't told you about how difficult it was to keep their love affair after the lightning bolt struck.

This situation is about a myth created by your parents that takes on epic proportions. The myth of "love at first sight" is that long-term relationships and marriages are made in heaven or through cosmic intervention and that you will recognize your soul mate as soon as you meet him. Only a small percentage of successful long-term relationships and marriages started in this way. Usually, successful relationships develop over time and require a lifelong commitment, and hard work.

Caryl and Sam, now age sixty, met when both were on a weeklong vacation in the South of France. Sam had a machine-tool company in the United States, and Caryl was a secretary for a company in England. The night before he was to return to America, Sam popped the question, and Caryl didn't hesitate when she answered "Absolutely." They have been happily married for thirty-eight years and have a daughter named Debbie.

Debbie, age thirty-three, has always watched her parents' unbridled affection with great envy. "That's the way I want my marriage to be—perfect," she told me. "When you meet the man who is right for you, you know it immediately." Although she has been actively dating for more than a decade, Debbie has yet to meet the one man who will sweep her off her feet.

Debbie's parents notwithstanding, the success rates for such hastily arranged unions are dismal. Most of us can cite examples of numerous couples who married before really knowing each other and divorced soon thereafter. Happily for Caryl and Sam, they beat the odds. The problem for Debbie is that their success has her believing such outcomes are the rule, not the exception. She, therefore, approaches her relationships with the expectation that if they are right she should know it instantly. After a week, or even a month or two, if she still isn't sure about a guy, her unconscious mind begins to feel that he must not be the one.

It is not usually wise or advisable to get married one week after you meet a man; you couldn't possibly know who the person is after such a short amount of time. Of course, romances blossom on widely varying timetables, depending on the people and circumstances. For many couples, a slow start, often following a period of being friends, can later build to a loving partnership, regardless of the way it might have happened for your parents.

Family Situation #8: You were Daddy's little princess.

Unconscious Messages You Might Have Learned
Men:

▶ Will love you unconditionally

▶ Should see you as perfect in all ways

▶ Should spoil and indulge you and make you the most important person in both of your lives

If you grew up in this situation:

▶ You need to understand that in the more extreme cases, such treatment by a father is emotional incest.

▶ You need to stop being demanding and childish with men; you do not deserve to be spoiled.

> You need to realize that you are not perfect; you can make mistakes (everyone does).

> You need to be aware that you are not automatically entitled to happiness or fulfillment; it is your responsibility to learn how to provide it for yourself.

> You need to critically examine the self-centered aspects of your personality.

Katrina's dad loved her mother, but he reserved all his special sweetness for his little girl. He was always telling Katrina how beautiful she looked, how spectacular her eyes were, what a joy she was to be around. When a necklace or party dress in a store window caught her eye, Dad raced to buy it and "make my little princess happy."

The problem is that her father was also making his princess unrealistic. No man a woman like Katrina dates will ever treat her as well as her father did. Her lofty opinion of herself resulting from such a fawning father translates into the belief that no man is good enough for her. (The fact that her dad will criticize each guy she introduces to him won't help matters either!) In seeking a "man like Daddy," Katrina will find herself with no one. She will remain a demanding, petulant child trapped in a woman's body.

Some women in Katrina's situation learn another, equally problematic, lesson. Since her father continually chose Katrina over her mother, she grew up with an exaggerated sense of self-importance and the idea that women who are wives are not respected. She may choose to avoid tying the knot for fear that will become her own fate. Sometimes women from this type of family become call girls to perpetuate "always" being that special other woman.

Such a dynamic between father and daughter can be a form of emotional incest. Women who overidentify with fathers who support the illusion of a specialness and intimacy that belongs more appropriately to Mom foster a delusional sense of self-importance that, in the end, no man can ever rival. If you grew up in such a family situation, you need to look at how this kind of dynamic with your father may have distorted your opinions of yourself. You must learn that it isn't a man's job to make you feel special, but your own. You need to manage unrealistic expectations and demands and look at what you believe men are "supposed" to give you as an adult and how these images are distorted as a result of your childhood.

If you want to become a Smart Heart woman, you must be willing to:

▶ Understand that your mother's choices have a large influence on your own partnership selections

▶ Work to expose the map your mother's choices created in your own unconscious

▶ Carefully examine the underlying dynamics at work in your own partners and relationships

▶ Look for ways your unconscious beliefs and images are undermining your conscious needs

▶ Work to eliminate those images that don't serve your objectives and enlist the help of a psychotherapist, if necessary, to help you do this

Exercises to Help You Identify Your Patterns

Exercise #1: Thoughts About Your Family and Relationships

In order to discover what some of your more specific beliefs and distorted images are, take a few moments to think about some of the beliefs you hold about men, women, and relationships. Make a quiet space for yourself to allow ample and honest reflection. Although you can just think about your answers, you will get more out of the exercise if you write them down. This is not meant to be a test, so write your answers quickly and spontaneously, as they come to you. Don't think too hard or edit what you think. If you feel blocked, write down the first thing that comes to your mind and keep going, even if it doesn't sound right to you. You will not be sharing these answers with anyone, so be honest with yourself. Feel free to approach the statements in any order, letting yourself wander first to those areas you feel are most important for you.

Your answers may be one word or a string of words, but they should be short and simple. You can answer the questions now and return to them again to add more to the response. For instance, the first time you complete the statement "I feel my mother is . . . ," you might write down: "sexy, creative, assertive, pushy, domineering, emotional." A week or a month later, you might complete it with "caring, loving, a good listener, strong."

There is no right or wrong answer—just your answers. Let your stream of consciousness flow. Come back to your answers a day or two later. You will be surprised to see how your feelings about these issues really influence your opinions, perspectives, and beliefs about yourself and others.

Thoughts About Women and My Mother

I feel my mother is _____.

I wish my mother could have been more _____.

My mother always told me to _____.

I always hated it when my mother _____.

The way I am most like my mother is _____.

My mother's view of men was _____.

I believe that women in general are _____.

The thing I love most about being a woman is _____.

The thing I like least about being a woman is _____.

In my marriage/long-term relationship, I hope I can be like my mother in the

areas of _____.

My mother made me angry when she _____.

In my marriage/long-term relationship, I hope I will never be like my mother

in the areas of _____.

The most difficult things about being a woman are _____.

Thoughts About Men and My Father

I feel my father is _____.

I wish my father had been more _____.

I never understood why my father always _____.

My father thought women were _____.

I believe that men, in general, are _____.

The thing I love most about men is _____.

I hated it when my father said _____.

It made me angry when my father _____.

I think that men are _____.

I hope that my husband/long-term partner will treat me as my father treated

my mother in the areas of _____.

I would never let my husband/long-term partner do what my father did to

my mother in the areas of _____.

Thoughts About Relationships and Sex

I believe relationships are _____.

The best thing about my parents' marriage is _____.

The worst thing about my parents' marriage is _____.

My most lasting image of my parents' relationship is _____.

My mother thought sex was _____.

My father thought sex was _____.

I wish I had/hope to have a partner who is _____.

The best things I can contribute to a relationship with a man are: _____.

What I want most from a relationship is _____.

I could end a relationship if _____.

The things that I like most about being in a relationship with a man

are: _____.

The things I don't know that I can contribute to a relationship are: _____.

I think sex is _____.

Exercise #2: Questioning Your Family

I have given examples of only eight family situations, but each one is unique with distinctive relationships that have an impact on our beliefs about life and love. It is possible that your personal family situation is not represented here. One of the best ways to discover which distorted images from your family situation have influenced you is to ask your family members questions about their own personal experience as a part of your family unit. For example, maybe you considered your mother to have been oppressed by your father. You might be shocked to learn that your mother didn't feel that way at all, that it was a conscious choice to say "yes" to him all the time out of concern and love for him. It's also amazing how things that we consider unalterable facts about our parents' marriage may not be shared by siblings who grew up in the very same household.

Moreover, others in your family may be open about issues that you may be hiding from yourself. For example, perhaps you see your mother as virtuous, but your older sister knows Mom had an affair with the next-door neighbor when you were a toddler; perhaps you thought Dad was a rogue, but he saw himself as a victim simply responding to your mother's prescription pill addiction and sexual frigidity—conditions you may have known nothing about.

Seeing perspectives different from your own doesn't change your reality, but it can help you understand more deeply and fully that there are other ways of looking at the same situation. The facts you believe are absolute truths may be just your opinions. You can shed more light on your family dynamics if you are willing to ask your parents, siblings, or other relatives (aunts and uncles, grandparents) for their impressions (both positive and negative) and their perceptions. This will help you expand your own thoughts and feelings. The best way to do this is to ask open-ended questions: for example, How did they see their relationship? or Why did they feel their spouse behaved the way he or she did? Be careful not to provoke them with your own recollections; just listen quietly. If their experience was radically different from yours, remember it doesn't mean that your thoughts and feelings are incorrect. It may mean that your siblings or your parents are in denial, or that they filter impressions through a different lens than yours. Remember, too, that the house your older brother or younger sister grew up in was different from the one you were raised in. When you were born, your parents were a different age than they were with your siblings. Their financial or emotional circumstances may have changed. Also, parents never treat their firstborn the same as they do a second or third child. With each child, they have learned different parenting skills, or their attitudes toward parenting have changed with each successive child. They, too, are growing and evolving as people.

Keep in mind that you are looking not only for problems that may have created unconscious distortions but also for the positive lessons and images from your parents' relationship. For example, any woman who acts as a doormat has also taught you to be cooperative and to get along with all kinds of people in various situations. If you've grown up in a household with violence, you can adapt to situations changing at a moment's notice. You've developed the ability to be very flexible. *Your family of origin, in spite of its negative aspects, has also given you positive characteristics and qualities.* Don't forget to notice these qualities and recognize how they've assisted you in becoming what you are today. Our greatest character defects accepted with enlightened consciousness and grace become our greatest assets when they are transformed. For example, my own father was very judgmental and critical. This was a quality I retained within my personality to my own detriment and that of those around me. As I expanded my awareness, I was able to use good judgment and perception to inspire others without being critical or making them feel inferior. Ideally, these qualities can be utilized and incorporated positively and consciously into your interaction with your own partner. You may realize, for example, that you are a generous, open, and loving person because that's how your father was, or that you are affectionate because your mother was always hugging you and patting you on back. Unfortunately, we often overlook the good qualities and attributes we have inherited from our families. These are traits that you should be actively seeking to mirror and bring to your own future partner.

71

Exercise #3: Making the Connection

Take a few moments for an exercise that will help you see the connections between your family of origin and your past relationships.

Think about the last few boyfriends you've had. For each man:

▶ List the qualities about him that attracted you in the first place.
▶ List the best qualities he brought out in you.

▶ List the cause of any obstacles that prevented the relationship from succeeding.

▶ List how **your** behavior contributed to the relationship's demise.

Look carefully at any similarities to your parents' partnership. Perhaps you seem to have attracted men who were prone to fits of rage, like your father, or maybe you even find gentle souls but provoke them to scream at you so that you feel loved. Also, look to see if your patterns repeat from man to man.

In order to become a Smart Heart woman, you must carefully examine the unconscious forces that may undermine your best intentions in a relationship. You must be willing to take a hard, sometimes painful, look at those aspects of your parents' relationship that you are unknowingly incorporating into your own relationships. If you choose not to examine them, they won't go away. Instead, they will continue to run your life behind the scenes. By exposing your unconscious agenda and beliefs, you will start the process of freeing yourself to make different, wiser choices. This, in turn, will allow you to create relationships that are more reflective of your unique needs and aspirations.

Media Myths (or Why *Ozzie & Harriet* Weren't Even Ozzie and Harriet)

Another powerful force that leaves equally distorted and detrimental images in your mind is the media. Your family didn't exist in a vacuum. In the United States, girls are bombarded with a series of myths about romantic life and marriage from all kinds of media images. For many little girls, it begins as early as age three, when they dress up as Cinderella for Halloween. Over the years, young women have been constantly bombarded with unhealthy and unrealistic ideas and images from a stream of sources: books (especially fairy tales), movies, television shows, and toys, such as Barbie.

Television, romance novels, videos, and movies are not reflective of real life, but most of us have lived with these images for so long that we have lost the ability to make the distinction. Many women in my psychotherapy practice spout what they believe to be truths about relationships, only to discover upon deeper contemplation that they're really talking about the characters in romantic comedies, soap operas, and romance novels.

The hard work of relationships is never part of the plotline. The standard Hollywood formula has the credits rolling immediately after the couple gets together and declares their true love. Difficulties dealing with religious differences, ex-girlfriends, financial setbacks, career conflicts, and overbearing mothers are conveniently left out of the picture.

Of course, the men who populate these media fantasies are wonderful. Career oriented, yet sweet and sensitive, doting on their woman and always putting the family first, these men are a woman's dream—but a dream they are. Real men are much more complex than any two-dimensional image can render them. It is unlikely that any man is like a romance novel hero—ruggedly individualistic yet astoundingly tender toward the woman who tamed him.

If, as an adult, you can't distinguish between reality and the unrealistic messages and images you may have processed internally as a child from television, movies, and romance books, you may be trying to create unrealistic scenarios dreamed up by entertainment sources without even realizing it. Who wouldn't like to believe that Prince Charming is going to take her away from all her cares? It can be dangerous to act on those distorted perceptions rather than seeing them for what they really are—entertaining distractions. We have to look at how these ideas negate reality and hold us hostage to idealistic expectations and demands. In order to *get smart with your heart*, you need to recognize the dangers inherent in being seduced by these media fantasies.

73

Media Myth #1: The Perfect Relationship

As perpetrated by:

Ozzie & Harriet

Leave It to Beaver

I Love Lucy

The Cosby Show

Father Knows Best

Unconscious Messages You Might Have Learned:

▶ Relationships are neat, clean, and controllable.

▶ There is such a thing as "happily ever after."

▶ People never argue with each other or have disagreements.

▶ Challenges and problems never occur in a "happy" household.

▶ There is no such thing as conflict, or at least any conflict that can't be resolved with a few jokes in under thirty minutes.

THE REALITY

▶ Relationships are complex because people are complex.

▶ Challenges are continuous; you must work with your partner to face them.

▶ There's no such thing as the perfect man, perfect relationship, or perfect family.

YOU NEED TO

▶ Learn how to forgive human failings and accept yours as well as others'.

▶ Learn how to be flexible and compassionate toward your partner's shortcomings and allow yourself and others to make mistakes.

▶ Learn that conflict is inherent in real life; sometimes we need to agree to disagree.

▶ Learn that love flows most fluidly between two people on equal planes.

▶ Learn not to diminish the connection between yourself and your partner by being overly critical because he doesn't live up to an ideal.

Media Myth #2: Love Conquers All
(Even Differences in Class, Background, Geography, and Impossible or Previously Existing Circumstances)

As perpetrated by:

An Officer and a Gentleman

Pretty Woman

Working Girl

As Good as It Gets

Unconscious Messages You Might Have Learned

▶ A knight in shining armor will come to rescue you from your life and hardships.

74

- A man's love can save you from the negative or immutable circumstances of your own making; e.g., wedding vows, children, or problematic personality traits.

- It's best to ignore life's difficulties because they are temporary and mutable.

- Differences don't matter.

- Love can overcome any obstacle placed in the path of your partnership, including geography, social status, race, and religion.

- Love can always change someone's negative qualities and severe personality disorders.

- There aren't any tangible or dangerous ramifications of casual, impulsive sex.

THE REALITY

- Differences exist and must be worked out, not ignored.

- All humans have flaws.

- You alone are responsible for creating your own happiness and successes.

- If you *expect* your dates to be handsome, rich, and ready to take you on worldly adventures, you will never be satisfied with an ordinary man who has a nine-to-five job and financial struggles just like you. The *Pretty Woman* scenario of being a hooker one minute and happily married to a millionaire the next is fiction; it is immature to believe otherwise.

- Sex, no matter what the circumstances are, can have serious consequences, from pregnancy to AIDS and other sexually transmitted diseases. Personality disorders, addiction, and abuse require professional treatment and are not cured by love alone.

YOU NEED TO

- Appreciate the man in front of you, rather than unconsciously scripting a fantasy with him.

- Avoid retreating into romance novels and other fantasies as a cure for the difficulties and differences in your relationship or to avoid relationships altogether.

75

- Allow yourself to be open to an exciting and fulfilling life, with all of its ups and downs.

- Know that you get back from life what you put into it.

- Do not allow yourself to be scared by a few bad relationships; be willing to get back out there. Remember, there are no failures, only those who quit.

Media Myth #3: Love at First Sight

As perpetrated by:

Cinderella

Sleepless in Seattle

While You Were Sleeping

Dharma and Greg

Unconscious Messages You Might Have Learned

- Love happens easily and effortlessly.

- Love will find you against all odds.

- You can fall in love with someone simply by seeing him or hearing his voice.

- You don't have to know someone to be in love with him.

THE REALITY

- "Falling in love" is only the beginning of a longer, larger, more involved conscious process of real love.

- The true test of real love comes after the "honeymoon phase" is over.

YOU NEED TO

- Date a variety of men and spend a long time evaluating the one you feel might be an appropriate long-term or marriage prospect.

- Stick with the relationship and learn how to do the real work of loving, even when it gets difficult.

- Understand that, unlike television shows and movies, life keeps on going long after the "credits roll."

- Know that real relationships are a result of conscious choices and commitment.

Get smart with your heart and set your sights on achieving relationship success in the real and existing world, not in the fabricated, fantasy world appearing on the silver screen, within the pages of a novel, or on television. The obstacles to success are greater in real life and must be dealt with consciously. When you allow yourself to experience the world as it is, your life becomes richer and more meaningful.

Mr. Right, or Mr. Right Now?

t is very important to pay attention, stay awake, be aware when you're dating, and listen to what a man is saying, as well as observing what he is doing. He may say all the right things, but his behavior may not reflect what he says. People make time to do things that are important to them, even men who are dedicated to their careers and work long hours, because that is their priority. If a man is truly interested in you, he will make time to pursue you and spend time with you. He may, however, go back to working long hours after you've established a relationship, despite the fact that he made time for the initial courtship/ approach. Depending on the stage of his development, he may be a workaholic, and you will need to be aware of that. It is important to learn how to make the crucial distinction between what he says and what he does so you can decide if he is what you want for your life and your relationship.

Every woman using the Smart Heart Partnership Process needs to learn how to stay conscious, pay attention, look, and listen, so she can hold out for someone who is truly a Mr. Right, not a Mr. Right Now who merely looks or sounds like Mr. Right.

Don't let desperation define your relationship design. Your relationship design emerges from the intention that you create by knowing what you want, being aware of the images, thoughts, and feelings that might be getting in the way of having what you want, and your willingness to take action and start dating. You must then be willing to take the next step and evaluate whether or not you are compatible with regard to personality styles, values, goals, and similarities on touchy topics or tough questions. Stay committed to your objectives, and don't settle for anything less than what you want. Trust that the relationship you've designed for yourself will occur as you become who you truly are. Keep trying until you succeed.

Brianna's story is a good illustration of how often women go unconscious, fuel themselves with magical thinking, and don't pay attention to clear warning signals. At the age of thirty-five, Brianna was tired of the dating scene. She decided she wanted a long-term committed relationship, but she was weary of bars and the boring, unattractive men she met in them, as well as the time and energy the dating ritual required. "I don't want one more date with one more jerk," she told a friend last year. "I want to be married just like everybody else."

Then she met Nick, a thirty-six-year-old single dentist who owned a large, very nice house in a fashionable part of town. Three of the four bedrooms sat empty, except for some half-filled storage boxes and trophies from his college baseball days. When Brianna first met Nick, she felt as if she should pinch herself to make sure she wasn't hallucinating. Tall, handsome, charming, and articulate, not to mention single, Nick seemed to be everything Brianna wanted in a husband.

When they went on their first date, he told her many stories about himself that detailed his accomplishments, trophies, skills, and intelligence. It bothered her that he never asked her once about her own successes or anything else about herself, but she was willing to let it slide. Even when he started dropping her off on the corner by her house so he wouldn't have to make a U-turn to get back to his she didn't complain.

When she described Nick to all her girlfriends, their disbelief about how lucky she was only made her desire him more. "You should see how much money he has. For his last vacation, he went across the world to Tahiti," she said, beaming. (That his holiday present to her was a beer mug or that he didn't invite her on the trip didn't really matter, she decided.) "He has the most beautiful green eyes," she boasted. So what if he never told Brianna that her eyes were magnificent, too?

As the months went on and the pair continued to date, Brianna began to flip dreamily through bridal magazines, selecting the colors her bridesmaids might wear and wondering how and when to broach the topic of

79

marriage with Nick. Eight months into the relationship, Brianna and Nick talked of going to the mountains for a weeklong vacation. He never made it clear whether he was treating or if they were going Dutch, but she figured she'd cross that bridge later. When the impending trip was just a week away, Brianna was distressed that Nick still hadn't definitively decided to go.

Brianna decided to confront him, sweetly, in her apartment one day: "Nick, I need you to make a commitment for the trip. It's getting kind of late." He stunned her when he turned to face her and replied dryly, "I don't believe in making commitments." Then, he walked out the door and never returned or phoned again.

Women who have invested themselves to this extent in a relationship and have deluded themselves with Brianna's kind of rationalization and denial aren't going to get over a breakup in a few weeks. Women like Brianna enter this kind of relationship with an unconscious tendency to blame the man for being a total jerk, rather than asking themselves why they weren't able to see the obvious signs from the beginning. Women who have been through a similar situation need to have the courage and willingness to look at their part in accepting and allowing this type of situation to continue.

When Brianna began to notice that she was making excuses for Nick's behavior, she needed to ask herself why she would allow a man to treat her in this manner and why she was involved with such a superficial, materialistic man. The hard question is why we aren't willing to look more deeply to discover the truth about who we are with, rather than allowing ourselves to be stunned when he walks out the door. We need to ask ourselves, "What is it about me that isn't willing to see what is actually occurring? Why don't I listen to what a man actually says instead of deluding myself with my own fantasies, hopes, and dreams?" What is clear from Brianna's story is that she was unable and unwilling to listen to and trust her own instincts. Rather than listening to that quiet internal voice nagging at her throughout the courtship asking "What about me?" she continued to ignore Nick's behavior until he made it painfully clear that he didn't care about her.

It took Brianna a long time to get over her anger over the way this relationship had ended. Once she realized how she had allowed Nick to humiliate her, she spent a lot of time and energy beating herself up emotionally and berating herself for her stupidity. How could she not have seen the signs? How could she not have had enough self-respect to stand up to him and demand to be treated better? With my help, she was able to admit to herself that she had an almost desperate need to be married and that it had blinded her to the reality of the situation. Although Nick may initially have looked good, how he actually behaved didn't match up to his appearance. It took Brianna even longer to realize that what she was angry about losing was what the relationship might have been, not Nick or actually having a relationship with him. Punishing and torturing ourselves for our mistakes once we realize our responsibility in the relationship only cause us to further doubt that inner voice.

We need to honor our growth process and learn from our mistakes. The goal is progress, not perfection. In loving and caring for yourself, you can be a Smart Heart woman who is willing to learn from her mistakes in order to make wiser and better choices in the future. It is much more productive to say to yourself, "I made this mistake. Thank you, God, the universe, or whatever, for revealing to me where I have a blind spot. I am now willing to be aware of that blind spot so that, instead of staying in another relationship for ten years that doesn't meet my objectives, I will be involved for only six months so that I can consciously determine if it is the right situation for me." The best way to grow and evolve is constantly to look at how you are making progress, rather than spending time and energy trying to be perfect. Remember to stop beating yourself up for being human!

All human beings must learn to listen to and trust their internal voice if they want to grow and evolve. Women should learn never to override their inner truth with romantic hopes, dreams, fantasies, or images that have been imposed on them by other people or even by themselves. They need to eliminate such notions of what they "should" be doing, what the guy they are with "should" look like, or what the relationship "should" be. If, for example, you come from a family of doctors and lawyers and the family expectation is that you should marry a doctor or a lawyer when your internal voice is calling you toward the saxophone player who lives on the floor below you, listen to your own voice and trust yourself. If you learn how to listen to and trust your own inner impulses, that powerful voice from your Higher Self will assist you in finding the person who fits with you and your relationship objectives.

Pay attention. Stop allowing feelings of fear, longing and loneliness, anxiety, or desperation to override your inner voice and letting distorted images control you.

If you have spent a lot of time and emotional energy on Mr. Right Now when you were convinced that he was Mr. Right, keep this idea in your consciousness and use it as your mantra: There is no such thing as failure, only a delay in the end result.

In order to meet your relationship objectives, you have to be willing to allow yourself the process of learning and making mistakes. If you make a mistake at work, you don't stop working and decide never to work again. You wouldn't stay in a job that was clearly wrong for you, costing you several years of your life; you would attempt to move on to another job. For some reason, many women who have wasted too much time in the wrong relationship will decide not to get involved in another one. Absence or abstinence is not the solution. If this sounds like a familiar situation, you need to be kind, compassionate, and gentle with yourself. Be willing to learn from your mistakes. Take risks, take action, and stop berating yourself for taking the time to get where you want to go.

Realistically, it may take some time to get past the hopes and dreams you held for a relationship that was inappropriate for you. People have to discover their errors before they can accept them. In the end, you will be grateful to be out of a relationship with a man who wasn't right for you. You may **feel** as if you had lost your hopes and dreams of happiness because you lost the man, but the **fact** is that your objectives, dreams, and hopes are still alive in **you.** As you become a Smart Heart woman, you learn how to keep yourself open and willing to learn while you move toward fulfilling your relationship objectives with the right man.

▶ You can never fail if you try and keep on trying.

▶ You can never fail if you risk and keep on risking.

▶ You can never fail if you keep on moving and taking action.
You're Worth Waiting for.

Is It Worth Waiting for Mr. Right?

If you've already been in a deep, committed relationship, remember how greatly the man influenced your life, both positively and negatively. When something sad happened, you probably longed to be comforted in his arms; when something thrilling occurred outside of his presence, you could hardly wait to share it with him.

A relationship is a vehicle for expanded consciousness as well as personal and spiritual growth and evolution. By being in a meaningful relationship with someone, we can become greater than we were before. If you are alone, you aren't encouraged by a partner to expand or do things differently. In a deep, committed partnership, that connection alone requires you both to expand in order to live together. M. Scott Peck, in *The Road Less Traveled,* says that the enlargement of the self that occurs in a truly deep relationship creates "a mystical union with the entire world." When a woman feels intimately connected to her partner, *if* the two are conscious, the whole of their union becomes much greater than the sum of the two parts. A loving relationship also brings a sense of security, continuum, intimacy, ongoing comfort, shared experiences and energy, as well as a chance to combine financial and other resources. A loving, reciprocal relationship is worth taking the time to find.

To operate under the fear that, as with a discount store sale, if you don't act now all the goods will be taken, is self-sabotaging. If you had big brothers who always emptied the cookie jar before you could get to it or you were shut out of your first-choice college classes because you went to a large university, you might be approaching the idea of marriage with the fear that there is a shortage of good men, and there are not enough good ones to go around. If this is a belief that you hold on to, you need to believe that, even if there is only one good man available, you're going to be the one who's going to have him. The facts don't reflect our fears, and pursuing any endeavor from a fear-based position weakens the possibility of manifesting what we want. You need to know that the clearer you are about what you want, the easier it is for the universe to bring that person to you.

If all the good men really are married, how can it be that a full one-third of all residents in just the borough of Manhattan have never tied the knot? Reality and census figures show that, if you want it, marriage is not only conceivable but also probable during your lifetime (Terry Lugaila, "Marital Status and Living Arrangements," March 1997).

When women don't use their heads to consciously pursue their relationship objectives, they are, in effect, accepting less than what is possible for them. When you compromise and capitulate in a way that doesn't reflect or celebrate what you want and who you are, you are essentially robbing yourself of the life you deserve.

Jeannie was a client of mine in her late twenties. She had been in an on-again–off-again relationship with a very handsome and charming guy who was crazy about her. He was also very oppressive, jealous, and an alcoholic and periodic drug abuser who would binge once a month. During these bouts, he would become totally crazed and out of control, scaring Jeannie, but afterward he was always repentant. He would buy her expensive presents, pledge his undying love, and vow that it would never happen again. She tried to break up with him, but he wouldn't let go. He even broke into her apartment a few times to beg her not to leave him. Jeannie was so distraught that she became suicidal, feeling that there was no clear way out for her. At the same time, she was torn because she was second-guessing herself, wondering if she would ever find anyone else who would "love" her the way he did.

Jeannie took some proactive steps to get out of this painful dilemma and to prove her own value to herself. She moved into a new apartment with an unlisted telephone number and, because she was in the process of changing jobs, she told her former employer not to give out her new address. Eventually, her old boyfriend faded out of the picture. Jeannie remained single for the following year. She spent the time working on her sense of self and succeeding in her new job. She dated a bit, but no one man really stood out.

After a time, Jeannie met a successful young attorney who was much more appropriate for her. He was stable, smart, and respectful of her. They dated for a while, got married, and now they have a child together. This man is a wonderful father to their son and adores Jeannie. They also share common values, and he doesn't have a problem with drugs or alcohol. Jeannie's husband is much more of a reflection of the lifestyle she wanted to live and the kind of relationship she was looking for.

It was extremely difficult for Jeannie to rid Mr. Right Now from her life and then have the courage to wait for her Mr. Right. She had to spend substantial time on her own, but in the end she was much better for having done so. Holding out is not easy. Listening to that internal voice is often difficult at first and usually requires immense personal strength, but it is always worthwhile. In the end, you get in touch with your authentic self, as well as finding a man who is suited for you.

It is hard enough to maintain a relationship when you know in your head and heart that it is *right* for you, given the pressures of young children, job problems, illness, financial woes, or just ordinary human failings. Women who choose a Mr. Right Now are not likely to find a relationship that will be satisfying or bring them happiness. Even if the relationship lasts, if it is not a high-quality relationship, the cost will be a damaged sense of self and well-being at a deep level. You probably know many people who have been married for thirty years but sleep in separate bedrooms, don't ever have sex, and rarely talk in a meaningful way. They are basically sharing living space, not their lives, nor are they bringing any energy or vitality to the relationship. You could have that kind of relationship, too, but you would certainly lose yourself in the process.

We may not be selling ourselves short for blenders and bright, shiny kitchen appliances as women in the 1950s did, but are we selling out for other outmoded images and ideas? It is interesting that most women would never support or encourage any of their friends to settle for someone less than they deserve because they know and honor who their friends are, but they are not willing to give themselves the same respect and support that they would give others. Emerson said, "Heartily know, when half-gods go, the gods arrive." You shouldn't settle for less than you deserve. If what you have isn't making you happy or meeting your objectives, it is far better to be alone. By letting go of Mr. Right Now, you create an opening and the space to greatly improve the chances that Mr. Right will enter your life.

Ask the Critical Question: "Do I Like *Him?*"

There's nothing more seductive than a man who is crazy about you, sends you e-mail every day, leaves you thoughtful messages on your answering machine, and gives you constant attention. You feel happy because someone is there to go out with on those formerly lonely Saturday nights. It's a wonderful and delicious feeling to be wanted by someone, but a woman using her head along with her heart must stop to realize that this is not enough.

Of course, it is exciting when a man is captivated by you, when he likes you enough to want to take you places, spend money on you, and spend his free time in your presence. It can be a real boost to anyone's ego. Unfortunately, too many women think that a man's interest in them is reason enough to start or stay in a relationship with him. It is not. As a Smart Heart woman, you need to ask yourself, "Am I interested in him? Do I like him?" If your objective is to find a mate or a partner and this man doesn't meet your relationship objectives, stop wasting your time and move on to someone else, even if his constant attention and seductiveness stroke your ego and feel great.

Valerie is a tall, big-boned woman who, although attractive, always had an inferiority complex about her looks. An executive in the film industry, she saw impossibly thin actresses daily. In comparing herself to them, she always came up short. According to those who knew her, she was bright, attractive, accomplished, sweet, and sincere, but that didn't count for much in her mind. She was under the impression that men wouldn't want her because she wasn't a bombshell.

When any man showed an interest in Valerie, she felt that she was the lucky one. As a result, she dated several bad-bet men, con men, and losers (in chapter 10, I detail the different categories of these bad-bet men), and she never broke up with a single one of them. As she told me in one of our sessions last year, "I always fear that if I let this one go, there will never be another."

By seeing herself as undeserving of a good man, Valerie was operating from a sense of fear and scarcity. If your perception is that you are lucky to have a guy (any guy), the fact that he is not someone you are truly interested in becomes less important than the fact that he is interested in you. In reality, although you might be better off with a man who is crazier about you than you are about him, you have to like him, too, for the relationship to be healthy and work.

As a woman, you need to know that men want to be with you. Women constantly underestimate the value of who they are and the love they have to give. No matter what your shape, size, status, or stature, there are many men who would want to be with you. If you don't believe this, test it out for yourself. Go into any bar just before closing at 2:00 A.M., and I guarantee you there will be men there who will be willing to go home with you right now. The point is not finding *any* man but finding the *right man for you*.

Why don't women understand that they are desirable to men? Often, by their very nature, women undervalue themselves. There's a body of psychological research called the "attribution theory" that explains what happens when you ask people to what their success can be attributed. For example, when a man is asked what accounts for his success on a project, he will say it is because of *his* talent and skill, whether that is true or not. Conversely, when a woman is asked the same question, she will credit external factors like luck or other people's help. Women tend not to believe that their own merits create their success. This mind-set is the reason why many women attribute their relationships to luck or fate. They fear their "luck" won't hold out a second time around. They don't realize it is also their own nature that will bring the right relationship to them—if not this time, then the next time.

The fact is that men love women—all different kinds, sizes, shapes, and styles of them. The problem is that women underestimate the value of who they are and the power of their love.

In order to become a Smart Heart woman:

▶ You need to *stop* undervaluing yourself.

▶ You need to know that there is no shortage of men who would want to be with you.

Never undervalue yourself and the power of your love. You are as desirable as any other woman, and you have the power to choose whether you want a relationship to continue or end. It is great when a guy is enamored of you, but relationships are only truly a blessing when the feeling is mutual. If the answer to the question "Do I like him?" is "No," then let him go.

Evaluate, Evaluate, Evaluate: Stop, Look, Listen, Then Evaluate Again

The Smart Heart Partnering Process is not a test that someone has to pass or fail. It is a means for you to become more conscious about yourself, as well as your partner, to determine if you are making a wise partnering choice. You learn to pay attention to the man you are with in order to evaluate him. Later, I will more specifically show how to find out critical information about a man's personality, values, beliefs, interests, lifestyles, and goals. From the first time you date a man, you should be alert and learning to determine if he might be right for you, if you wish to date him for fun and common interests, or if you want him for a long-term partner.

The process of evaluating him should begin from the first encounter and continue over the entire course of the relationship. By the end of the first date you should be able to answer some important questions, the answers to which may tell you enough for you to know you don't want to go out with him a second time. Other answers may take months to discern. After three or four dates, you should ask (in a provocative way) enough pertinent questions, truly listening to the answers, so that you know more about him than if he likes action movies and Russian dressing on his salad.

Generally, people in a new relationship are on their best behavior for the first six to eight months, after which time who they really are starts to become evident. Everyone knows a couple who fell in love and married after five or six dates whose relationship worked out beautifully, but those lucky exceptions only underscore the rule. For the rest of us, it can take up to a year (or longer, if you are in your twenties and still evolving, or if the romance is being conducted long-distance) to learn enough to determine whether or not a man is the right one.

Don't wait for a man to volunteer the information you need. If he is a big talker, some of the answers to your questions might emerge naturally throughout the course of your conversations with him, but this is not usually the case. It then becomes your responsibility actively to ask for answers.

I am not advocating interrogation until he breaks. There are more subtle ways for you to incorporate these topics into the natural progression of conversation. Try bringing up a topic by telling him how you think, feel, or relate to a given issue. You could say, "I am living in a small apartment right now and don't have a lot of privacy or outdoor space. I hate having my neighbors know my business. Someday I would like to move out of the city and perhaps live in a house. Where do you live now? Are you happy with that situation?" Of course, if he invites you to his house, you can observe much for yourself. Pointed questions or conversations may not be necessary. It doesn't necessarily matter how the answers come to you, as long as you gather important, concrete facts about his life and are willing to be proactive in drawing them out if they are not readily forthcoming.

Here are some guidelines for questions that might help get your brain percolating.

What Is He Like?

▶ Where and how does he live?
Does he live in his car? A penthouse? With five roommates? What is the ratio of beer cans to bookcases? Is his place decorated and arranged comfortably, indicating that he cares for his living space; or is there junk everywhere with milk crates holding up the stereo and TV, indicating that he hasn't put a lot of thought or money into how he lives?

▶ What is his lifestyle?
Does he like being out late every night drinking until the early hours?

Does he get up early in the morning to exercise, read the newspaper, and drink coffee before the day begins? Does he seem overly materialistic or concerned about his possessions?

▸ What is his attitude toward work?
Does he have any career goals, and, if so, what are they? What kind of work does he do? Does he enjoy his job or would he rather be doing something else? What has he accomplished thus far? Is that on a par with your past achievements?

▸ What is his financial situation?
Are his finances in order, or does he squander whatever money he has? You might want to ask yourself if you're happy with who he is now, or are you attracted to his potential? (I discuss this question in more depth in chapter 10.)

▸ On the surface, do your personalities seem compatible?
If you're still in the early stages of a relationship, you need to make a simple, quick assessment to determine if your personalities might be compatible. For example, is he generally taciturn and argumentative, or is he usually friendly and in a good mood? Is he cynical, skeptical, or sarcastic while you're happy-go-lucky? Take a broad-brush look at how he is when he is with you and how that feels in relation to how you are with him. Later on, as the relationship progresses, you might want to have him fill out the Personal/Partner Profiler so that you both get a more in-depth look at each other.

▸ Are your sexual appetites harmonious in terms of frequency, risks, fantasies, etc.?

▸ What are his friends like?
Does he have many friends? Do you seem to be his only friend? If so, are you willing to fill that role? Is he reluctant to introduce you to his friends? If so, this could be a major danger sign. Does he have deep friendships with other men and women? Does he seem to be with friends out of genuine affection, history, or common interests?

▸ What are his ethics, values, and spiritual beliefs? Are they similar to yours? Was he raised in a particular religious tradition? If so, does he still practice those beliefs?
Does he attend worship services regularly and does his daily life reflect

89

those beliefs, or does he exhibit contrary behavior during the rest of the week?

▶ How does he relate to others—women, colleagues, relatives, children? Does he demonstrate a standard of good behavior, both professionally and personally?

▶ How does he deal with authority? How does he relate to subordinates and superiors?

▶ What are his attitudes toward the elderly or the handicapped and disadvantaged?

▶ Does he have a philosophy that serves as his moral compass? Does he seem to maintain his dignity and integrity?

▶ How does he treat you? Is he polite? Does he open the door for you? Does he call when he says he's going to call? Is he consistent? Do his words match his behavior?

▶ What does he value? (country, religious or spiritual beliefs, community)

What Are His Past Influences?

▶ Where and how was he raised? If you've met his family, do you like what you see? Are they nice to you? Is he nice to you in front of them? How does he treat his mother? His behavior toward her could reveal a lot about his attitude toward all women. If he behaves negatively toward his family, does he blame them for things that are not working in his life today? Due to his upbringing, is he used to a particular lifestyle that is in direct conflict with the way you were brought up or how you would like to live? If there are vast differences, do you think you will be able to surmount them? Are you open to a different lifestyle? Would you be willing to merge your styles of living? If you haven't met his family, does he speak about them in a positive or negative way?

▶ What do you know about his past relationships? If he says all the women in his past were bitches and bimbos, guess who the next bitch and bimbo is going to be? If he says nothing, you should wonder what he might be hiding. Most men won't offer this information voluntarily; you need to ask them. *A word of caution:* Don't start the conversation by revealing all the details of your relationship history as a way of getting him to share. Women do need to know about men's histories and can usually handle the truth; in contrast, men don't want to know about your past because picturing you with other men often bothers them or hurts their ego. (This is one double standard that is probably here to stay.) You need to ask him things like "How did the relationship end?" "What was your part in how and why the relationship ended?" "What did you like or not like about the person with whom you had the relationship?"

▶ What life experiences left a mark on him?
Has he been victimized by great losses, either financially or personally? I was in a relationship with a man for two years before I found out that his father had committed suicide. If he has suffered life-shattering trauma, what has he done to heal these wounds? Were his parents divorced? Were there suicides or premature deaths in the family? If he's done nothing to work through them, these experiences will most certainly affect you and your relationship with him.

▶ Does he have any major illnesses, genetic predispositions, or sexually transmitted diseases?
Try to discover what his health history is on both sides of his family. Is there a history of premature death, heart attack, diabetes, high blood pressure, fertility problems, emphysema, mental illness, or substance abuse?

▶ Is he battling any addictions?
Drugs, food, sex, and gambling are all major addiction problems in contemporary society. It is important to notice if he's always taking pills, if his moods alter radically, or if he spends extended periods of time out of contact with you. Watch and notice what is going on. There are some specific behaviors outlined in chapter 10, "Bad Boys Are Bad Bets," to look for if you suspect a problem. If he does have an addiction, is he involved in a twelve-step program that is helping him overcome it? If so, how long has he been involved in such a program and to what degree does he participate? Does he regularly attend meetings, go to therapy, or meet with a spiritual advisor?

If you are involved in a relationship that has become increasingly serious but have nagging questions or suspicions, you might consider the decidedly unromantic notion of hiring a professional to investigate him. Especially when things are going well, women often lose their clarity and objectivity. Offhand comments referring to mounting debts or multiple ex-wives often go unexplored. A typical background check can reveal criminal convictions, prior marriages, employment history, and IRS debt, among other useful information.

If you are a successful woman with income and assets—e.g., property, inheritance, investments, or life savings—you need to be responsible about protecting them. Women have this feeling that is it unromantic and distrustful to take action without a man knowing that you are checking out his history and financial situation, when the fact is you cannot be responsible for your situation if you don't take action to protect yourself.

I wish I had more thoroughly checked out one ex-boyfriend, who claimed to be a highly successful investment banker when he actually was a low-level clerk at the firm where he worked. Only after months of dating did it become painfully evident that the man was broke and not all that he had claimed to be.

If the search yields positive results, you will feel more comfortable knowing that you and your assets are safe. If something negative is revealed, it is better to leave quickly to avoid dangerous and costly consequences in the future. Licensed private investigators are listed in your local phone book and on the Internet.

Finding Mr. Right Takes Clear Intention, Commitment, Footwork, and Faith

Smart women grow up feeling that they can make things happen at will. As children, when we wanted to do well on a test in school, we studied to pass it. As teens, if we wanted to purchase a stereo or a car, we would get an after-school job to save money for it. Even in college, if we wanted to get into a sorority, we did what was required to be accepted by the group.

Finding the right husband or partner isn't like that, however. Settling for the wrong man just because he is handy or we are ready isn't the hallmark of a woman using her head to make relationship choices. You need to accept that finding the right man takes time and effort—time to evaluate him, effort to seek him out, plus the willingness to let go and start all over if he turns out not to be the one for you. The process isn't as quick or easy as we might like, but our efforts can result in years of happiness and a satisfying relationship. It is worth the work and the wait.

Even someone like Jamie, a successful screenwriter who believed the hype that her chances of getting killed by a terrorist were greater than the odds of getting married, benefited from this process. Jamie had never been married or proposed to. Now that she was forty, she wanted to get married. She had spent so much time building a successful career that she hadn't previously thought about being involved in any meaningful, long-term relationships. Jamie admitted to me that she was fearful that, now that she was older, her chances for marriage were slim to none. She had been dating for a long time, but even though she was meeting a lot of men and getting asked out, she wasn't meeting anyone she truly responded to, which only added to her discouragement.

Jamie needed to decide what her relationship objectives were. She needed to discern what kind of man she was looking for—i.e., what his qualities, values, concerns, and characteristics were, what he looked like, what kind of work he did, how he would contribute to and complement her existing lifestyle. We discussed what she thought she needed and wanted so that she could come up with a clear relationship objective.

She decided that she wanted to be with someone who was creative, like herself. Even a nine-to-five job, if it's the right one, can be creative and utilize an individual's talents. It was important to her that her partner understand her creative needs. She also wanted to be with someone who didn't have children from a previous marriage, preferably a person who hadn't been married before at all. Because she was Jewish, she wanted someone else who was Jewish. In addition, she was interested in finding someone who was physically attractive.

Once Jamie decided what she wanted, she designed her relationship objective. Then, she had to declare it. She told all her friends that she wanted to get married and what kind of guy she was looking for. She held that intention in her heart and mind. She had to change her old belief pattern, which insisted that, all evidence to the contrary, there wasn't a man out there for her. Holding an intention is like keeping faith alive in a conscious way, which is what Jamie did for the first time in her life.

I also suggested that she write down these objectives on nice paper and put it in a special, beautiful box in her house so it could be near her to gather and draw energy toward her. I call it a "God Box," "Intention Box," or "Universal Energy Box." You might want to do something similar. Write down your intention and put it somewhere special—in a box, special bag,

93

folder, envelope, or journal somewhere near you to look at and draw inspiration and encouragement from whenever you feel your resolve waning.

Jamie began to go out on dates again, but her objectives were never far from her consciousness. She became more courageous about asking direct questions of these new men. She learned how to evaluate men more quickly and separate the facts from her fears and feelings. If she met someone who was clearly looking for some casual fun or didn't fit in with her plan, she lovingly and respectfully let him go and moved on to someone else. This is something she never used to have the courage to do because of the fear that no one better would come along.

Almost six months after she made her list, Jamie went to an art opening at a local gallery where she met an attractive Jewish architect who had never been married and didn't have any children. He happened to be at the opening because his firm was in the same building as the gallery. He had run down to take a quick look at the show and have some wine and cheese. He met Jamie and they started talking. They dated for seven months. During that time they both shared with each other that they wanted to be married and to start a family. They knew they shared the same objective, in addition to their common interests and values. Ten months later, they were married.

Jamie's story illustrates how being clear about your objectives, stating them to yourself, your partner, and the world, and holding out until that objective manifests itself has true power. You can see what happens when you are open to the outcome and keep practicing evaluating the people in your life to discover whether or not they are appropriate for you. You also have to practice, as Jamie did, disengaging from relationships that don't meet your objectives, so that you can find Mr. Right rather than settling for Mr. Right Now.

6

Conscious Dating: How to Make Him Squeal, and What Not to Reveal

The Smart Heart woman shares her dating objectives with the people who most need to know them—her dates. Even on the first date, you must let your man know what your relationship objectives are. A woman using her head, along with her heart, in dating must realize that, although it may feel awkward or uncomfortable at first, telling a man the truth is a critical step in getting to your objective. Practicing being honest with your next few dates will make you into a life-long pro.

Why is it important to share your dating objectives? It's the only way you can know if he has similar goals. Being forthright is the only way he will know what you are looking for. You can subsequently avoid any games, guessing, and misreading of confusing clues. In order to become a Smart Heart woman, you must know what you want in a relationship and learn to feel comfortable asking a man if he wants the same thing as well.

When I tell many women in my practice about this crucial part of the process, some of them act as if I were asking them to walk naked down Rodeo Drive on Saturday afternoon. The fear they have about stating their objectives up front goes beyond the fear of revealing this information on a first date. Many women have been in relationships for years and still have not made it clear to their partners what their true objectives are. It is astounding that smart women behave in such a manner. This self-destructive behavior doesn't help you reach your objectives and it can cost you years in unproductive relationships.

Why do so many women feel uncomfortable being honest about what they want in their relationships? One reason is that they don't feel that they deserve to get what they want. Another reason is that many women fear that if they tell the truth, men will leave them. If you are truthful with a man and he leaves you, it is better that he leave on a second date rather than after you have invested a lot of time and energy in trying year after year to make something work that won't.

How and when do you express these objectives to your man, date, or existing partner? The answer is simple. Tell him what it is you want and ask him what he wants. The sooner you clarify what you are looking for, the better.

Honesty isn't just the best policy; it is the only policy. It will save you a lot of time, energy, and heartbreak. Remember—tell, ask, listen.

Don't Be a Banana

When you know who you are and what you want, you can't share that information too soon. If you ask a man, although he may never volunteer this information, he will tell you the truth more often than not. Generally, a man is not interested in withholding information or in playing games, unless he is a really bad bet.

The clearer you are about yourself, the more efficient and effective you will be at evaluating men, starting with your first conversation with them. Certainly, within two or three conversations and one date, you can assess if you are on the same page in terms of what you are both looking for. If a man is looking for a partner with whom he can have a long-term relationship, he'll tell you up front, if you ask. By directing the conversation and asking him pointed questions, you will probably hear: "Yes, I am interested in marriage" or "No, I don't want to be married" or "I just want a ski buddy and a dinner date right now" or "I'm just starting my business." By the way, when a man makes a statement about business commitments, he is **not** usually interested in starting a long-term relationship. You will have to extrapolate the meaning of such a statement. Chances are, if he says "I'm focusing on building my business right now," it is unlikely that "I am really looking forward to settling down with someone" will follow. It is important

to listen to him and believe him because nine times out of ten he is telling the truth.

You mustn't pretend. After hearing what a man wants, if a woman really cares for him, the tendency is for her to bend or compromise her own needs in order to meet his. Alternatively, she may suppress her needs in the hope of eventually changing his mind or in the expectation that he will come around to her way of thinking.

There is a story I share with women in my practice that is very helpful in explaining the importance of being your true self in a relationship and of being able to sever a relationship, if it is not what either party wants. I call it the "The Banana and the Peach."

Let's say you go to a party and you see a fabulous guy across the room. You look at him and flirt with him with your eyes and body language, signaling that it's safe for him to approach. He makes his way over to you and starts talking. After some conversation, he says to you, "Wow! You are the most fantastic BANANA I have ever met!" In your heart of hearts, you know that you are no banana, you are a PEACH. Still, you think that this is the greatest guy you've ever come across.

You then run down to the costume store and get yourself a banana suit and zip yourself into it. For the next six months, you try to pretend that you are the best banana ever in order to stay with this fantastic man. Ultimately, he is going to peel down your skin, bite into you, and discover you are not a banana but a peach. You will honor yourself and save a lot of time and energy if you are able to tell the man when you first meet him, "You know what? I'm not a banana. I'm a big, delicious, juicy peach. If what you are looking for is a banana, you should really go find one because I deserve someone who loves big, delicious, juicy peaches."

By stating who you are and what you want up front, you save yourself heartache and anxiety. In the end, he will find out the truth anyway. If you pretend to be something you're not, you put yourself in the precarious position of being taken advantage of by any man you are with because you have demonstrated that you are amenable to pretenses and open to any suggested change. For instance, he might say, "Honey, you are so beautiful, but you would be even more beautiful if you got breast implants, or cut your hair short, or lost some weight, or wore different clothes, or stopped talking so much." I see this happen to women all the time. While you must be willing to make small changes to please your partner, just as he should be willing to make small changes to please you, major compromises should be avoided. Women initially agree to make such changes because they think, "Well, he wouldn't ask me to do this if he didn't love me." If a man asks a woman to make major changes in her appearance or personality, she should say to her partner, "You know what? If that's what you want, then you should have it, but you are not going to have that with me."

Sally is a thirty-year-old southerner who adores spicy Cajun cooking and steamy jazz. Her wild side often got the best of her, and she was prone to embarking on spur-of-the-moment adventures. Once, she and a boyfriend drove all night to an amusement park so they could be the first to ride the gravity-defying parachute drop. Fun was a very important aspect of her life, but now that she was getting older, she decided it was time to start being serious about getting married and starting a family.

Two days after her thirtieth birthday, Sally met a handsome, charming accountant from a conservative New England family who clearly had never applied the word *adventure* to his own experiences. Sally decided she would have to tame her sizzling streak if she wanted to have a relationship leading to marriage with Ted.

When he took her to a "steak and potato" restaurant on their first date, she heartily ate a steak, even though she usually ate only fish and vegetables. When he took her to the opera, she tried her best to seem interested but spent half the time trying to stay awake. When he took her to a polo match on a sunny Saturday afternoon, she put on her most conservative skirt and went along, even though she had had her heart set on a hike to a breathtaking waterfall. Not once did she admit to him that steak wasn't her favorite food, that opera bored her to tears, and that she couldn't stand watching those poor horses in a sport she felt bordered on animal abuse.

It took Sally seven months to realize that she had transformed herself into something she wasn't. No matter how great this man may have looked on the outside, if she couldn't be herself, there was no point in being with him simply to fulfill her longing for a committed relationship or because he fit some idealistic image she held of a potential partner.

When you contort your true nature, you can't relax and enjoy your time with the man you altered yourself for. Inevitably, burying your true identity leads to resentment at not being able to let your real self and interests show. What's more, when you finally do get "peeled" and are discovered as the peach you are, the man will inevitably feel duped and disappointed. Don't be a banana just because he wants a banana. Be a great, juicy peach with a man who thinks that fuzzy fruit is the most delicious kind of all.

Exercise: Are You Trying to Be a Banana When You're Not One?

Which of the following statements describe you?

I act as if:

- I don't want children when I really do.
- I like going to and watching sporting events when I really don't.
- It is okay with me when he dates other people when it's not.
- I love his mother when I hate her guts.
- I'm happy playing second or third banana to his business and his friends.
- I am easygoing about the casual status of our relationship when all I really want is a serious committed relationship.
- I am serious about marriage and kids, when I'm really just looking for a good time.
- Going trout fishing in Alaska is my idea of a good time when touring through European cities is more my speed.

Although a man will usually openly and honestly state where he is and what he wants, he will seldom ask you what you want. Don't sit there talking on the phone or across the dinner table from him waiting for him to give you the perfect opening to state your objective. I've rarely heard a man say, "So, Suzanne, tell me what you are really looking for in terms of a relationship." If you are holding your breath for that to happen, you will either turn blue from not breathing or grow old waiting. You have to be proactive and just say it. He will undoubtedly not make the correlation between this pleasant dinner date and his search for a long-term, meaningful relationship, even if that is what he wants. A man may be hunting because he is hungry, but if you ask him, he will just say that he is hunting. A man will respond to you truthfully, as long as he doesn't feel trapped or put on the hot seat. The best way to state your objectives and gather information is to:

1 Share your own experiences (although not in great detail) using "I" statements.

❷ Ask him how he feels.

❸ **Listen** to what he says.

For example, you might say, "My business is doing great. *I* really love what I am doing, and *I* am excited and interested in creating the next chapter of my life. *I* would like to meet someone special and settle down. How do you feel about your life right now?"

He might respond, "Well, I'm starting a business now and it's a lot more time-consuming than I thought." How this translates from "man-speak" is: "I don't have enough time to be in a long-term relationship right now because my first priority is my business." If he is not able to continue with a conversation about future plans, move on.

Special note of warning: Discussing your old boyfriends and past relationships in detail can be hazardous to any relationship.

Men never want to hear about your old boyfriends or past relationships in any detail, but you need to hear about his past relationships so you can evaluate how he was with women in his life. If you ask him, he'll probably be more than happy to tell you, but if he asks you about your past relationships never interpret this question as a sign of genuine interest in the answer, or his ability to hear or handle this information. He isn't really interested in the truth about your past relationships and boyfriends. He wants to think that he is the first one ever to be with you, although rationally he knows that couldn't be true. Your support of this illusion will be beneficial to your future with him. It is a paradox that a man wants you to have the experience of having been with other men so that you will know how to pleasure and support him and he won't have to teach you everything. Nevertheless, he wants to believe that you have magically obtained this knowledge and experience without having been with anyone else.

When he asks you about past boyfriend and relationships, you need to deflect his questions carefully. You might say something like "Of course I've had other relationships, but none of them compares with you." The key is always to make him feel that he is the important one in your life now. Never say anything like "I've slept with fifty guys, and you are the best so far." Even if you believe that, by comparison, it's complimentary to the guy you are currently dating to tell him how bad your last boyfriend was, men never see it that way.

A man is visually oriented by nature, and the last thing you want to do is give him a clear mental picture of you with someone other than him, even if that other guy was a loser. Try "I have been with a few men, but being with them was all about getting myself ready for you, because you are the one for me. You are the best man I have ever been with." He might respond, "Oh, come on, you've been with other cool guys," but you could then say, "They are not important to me now. What's really important now is you."

Another warning: Especially in the beginning, it is better not to reveal negative and dramatic/traumatic personal histories, whether they have to do with your childhood or past boyfriends. I am not advocating lying about your history, but I do recommend avoiding specifics and then turning the conversation back to him. For example, there are certain kinds of things you don't necessarily want to reveal on the first date—e.g., if you grew up in an alcoholic home, were beaten and raped by your father, are a recovering alcoholic and drug addict, used to be a prostitute, or were living with a guy who beat you, ripped you off, and left you without a dime. Often there are circumstances that have shaped your past and created who you are now that it may not be advisable to reveal to the man you are with. You might feel it is none of his business if, in fact, you have dealt with these issues and they are no longer a part of who you are today. He doesn't need to know what your past negative struggles were as much as you need to discern if he has dealt with his past struggles. It is our tendency, as women, to want to reveal everything all the time and to bare our souls to someone we love. Information of a sensitive nature, however, is often difficult for men to handle. It is preferable to process this type of experience with a therapist, spiritual counselor, or some other professional or neutral party. You don't want to lay these confessions at the feet of your partner who, by his masculine nature, might feel prompted to do something about them. He may feel threatened, intimidated, or fearful that the "old you" might resurface in the relationship and he would be incapable of dealing with it. Perhaps, over time, if you become involved in a long-term, intimate relationship you may want to share certain aspects of your life with him, but it is very burdensome for men to hear specific negative things about which they can do nothing—and sometimes they are scared away.

Here's a sample conversation that you might find helpful in laying out your relationship objective:

You're out on your first date with a great guy whom you met through a friend. After some pleasantries, you could begin by saying, "At this point in my life, I am really interested in having a long-term relationship with some-

101

one (I'm not particularly referring to you). I really don't want to be dating just for casual sex or to have someone to go Rollerblading with. How do you feel about this? What are you looking for?" If he says "Yeah, I'm looking for that, too. I've been single for a while and I want to have someone to share my life with," you could ask, "Well, how long have you been single?"

He might answer, "Over twelve years."

You could then ask, "Well, if you've been interested in settling down for twelve years, why haven't you made a connection yet? What do you think is stopping you?" In this case, his answer might alert you to some danger signs because you have to wonder what it means when he says he has been trying to find a partner, but after all that time it hasn't happened. What has been going on in his life and mind that has kept him from meeting his own stated goals? **Carefully listen to his answers.** Conversely, if he has been single for the last year and a half, has been out of a relationship, and now wants to make a commitment, chances are he actually is ready and has been going through his own stages of personal development.

The goal of having such a conversation is threefold:

1 You state clearly and confidently where you are on the relationship continuum.

2 You find out where he is on the continuum and then determine if you are in the same place or at opposite ends of the spectrum.

3 You get valuable insight into his personality by finding out about his relationship history and discover what might manifest itself in the future, if you choose to proceed with the relationship.

Another major advantage of these early exploratory conversations is that whatever answers you get from him have nothing to do with you, because you just met him. His answers won't yet be colored by how he feels about you, and your perception of his answers won't be colored by how attached you might have become to him.

If the Answers Point to "No," Let Him Go

Most women have the ability to get into a relationship but not get out of one, even when it is wrong for them. You must learn how to extricate yourself from a relationship as quickly as possible if it isn't working or meeting your relationship objectives. Women need to practice getting out of bad relationships rather than staying in them because they are afraid of hurting men's feelings.

Why is leaving a bad relationship so hard for women to do? Because, not knowing what their goals are and not valuing themselves enough, they are more comfortable staying in a relationship until the man decides it is time to release them. When you allow a man to decide when to end a relationship, even if you also want it to end, you give away your power.

There are many excuses women give as legitimate reasons for not breaking up with men. A great lament is "He's so kind; I don't want to hurt his feelings." Just because a guy is nice doesn't mean he is romantically right for you. It just means he is nice. No matter how many positive characteristics a man has, if he is not the right partner for you, if you don't want the same things, you must end the relationship. Keep in mind that he is a grown-up and he'll get over it; you're a grown-up, too, and you'll also get over it.

"It isn't the right time to tell Ben I don't want to see him anymore," twenty-seven-year-old Clara laments. "He just started a new job, and I don't want to unsettle his life any more than it already is."

It can be harmful to take Clara's approach. When you don't leave relationships honestly, your subconscious often removes you in other ways— e.g., by generating negativity and big dramas, overeating and gaining weight, having affairs, creating conflict, lying, or seeking refuge in alcohol or drugs to force the person to leave you. These behaviors are manipulative and immature. More important, they are self-defeating and self-destructive. Why suffer, torture, or hurt yourself because you are no longer interested in being with someone and are afraid of hurting him? You need to learn how to manage your own fears and anxieties, as well as take responsibility for them, not leaving it up to the other person.

Know That There Is No Right Moment to Tell the Truth

Some occasions are more optimal than others, so exercise tact and good judgment. There is, however, a preferable way to go about telling the truth. It is more effective to use statements that begin with "I." When letting a man go, you need to:

1 Be complimentary and appreciate him for his positive traits.

2 State that the relationship isn't working for you.

❸ Support and acknowledge what is great about him. Let him know that you believe that the right someone is going to choose him, just as the right person is going to choose you, and this will be better for both of you.

Don't begin with an inventory of all that you didn't like about the guy. Don't say, "I'm not going to be with you because you are an abusive, arrogant, selfish jerk" (even if it's true). It's unnecessary to assassinate his character or hurt his feelings simply to make an exit. It dishonors you and him and, in effect, only makes things worse. The most effective, least hurtful way to say good-bye is to speak about your own experience and to acknowledge his positive qualities, no matter how minimal they may be.

Some examples are as follows:

❶ "You are a bright, successful man and I'm sure that there is a wonderful woman out there who is perfect for you, but this isn't really what I'm looking for. I honor and respect you too much to waste your time and I honor and respect myself enough not to want to waste my time. I'm sorry, but this isn't going to work out for me."

❷ "You have been really fun to hang out with, but I see that you want this to get more serious. I don't feel we're right for each other for the long term, so I don't think we should see each other anymore."

❸ "This relationship isn't what I need right now. I'm interested in getting married, and you're not the right person for me. I'd prefer that you didn't call me again."

❹ "I'd like to marry someone with whom I have a lot in common. You are a really nice person, but I don't feel we're compatible."

Don't leave the conversation open-ended by saying something like "I don't think this is going to work out for **you**." He will feel compelled to give you all the reasons why you are perfect for him. I have known many women who tried to get out of relationships by saying "I'm not the right person for you," and the men inevitably say "No, you are great! You are exactly what I want." No one wants to be told what is or is not working for him. People want to make their own decisions.

You might say, "I am flattered that you are interested in me, and I've enjoyed the time we have shared. You are a lot of fun and have a great sense of humor, but this isn't right for me. It is not what I want for my life at this moment. I know there is somebody who right for you, just as I know there is someone who right for me, but this isn't the right situation for either of us."

The Sooner the Better

If it becomes clear that the two of you are on divergent paths and you realize that it is time to end a relationship, tell him right away. Do it briefly in one conversation. Don't delay or string out the process, dropping a few hints each week in hopes that he'll catch on. Making a smooth, clean break will allow you both to move on, heal, and be ready for the next opportunity. When you first let him go, his feelings might be hurt, but ultimately you are doing him a favor by giving him the space to get over you and find someone else.

Coming to the end of a relationship is difficult, but it is harder to stay in a bad one longer than you'd like to. Leaving will be hurtful, but that is a part of life. Your responsibility is to remain true to yourself and keep your objectives clear within your heart and mind.

You cannot be available to meet someone else if you are spending your time with the wrong man. Mystics and seers believe that when you close one door, another opens. Have the courage to open the door of your heart to the universe. With diligence and a sprinkling of luck, the right man *will* turn up soon.

Never use breaking up to threaten or manipulate a man into changing his mind or to force him to give in to your desires.

Don't break up with him if you want him to say "No, don't go! I love you. I need you. I'll do anything to stay with you." Believing this will happen is magical thinking. A response like that is rare. If it does occur, it is usually insincere or reactionary. If you need the reassurance of a commitment, request it. Ask him to express his deeper feelings, rather than creating an immature, negative drama that will shake the foundation of trust between you.

Before You Let Him Go, Make Sure
the Answers Point to "No"

Even if all or most of the answers point to "No," you need to make sure that there aren't more "Yes's." *It is important not to overreact immediately and dump him before you see if he displays a willingness to change. What initially seems like a "No" may be alterable if he does want to change and realizes this is better for both of you.*

Remember Tim and Janine from chapter 1? Things were going well for them. He set appropriate boundaries with his ex-wife as Janine had asked him to. They became more intimate, and, after seven months of seeing each other, Tim told Janine that he had herpes, which he had contracted a long time ago and had kept under control. He explained that he had been really safe with her and had done everything he could to protect her, but he knew that he was on the verge of an outbreak and felt that he should tell her because he didn't want to expose her to this sexually transmitted disease.

At first, Janine felt betrayed and horrified. She was incredulous that he had waited seven months into the relationship to tell her about his condition. I told her, "You can choose to be upset and hurt by the news, but let's first look at the good things. Why would he wait to tell you? If he really liked you, he would be worried about telling you too early for fear you might leave him. He has been respectful and hasn't directly exposed you to the disease. Although it feels as if he has betrayed you, he is coming forward to let you know that you need to protect yourself. You can choose not to trust him at all and leave him, or you can choose to have compassion about his fear and his inability to trust in your love for him. If this were a situation in which someone exposed you to a deadly sexually transmitted disease such as AIDS, or another serious sexually transmitted or communicable disease, it would be a completely different situation. Obviously, there is a distinction between life-threatening circumstances and those that, although they may be disappointing and hurtful, need not necessarily be cause for ending the relationship. You could focus on the betrayal and distrust, but isn't it better to look at what is working and is good about him and your relationship?"

Here is an example from my own life: I had been dating a certain man for about a month and a half. On Valentine's Day, he gave me a card and a tiny bottle of perfume. When my birthday came up a few weeks later, he gave me a very sweet, thoughtful card but didn't make any plans to take me out to dinner or do anything special. I gently and lovingly told him, "I really like you and think you are a wonderful man with many great qualities. I am grateful for the cards and perfume, but I have to be honest with you. Valentine's Day and my birthday are both special occasions for me. Not making a special effort to extend yourself and do something extra has hurt my feelings. It is important to me that you respect me enough to make plans on special occasions in advance. If you don't want to or you can't because it's too much for you, that's okay; but if that is the case, then I am unable to continue seeing you."

He listened to what I said and admitted I was right. He said that he had spent over an hour choosing just the right card to express his feelings for me, which I thought was very sweet. I was glad to know he had taken that kind of care and gone to so much effort. Although he didn't bring me champagne and flowers on every date after that, he did start to make changes and begin to call more frequently, make plans in advance, and, several weeks later, he took me to a luxurious hotel for a long, beautiful weekend.

I could have ended the relationship as a result of my hurt feelings and his lack of awareness concerning special occasions, but after I lovingly explained to him what my needs and wants were, he was able to respond in a way that was more satisfying for me. As a result, we both enjoyed our time together even more. He was pleased because I was happy and felt special, and he became more considerate and aware of what brings me pleasure. As our relationship continued to grow, so did our ability to communicate with each other. He benefits from being with me because I greatly care about him. He feels that love and caring through my direct action and acknowledgment of the truly loving man he is. In the beginning, give your man the benefit of the doubt since he may not readily be aware of what is good, bad, right, or wrong in caring for you.

It doesn't occur to many women to say what they want, even concerning the small things. You need to decide what is important for you; i.e., how you want to be treated and what constitutes respect, attention, and caring for you. You then need to communicate these things to the man you're with. Before you let him go, give him a chance to respond, evolve, and grow into a new way of being. He just may surprise you.

This idea doesn't just apply to birthday cards and long-weekend getaways. You need to take a stand for whatever you think is right. If an abusive man is not allowed to be abusive with you, he becomes a better man. If you don't allow a man to be inconsiderate of you, he can become a more thoughtful man. If you let him know that rude behavior doesn't work for you, he has an opportunity to become more sensitive and respectful, not only to you but also to all women with whom he comes in contact.

Conscious Dating

When you decide what your relationship objective is (i.e., Are you dating for companionship, fun and sex, long-term relationship, parenting and partnering, or just friendship?), you must be courageous enough to take risks to go out and get it. Taking risks means getting into the action. In order to do this, you need to date. You might need some tips, however, especially if you've never really dated before or if you are recently back on the dating scene after a lengthy absence (due to, for example, divorce, being widowed, or a self-imposed abstinence to focus on your career).

During an era like the seventies, which was freer sexually, many women fell in love and fell into bed by the second or third date. Even today, despite greater sexual caution, a man who comes over to watch a video and have a pizza may end up spending the night with you and never leave. By consciously dating, using your head as well as your heart, you can enjoy getting to know someone new and be able to discern whether or not he is worth spending time and energy on and if he is in alignment with your prospective goals.

Fun and Fundamental Tips: The Importance of Flirting in Creating an Open Path for a Man to Move Toward You

Flirting is not old-fashioned, manipulative, or stupid. Nonverbal flirting with a man with whom you're unacquainted is the only way to let him know it is safe to approach you. If you don't give him some signal that he is more special than the thirty other guys who are in the room, he will not know that you have your eye on him. Don't wait for him to notice you first. If you pay some attention to him, he will notice you and will probably be interested in meeting you.

When a young man is interested in the opposite sex, he's willing to take many risks. When you were nineteen or twenty, didn't it seem as if more strangers approached you in social situations? The truth is, as men get older, they don't retain their former brazenness and testosterone-driven urge to make the first move. Most men over twenty-five have been rejected by women numerous times and are weary and wary of taking the risk of putting themselves out there if they don't have some kind of sign that they won't be rejected. They have already had sex. They know what it feels like and enjoy it, but they are less than likely to approach someone who is not approachable, who has her nose in the air, is averting her eyes, or is hiding among a large group of friends. Some women may be inviting and receptive to men in whom they have no interest, but when they spot someone they would like to meet, they suddenly turn shy and look down or away. If this is your tendency, you need to practice changing that.

How do you get a guy to approach you? Here's the secret formula: Look at him directly, making eye contact, while you smile and count to ten slowly. Then, keep smiling. That's it! If you continue to look at him and smile, he will eventually walk over to you and begin a conversation. Invite him in with your eyes and an open demeanor, or else he won't risk an approach. If this is something that you don't think you can do naturally or without being self-conscious, you can practice in low-risk, inconsequential situations. Smile and count at the man behind the counter at the dry cleaners. Smile and count at the bus driver as you step on the bus. Smile and make eye contact with a man in the produce aisle of the grocery store or the guy next to you at the gym. I smile at men when I am walking through airports. If a man is walking by me, I will smile at him as he passes by and then watch as he trips over himself.

Another reason to smile at a man is because men want to be with women who are happy and confident. A smile is the best way to convey that. People gravitate toward those who appear self-assured. You need to project outwardly what's on the inside. Even if you don't feel you have it together, it doesn't matter. *Smile and act as if you do.* You'll be surprised how quickly you really start to feel that way.

If you meet someone through mutual friends or colleagues and you're interested, tell those friends you would be happy to go out with their friend. He might need to know that you would definitely say "yes" if he were to ask you. Often, the mere power of suggestion will encourage him to ask you out, even if he wasn't necessarily thinking of doing so before. Plenty of relationships have started because a well-meaning acquaintance hinted that the other person was interested in him or her. Flattery works. It costs you nothing; it is a generous act; and there is no harm in using it to be proactive.

Men constantly need reassurance that it's okay for them to approach, and an invitation from you in the form of a nod, a smile, or a look implies "Yes, it's safe."

Use your inherent feminine wiles to interact with men, and bear in mind that men need as many green lights as you can possibly give them. They won't automatically take a risk on an unsure bet. You need to be open and willing to take action, giving a clear signal to men in whom you are interested that it is safe to proceed. Initiate interactions so that you can begin to determine if that person meets your criteria for a relationship. If you never get to meet him or know him, you will never discover if he will fit into your relationship design.

This part of the process requires you to be **open, not attached to a specific outcome.** Just because you meet a man at a party doesn't mean you *have* to marry him and have his children. Neither does it mean you *will* marry him and have his children. **Stay in the moment.** Concentrate on being open and observant. Watch what he does and listen to what he says.

When You Are Dating, Always Let the Man Pay

This might sound like a throwback to the 1950s but, in the beginning at least, always let men pay. When you don't, it denies an important aspect of their nature; i.e., that men like to provide for their women. When a man is courting you, the way he provides for you is not by dragging in a slain buffalo he took down on the plain but by picking up the check. If you feel uncomfortable about a man contributing in this way or you feel that if a man pays for dinner, somehow you owe him something, i.e., sex, then you need to change your way of thinking now!

When a man picks up the check, he is thanking you for the pleasure of your company. If you know your own value and worth, you should know that you are worth at least the price of dinner! Have you thought about what it costs you to prepare yourself to go out on a date? Whether you are a high-style or casual woman, you still put in substantial expense, time, and energy to prepare yourself. Things add up. For example:

stockings: $10

manicure: $10

perfume, lotion, makeup: $100

new outfit: $100–$300 (even jeans are $65 today. Throw in a Gap T-shirt, and you are up to almost $90!)

shower and prep time: one to two hours (maybe you left work early, which costs you even more)

This doesn't mean that a man may not have spent $90 for jeans and a T-shirt, or $500 for a new suit, to take you out. In general, however, men tend to wear what they have in the closet. They may iron it or clean it to prepare for you, and, I hope, take a shower, but the lengths that they go to are, by and large, a great deal less significant than our time, effort, and expense. If you find that you're dating someone who believes that because he's taken you to dinner, he has paid for the right to have sex with you, it is likely that you need to move on to another man. If his archaic way of thinking depicts you as a sexual object, he should pay directly for a hooker, rather than try to ease his conscience about that aspect of himself by buying you dinner in order to get you into bed. If you think it doesn't cost you anything, think again.

On the first few dates, leave your wallet at home. You might want to take along $10 in "mad money" to ensure that you can call a cab and get home if you need to, but don't bring credit cards, no matter what! If this makes you anxious, manage your anxiety. By sharing the cost of your dates or insisting that you pay, you stop a man from doing what he was built to do, which is to care and provide for his woman. This is not to say that, over the course of time, you shouldn't be contributing to your joint activities, especially if you are a successful woman. You can return the favor in many thoughtful ways—cook him a nice dinner, give him a gift in return for his taking you away on a nice weekend trip, but a good general rule of thumb is to let him pay, particularly in the courting stages of your relationship.

Men LOVE to Do Things for Women, but They Don't Want to Be TOLD *What to Do!*

For many independent, successful women, this may feel like a throwback to less modern days because women today tend to open their own doors, carry their own groceries, set up their own VCRs, and bring their own cars to the auto repair shop. Women need to understand, however, that just because they *can* do those things doesn't mean they always *have* to do them, especially if they have a man in their life. Allowing a man to contribute to you and your well-being by letting him do those kinds of things for you (even though you can do them for yourself) doesn't make you any less than who you are. Fending for yourself doesn't prove anything or make a man be more attracted to you because you are so independent. Letting a man do things for you actually makes him feel good about himself because he is contributing to your welfare. It also puts you more in touch with your feminine energy. Feminine energy is receptive, rather than dynamic; passive, rather than active. During impregnation, a woman can be physically passive while a man actively releases his sperm into her, and the embryo grows within her. Many women today have lost connection with their feminine energy. Of course, you need to exercise your male energy out in the world in order to survive and be successful, but when it comes to relationships with men, it is really important to remember that you can't have TWO men in the relationship, energetically speaking. Stop being the other man, energetically speaking, and practice using your feminine energy.

I know how to fill my car with gas, hang a picture, or talk to a contractor, but when I am with a man who is capable of these things, I let him handle them. I am not lazy or incapable, but relinquishing control over those things allows me to be more feminine and, frankly, it makes him feel good. Allowing him to open the door or pull out a chair enables him to extend himself and contribute to me. Graciously accepting a man's courtesy and contributions actually makes you more appealing and feminine because he feels needed. If your man isn't doing these things because it has never been requested of him, you need to ask him politely to make those kinds of contributions. I am not suggesting that you feign ineptitude as a way to manipulate or be dishonest. If he isn't good at negotiating with a contractor and you are, you can show him how it's done. Allowing him to see what you know how to do contributes to him. Don't have things done incorrectly simply to preserve his manhood, but allow him to assist and contribute in the ways he knows how.

Nonverbal Communication with Men

Regardless of how you feel about it, the fact is that there is a major distinction between men and women. Men, particularly from the ages of eighteen to forty-five, are visually oriented. In my practice, I repeatedly hear women say that it shouldn't matter how they look, what kind of physical shape they are in, or what kind of clothes they wear, because a man should be able to see through all that to the person they are inside.

The **fact** is that men cannot help that they are neurologically and genetically wired to be attracted to women, initially, by how they visually present themselves. Men are hooked for reasons they can't explain. A man will find himself attracted to a particular woman, but he won't know why. Conversely, a man can't force himself to be attracted to a woman if he's not. When it comes to finding men attractive, women usually have a variety of reasons (including looks), but they can also become increasingly more attracted over time as they become better acquainted.

It is important to look the best you can by taking care of yourself physically, making sure you are attractively dressed, neat and clean, and highlighting your best attributes. Make sure that your hair looks nice, whatever your style is. This doesn't mean that you have to be rail thin or strikingly beautiful to attract a man's attention. Whether you are a casual-jeans-and-T-shirt kind of woman or one who wears dresses and immaculate pumps, enhance what you have. Men like to be able to see what your body looks like. Don't underestimate how much energy and power of attraction a positive attitude holds. If you have a positive, optimistic outlook, not only toward men but toward life in general, men will pick up on it, and you'll be more appealing as a result.

If you want companionship, contact, and connection with a man, there are some things you must accept about the basic differences between men and women. It is important for you to know that allowing a man to contribute to you, either monetarily or energetically, does not diminish you in any way. The successful women in my practice who have been willing to step back, be still, and allow men to do things their own way and in their own time find that their lives become easier. The men that they are with keep trying to expand their contributions to them. If we allow men to use their power for us, rather than trying to control it or feeling threatened by it, we acknowledge who they are and what they can contribute to the relationship. You are a vibrant, independent, smart, successful woman who can become a better one by allowing the man you want to be with the space to become a better man. This creates a win-win situation for both of you.

PART 2

Detours, Dangers, and Disasters

As you move through the Smart Heart Partnering Process, becoming clearer and clearer about what you want and need from relationships with men, you gain the awareness that you are the one who creates your reality and generates your relationship experiences. You can choose whether to date for fun and pleasure or to commit to a more long-term relationship. This stage of the Smart Heart Partnering Process is going to help you stay on track and avoid the dangers that derail many promising relationship possibilities. To prevent your love from crashing and burning, we'll look at the kinds of people, circumstances, and thought patterns that can lead to relationship disaster and explore how you can learn to avoid them in the future.

What's Love Got to Do with It?

The answer to the question "What's love got to do with it?" (particularly as it relates to the success of a long-term, intimate relationship) is: **everything and nothing.** Part of the challenge that women face in trying to understand the nature of mature love is the limitation of the English language. Our language doesn't give us many terms for the diversity of love's expressions—e.g., love of life; love of the spirit; the love of a mother for her child or a child for his mother; the love of friendship; the burning, passionate love of an idealistic, young romantic; or the mature love of grandparents celebrating their fiftieth wedding anniversary together. Each type of love is vastly different, but we speak of them by using one generic English word—*love*.

Why does this matter? After all, we know that our love for our mother isn't the same feeling we have for a guy we've just met and can't wait to see again. By not having the proper, precise words to differentiate among the variations of love, even though we feel them naturally, we are unable to discern love's more subtle distinctions. This is one way women get themselves into big trouble. The challenge we face by not having adequate terminology for these distinctions lies in being able to comprehend the dynamics of an immature, romantic love versus a mature, adult, sexual love. Women are generally so focused on idealized, romantic concepts of love that they are unaware that these distinctions exist and what they are.

The Three Forces of Love: Eros, Sex, and Love

For love to mature, all three aspects must be operative. First is Eros, followed by Sex, which acts as an energetic bridge to the third phase, which is mature, conscious Love. Both sexes are affected by these three forces, but we are often unaware of their existence, let alone the distinctions among them. This makes it difficult to make wise choices in relationships. My teacher Dr. John Pierrakos says in his book *Eros, Love, and Sexuality*, "To love another, we must love ourselves; we must heal the split within. Eros, sexuality, and love present the possibility of unifying the masculine and feminine within each one of us and at the same time allow us to unify our soul with another being."

Eros: The First Aspect of Love

In a romantic relationship, we often feel an overwhelming, passionate desire to be with a person. It's as if Cupid had shot us with an arrow and we were powerless to do anything other than be with our beloved. We may think that this erotic feeling is the totality of love. It is erotic and exhilarating, but it is only the first stage of love, Eros.

Eros is the Greek name given to the mischievous god called Cupid by the Romans. He represents the lusty, unconscious, chemical attraction that forms the bulk of our myths and fantasies about romantic love. You may have been "struck by Cupid's arrow" in high school or college, when you fell for your first true love. It might have happened when you saw a handsome stranger across a crowded room, or perhaps with an acquaintance you've known for a while and are suddenly aware of a pulse-quickening sensation. Eros is responsible for that giddy feeling most of us experience when we first get involved with someone. We feel a quickening of our heartbeat, flushed skin, a nervous stomach, a sudden loss of appetite or ability to sleep, and an inability to concentrate on anything other than him. "Eros is a unique experience, but it is not love itself . . . it is the bridge that connects sexuality and love. Eros must be continually rekindled because it burns out just like a meteor entering the atmosphere" (John Pierrakos, *Eros, Love, and Sexuality: The Forces That Unify Man and Woman*).

The erotic force is one of the most potent energetic forces in the universe. It has incredible power and impact. It ideally serves to connect the other forces of Sex and mature Love. Once you have been struck by Cupid's arrow, this irresistible chemistry causes two bodies to merge in heightened sexual pleasure, allowing the individuals to declare their love and choose each other. Most immature interactions end at their sexual peak, and the pleasure is short-lived. In a more highly evolved connection, the pleasure of sexual contact, enhanced by the erotic experience, transports the lovers from the temporal pleasure of the erotic into a permanent state of pure love based on choice, as well as feeling.

Eros is the closest thing to real love that an unevolved individual can experience. It is like a ticket to an amusement park; it is exciting, but it's not the main attraction. When hit with this force, even the most base personality is able to rise above his primitive nature. A lout or a criminal may temporarily be able to experience a conscience and express goodness; a selfish man will become magnanimous; a lazy man will show initiative; an inflexible man will become spontaneous. The powerful force of Eros removes our feeling of separateness, if only for a short while. The erotic force gives our spirits a taste of union and ignites a longing for love. The more deeply and strongly one has felt Eros, the less one can be content to settle for being apart from either others or from life itself.

When we are under the influence of Eros, it is as if we enter an entirely new world, a paradise we cannot believe has been concealed from us for so long. Suddenly, we are consumed by thoughts and feelings for a person who may not even have been a part of our lives previously. We think about him constantly. We want him near us every moment of the day and night. Sitting across a table seems too far away. We want him beside us where we can feel his breath and touch him. Our boundaries quickly disappear and we are unsure of where we end and he begins. We are filled with delight from the pleasure of this erotic force.

Natural chemicals in the body, like dopamine and endorphins, are released in our brains. We feel an explosion of energy fueled by erotic fires, and we are enveloped in the natural high that characterizes this stage of love. These chemicals are at least partially responsible for changing our perception of the world and heightening all our senses.

Eros is a wonderful gift that the universe allows us to experience through opening our heart to another. Eros dissolves our defenses, giving us the opportunity to connect at a deeper, more intimate level.

Some men and women become addicted to the intense emotional and erotic experience of Eros. Eros junkies stay in a relationship until the erotic fire diminishes. They are quick to leave in search of another erotic experience once the initial sensation subsides. Some psychologists label these individuals "ninety-day wonders" because they tend to remain in relationships for only three to six months, typically the amount of time the initial erotic fire stays lit.

In contrast, mature and conscious love is a continuous expression. Mature love is learned and manifested as a result of creating a foundation over time, through personal evolution and commitment. Love doesn't randomly appear the way that Eros often does.

Eros can strike with surprising, unexpected force. If our spirit has prepared a foundation upon which to build a loving relationship, Eros can link men and women in a profound and sacred union. In this respect, Eros is immensely important. It frees us from the inertia of a solitary, safe existence. It rekindles an awareness of longing for connection with another being. The universe plants a seed in our souls from which we grow toward a destiny of union, rather than living out a lonely, unhappy fate.

The Erotic force can powerfully propel us into expanded levels of awareness. Eros can be enjoyed for its own sake, while it lasts, but an unevolved personality will not utilize the erotic experience to cultivate mature love. Rather, by using one partner after another, until Eros has worn off, an unenlightened individual will be emotionally ignorant when it comes to understanding a deeper meaning of the true gifts of Eros.

Some women may think it's time to end a relationship after Eros diminishes. They don't understand that Eros is not synonymous with love. They mistakenly believe that if they don't feel the rush or passion of Eros, they're no longer "in love."

One client of mine, Danielle, was a travel agent who, thanks to the perk of discount tickets, has traveled all over the world. At the age of twenty-seven, she had probably had that many boyfriends during the last five years. Then she decided she wanted a husband and children; at the pace she was going, however, she didn't see how marriage and settling down were possible. "It always seems to go the same way," she lamented. "The places and faces keep changing, but the ending is always the same."

Because she traveled so frequently, Danielle generally would meet guys on her trips. Eric, a man Danielle met several months ago in the French Virgin Islands, was typical of her dating situations. Even though Eric lived in

Philadelphia, he had been to the islands many times before. He knew all the charming little bistros, bars, and hidden romantic spots.

The flirtatious courtship of the first few days gave way to intense passion by midweek. When they consummated their relationship sexually, the lovemaking was spectacular. Danielle felt that Eric was truly different from the men she had known previously, and she couldn't wait to bring him home so he could see her new apartment, her successful business that she had built up from nothing, and her favorite neighborhood restaurants.

When the vacation ended, the pair kept up their fervent romance by telephone and e-mail during the week, and Eric went to New York nearly every weekend. About three months into the relationship, however, Danielle found herself looking at the clock, as she usually did, on Friday evenings. Instead of wondering with restless anticipation when he would finally arrive, she began feeling a twinge of anger when he wasn't there at 7:30 P.M. as he had said he would be. When he finally arrived at her apartment, the evening went fine, but the next day when she told Eric she couldn't spend the afternoon with him because she had work to do in her office, his annoyed reaction irritated her.

She started to fear that the glow surrounding him was beginning to fade. During the next few weeks, Danielle could almost sense a physical difference when it came to Eric. The headiness was gone, and the magnetic pull to be with him was weakening. The excitement no longer welled up inside her whenever she thought of him. She was sure this was a definite sign that it was time to move on. Because she didn't have the same feelings as before, she was sure this meant that she was no longer in love with Eric.

The diminishing of the erotic force can be upsetting to women who don't realize that their relationship isn't dying simply because the feelings have changed. Rather, it is progressing to the next, more enduring phase. When people are initially filled with the erotic force, they are on their best behavior with their new partners, treating them as if they're the most important people alive. During this stage, you don't burden your lover with your troubles, force him to submit to your desires, or berate him for forgetting your birthday. Those unromantic actions might scare him off and end the marvelous moments we enjoy so much.

Erotic passion is a sensational experience, and it is understandable why women like Danielle are always looking for it. A Smart Heart woman who wants a long-term, meaningful relationship will never find it flitting from one erotic experience to another. Eventually, even the most high-voltage charge between a man and a woman begins to subside in the normal progression of mature love. Most of us, however, are unwilling to make the effort to keep the spark of Eros alive by learning to love in a mature way. Without love, the erotic force will burn itself out. I perpetually hear the lament "I must not love him anymore. It just doesn't feel the same."

The erotic force is often confused with what we normally perceive as romantic love. It is also easily confused with a sexual drive that can overpower us with a seemingly uncontrollable sexual instinct. Eros is, in actuality, very different from the love and sex forces we mistake it for. On a spiritual level, it can be a gift from the gods. Without it, most people never experience the intensity of feeling and beauty that are inherent in real love. Without the taste of Eros, the desire for genuine and enduring love would remain hidden in the depths of our souls, prevented from expression by a fear of truly loving and being loved.

Sex: The Bridge Between Eros and Love

Sex is a mature, healthy component of adult love. It is generally an extension of the erotic force, but not always. During eras when sexual desire was taboo and repressed, two people might experience a tremendous erotic force, but sexual activity didn't necessarily follow. In modern life, sex generally follows the initial impact of Eros. We consummate that erotic feeling through sexual expression. From that expression, we hope to move into Love.

Sex fuels the erotic fire, deepening your emotional connection to your partner. Sex in conjunction with Eros opens your heart to the universe through your pelvis. It is an act that can create new life, provide relaxation and revelation, and feel great. If it didn't, teenagers wouldn't be so anxiously compelled to do it, and neither would we.

When we are in the Erotic stage of our relationship, sex is one of the ways we choose to put that feeling into action. Sometimes, we feel so much passion toward our partner, we can hardly wait to get his clothes off. If you are looking for a terrific physical experience, having sex in the early erotic stages of a relationship can be exhilarating, an erotic flame that burns to an even higher, more sensational level of passion.

However, if your relationship objective is a long-term relationship or marriage, I recommend that you abstain from sex until you can better assess the relationship's potential. Sex has a way of prematurely bonding a woman to a man. You may know in your head that a particular man is a terrible match for you, but if you have sex with him you may soon find yourself counting the hours until you can be together again. If it is clear in your mind that you are looking only for great sex and not a long-term pairing, by all means jump in. The combination of sex and the erotic force can be a delicious experience.

Is it possible to have Eros without sex? Of course. The desires that come with Eros can be satisfied in other ways, including late-night talks on the phone, romantic e-mail (if you have a secure, private system), long walks on the beach, and sensual touching and kissing without intercourse.

Sex can, in fact, help you move from Eros to love because the erotic force, when combined with sex, can transform you so you can make the decision to love. A sexual relationship with a man can open up your heart by keeping the loving energy moving through your body, thereby deepening your desire to act in loving ways. In this way, sex can truly deepen the experience of love.

"After we first made passionate love in his office late one night, I would have said sex with Peter was the best it could ever be," my client Janet confided to me. "But as the months went by and our relationship became more committed and loving, the sex actually got better and better."

Janet discovered what sex therapists have known for years—that the best sex happens in the context of love with ongoing practice and deeper intimacy. The deepest, most satisfying sex occurs with a man with whom we have made a commitment to love and who has made one to us in return. That's why some couples who have been married for decades can honestly say they are not bored in the bedroom. The love they feel for each other revitalizes the sexual act and keeps the erotic force flowing.

When deciding to move from Eros to sex, women should be aware, especially if their eventual hope is for long-term love, that men will often use a mask of love in order to satisfy their sexual desires, even when it is really only an erotic outlet for them. A woman may give in to participating in a sexual activity she is not comfortable with because she "loves" the man. She will engage in sexual activity, even if it really doesn't feel right for her. It is very important that you receive pleasure and enjoyment from any sexual activity you engage in with a man. You should never compromise your own beliefs and values or do something about which you are uneasy just because you "love" somebody and it is something *he* wants to do. Unless you feel an openness to experiment and are interested in his suggested activity, don't do it.

True Confessions

Many smart, successful, mature women in my practice say they feel horrible when a partner, under the guise of love, makes requests for them to perform sexual acts that fulfill fantasies, although these acts may be in opposition to the woman's own beliefs. If a woman resists her partner's sexual requests and is then told that if she loved him she would participate, that is a form of emotional coercion. Lovemaking then moves from the realm of eroticism and sexuality into perversion—perversion because sex is no longer a mutually shared pleasure. The situation becomes a power struggle of dominance and submission. Experimentation and acting out of sexual fantasies between two mutually consenting adults are perfectly healthy and normal. The sex act, whatever it may be, is not necessarily perverse in and of itself, but if both partners don't receive pleasure and enjoyment from it, it is not a healthy, freely given exchange.

The person making a sexual request often believes there is no harm in asking "in the name of love" in order to get what he wants. This is problematic. For instance, he may ask you to engage in a *ménage à trois,* rationalizing that if you love him and want to satisfy his needs, then you will agree. If you are uncomfortable with his request, he won't acknowledge that. If you confess to him afterward that it wasn't something you were comfortable with, that you didn't enjoy it, that it was either frightening, humiliating or painful for you, he will act as if there is no harm in what you did for him. If he is unwilling to see the difference between loving sex and perversion, either by not asking you in the first place or not dropping his request once he senses your discomfort, he won't care that you didn't want to do it or that it felt shameful to you. He will ask you again and again.

The Sex Force

The Sex force is the most creative force in the universe on any level of existence. When it is combined with Eros and Love, it can reach its highest expression. If it exists without the presence of its companion forces, then very different relationship situations result. A highly evolved sexual force is generative and will create spiritual ideas. In a less evolved form, the sexual force is purely organic, with the primary purpose being procreation. Its impulse is totally selfish. Sex without Eros and Love is often expressed and referred to as animalistic or instinctual. As we view nature, the drive for reproductive sex manifests itself in all living creatures for the perpetuation of their species.

In rare cases, Eros without Sex and Love can exist for a limited time in the form of Platonic love, which is not consummated by the sexual act. Sooner or later, though, if one of the participants in a Platonic relationship is healthy, the sex force will be ignited by Eros. The longer the three forces of Eros, Sex, and Love remain separate, the less healthy and functional a person becomes. The more one is able to integrate the three forces, the more balanced and vital one is.

Friendship between a man and a woman is another permutation of these forces. Although erotic or sexual force will inevitably try to sneak into a friendship, by means of reason and will the energy can be directed in a properly balanced way, so that none of these forces is expressed inappropriately or in a way that is detrimental to other commitments.

Another frequently seen combination in long-standing relationships is the combination of Love with Sex, but without Eros. While able to share companionship, affection, mutual respect, and sexual relations devoid of an erotic spark, couples in this kind of sexual relationship get stale out of habit and familiarity. They often can't articulate exactly what is missing—they just know that that sparkling feeling of energy they had at the beginning of the relationship (Eros) is gone.

Love

Mature love isn't the instantaneous occurrence depicted in movies, books, or on television. Eros and Sex are integral to Love, but Love also involves consciousness and work. "When we allow love to flow through our life, we feel a powerful organic reaction in the body: deep breathing occurs, the heart expands, the pulse strengthens. In the state of love . . . we are infused with a divine energy, one that permeates all existence" (Pierrakos, *Eros, Love, and Sexuality*).

Love Is a Choice, Not a Feeling

Your feelings will change like the weather, particularly when you are involved in a long-term relationship. One day you are going to wake up and look over at him and think that the way he drools on his pillow is the cutest, most endearing thing you ever saw. The next morning, you could wake up and wonder, "How did this person get into my bed? Look at the way he

126

drools and snores! Disgusting." The conscious choice to love in spite of how we feel is what creates mature and lasting love.

Part of becoming a Smart Heart woman is understanding that, unlike Eros, Love is a **choice**, not a **feeling**. This can be problematic for both men and women, and lack of understanding can encourage a "Peter Pan Syndrome": people search constantly for that erotic charge, but when the feeling diminishes they think, "I'm not in love anymore." In actuality, they've moved out of the erotic stage and into a phase of the relationship when real work and commitment begin. This is the substance of conscious loving.

Love is a capability that we develop over time: we decide to act in loving ways, even when we don't feel like it. It is very easy to love someone when he is being lovable, but it is a greater challenge to love him when he is being unlovable.

The experience of love is a vibrant expression that moves outward from within, reaching out to touch the people around you. Loving energy is emitted in a free-flowing and open way. Loving is an act of will, motivated and guided by intelligent choice that results in conscious awareness. Complete, mature love will include not only your mind but also your body and spirit. When you give loving energy, you feel alive, vibrant, and connected to the world, as well as to your partner. Love is a commitment to be of service to each other and a sincere desire to give of ourselves. Mature love isn't just about being loved; it is about choosing to be loving.

Stop Searching for Unconditional Love

In my psychotherapy practice, I see women who want their men to love them no matter how they behave. They mistakenly believe that a man should always put a woman's desires before his own and that he should love her unconditionally. Let's be absolutely clear about this: Unconditional love does not exist in a romantic relationship or in adult life. Women who search for men who will love them unconditionally and meet their every need will be spending their lives alone. Such a man is a fantasy. He can't be found in the real world. Many of us get hooked into that belief because we are trying to re-create an infantile time when we got our first (and only) taste of unconditional love.

When a child is born, he or she is entitled to unconditional love and protection by parents because that is not only the parents' obligation but also a matter of the infant's survival. Children who are not given unconditional love when they are young try to find it all their adult lives.

127

They hold a distorted and inappropriate image of love that is impossible to create.

If you are seeking unconditional love as an adult for whatever reason, GIVE IT UP. **Love between two consenting adults is CONDITIONAL by nature. It requires appropriate, mature behavior. It must be earned, and it must be maintained.**

If your experience as a child was abusive or neglectful, then you know how it feels to have parents who didn't love you. You may still be seeking to be loved and accepted as an adult. This is not a defect. It merely highlights the fact that the ability to love and be desired has not been erased from within you. If this is your history, you must choose your partners carefully so that they don't mirror your parents and re-create the same experience of rejection. You must work hard to evaluate and search, perhaps resolving to be alone if you can't find a man who will treat you with the (conditional) love, respect, and attention that you deserve.

You need to realize that bonding with the object of your affection is of no value if he can't return that love. The flow of love needs to go in both directions. You must come to terms with the fact that you are not *entitled* to the unconditional love of which you were robbed as a child. Accept that you were cheated. If you devote your entire life to bitterness and obsession over the love that you were denied, you are denying yourself the possibility of achieving happiness and fulfillment in a loving, adult, mature, and balanced relationship, either now or in the future. Ask yourself how strong your commitment and willingness to change your old beliefs are, because handling that is your responsibility, not a potential partner's.

Unconditional love does play a role in our adult lives. Rather than futilely hoping to receive unconditional love, we can learn how to give it. By accepting our mate's human foibles and trying to live in a state of grace and forgiveness, we can open our heart to loving our mate. It isn't easy, but the rewards are worth it, not only to our partner but also to our own spirit.

Having children provides an opportunity to love unconditionally. When you become a parent, if you aren't one already, you will find that your baby will undoubtedly cry at a time when you feel too weary to get up from the chair. Nevertheless, you will find it in your heart to go to your child with love and understanding, even if you aren't feeling compassionate at that moment, simply because you have made the commitment to act in loving ways. You will find it in your heart to be loving and understanding with your belligerent daughter (or son) years later when she is a defiant teenager, because you have consistently chosen to love her in spite of her obnoxious behavior.

In the best of all worlds, in a partnership between two people, all three forces (Eros, Sex, and Love) would be active, pulsating, and present. Even if the erotic force lasts just a brief time, how can you bring it back into your relationship?

You can reignite Eros over and over again as long as you are willing to reveal yourself to the other person sexually, emotionally, and spiritually. Whenever you think you know everything about your beloved and there is nothing left to be revealed, Eros will be gone. The erotic force allows you to reveal yourself at a deeper and more intimate level both emotionally and sexually. Couples unwittingly stop the erotic flow because they erroneously believe that there is a limit to the revelation of another person's soul. All the great spiritual teachers and philosophers propose that you could spend a thousand lifetimes and never truly know the depths of someone's soul.

Keeping the erotic force flowing depends on your willingness to learn how truly to love—to move past the superficial, day-to-day existence to live a life of revelation and exploration. If you are willing to go deeper into the soul of your partner, experiencing him and sharing yourself, you can find these three forces working together in an integrated and fulfilling expression. You can use Eros and Sex as a bridge to Love, depending on your development, courage, commitment to love, and your ability to reveal yourself fully.

Using Sex as a Bridge Back to Eros

When you first become involved with a man, Eros, then Sex, acts as a bridge to Love. After you have been in a long-term relationship for a period of time, you can use Sex as a way back to Eros. Sexual contact is a way to recapture and rekindle the erotic force that first brought you together. People who are married or in long-term relationships need to keep fueling their erotic fire through continual and ongoing sexual contact.

One of the first questions I ask couples who come in for counseling is "How is your sex life?" Sex is usually where many relationships start to break down. One or both parties start withholding sex, making it impossible to rekindle the initial excitement and erotic feeling. Sexual energy flows in both directions in a committed, loving relationship. Sex brings us back to Eros and back to Love, over and over again. Women find that the more they have sex, the more they want it, and the more open they are to choosing to love, which is why a healthy sex life is such an important part of any loving relationship.

There is a long-term benefit of continually using Sex as a bridge back to Eros within an ongoing, committed relationship. A circular, complementary dynamic begins to emerge. By coming to a woman with his sexual energy and inserting his penis, a man helps a woman open herself up to feel the power of her own pelvis. A woman wants a man to want her for her heart, so she helps him to open emotionally. The exchange occurs as she gives her heart to the man, thereby assisting him in opening his heart. His penis will come into her pelvis, allowing her to feel the pleasure and energy of her own sexuality. These sensations and feelings of love and pleasure progress to her heart which, in turn, goes out to his heart. His capacity to open his heart expands out of the deepening expression of mature love and desire. This creates a circular, balanced, harmonious flow of yin-yang energies within the man and woman.

Many women feel negatively about men always wanting to initiate sex prior to a satisfying display of love and affection, but when Eros and Love are combined, having intercourse is the way a man first makes the connection. The sexual context helps a man open up his heart to a woman. There is a distinction for men between sex as an activity and sex as a bridge. Women need to understand that by utilizing these energies, during the right situation and at the right time, she can get what she wants, which is a man to open his heart to her.

Sex can also help to open the heart of a woman who is feeling angry or unhappy with her partner. I advise my clients to consider having sex with their partners even when they are not feeling particularly sexual or loving. In fact, they should consider it especially when they are not in the mood. When you are angry, that anger keeps love from flowing, causing your spirit and energy to contract. By continuing to have intercourse with your partner even when you are angry at him, you can open your heart and get the love flowing again and reenergize your commitment to love.

The most fulfilling relationship is when a continual flow of sex and loving action energizes our hearts, heads, and pelvis in a way that helps us constantly regenerate the passion of Eros. A Smart Heart woman understands that she is equally responsible for keeping the flame of Eros alive, both through its expression sexually and through her commitment to loving action.

How to Act on Our Decision to Love

How do we act on our decision to love our partner? There are innumerable ways, day in and day out, in which we can act with integrity, behaving responsibly, and find it in our hearts to be forgiving and generous with our mate.

Is it easy? Of course not. Opening our hearts to express love continually is one of the most difficult things we can do. When we get married, we may vow to love and honor our partner "for better or worse," but most of us naively expect the good times to last forever. Difficult times in a long-term relationship are as inevitable as joint bank accounts or a double bed. Keeping our hearts open during the trying times is the truest test of a commitment and one of the highest spiritual practices we can undertake. Once a Smart Heart woman makes the choice to love, honor, and cherish, she needs to consciously put that decision into action.

Smart Heart women understand that love means having to say you're sorry.

131

Taking responsibility for your actions is a primary component of being a mature adult and of choosing to love. You are not merely a passenger in your life; you are the driver. Everything that happens in your life and in your relationships is largely a reflection of the decisions you make and the actions you take. Instead of blaming your partner and external forces when things go wrong, acknowledge your part and actively work to correct any problem situations.

Smart Heart women understand that love means sharing negative feelings such as anger, jealousy, insecurity, or confusion.

Sometimes you're also hurt, sad, happy, hopeful, or nervous. It means telling your partner the truth, not a whitewashed truth, but the truth in all its detailed glory, no matter how unpleasant, inconvenient, or painful it might feel—the truth about how you feel, what you did, and what you think. Telling the truth always is tough. Most of us aren't necessarily accustomed to doing it, and our honesty can sometimes bring pain to our partner. Acting in a loving way, however, means not withholding ourselves from our partners. One note of caution, however: Don't bludgeon your partner with the truth. Be direct, but also be kind, compassionate, and gentle. When you can reveal your own fears and follies—your human failings and frailties—to your beloved, you create a greater intimacy.

Smart Heart women understand that love means honoring promises.

When you make a promise to your partner, view it as a binding contract. Keeping a vow shows your partner that he is valuable to you, that you do not take him for granted. Whether it's a promise to drop fifty pounds or merely to drop off a letter at the post office, once you make a commitment, nothing short of an emergency should keep you from at least making your best effort to fulfill it.

Smart Heart women understand that love means respecting their partners' opinions.

It doesn't matter if you studied political science in college and have worked on the last two presidential campaigns. You may be convinced that electing the independent candidate would be the worst thing to happen, but if your partner genuinely disagrees, you owe it to him at least to respect his right to an opinion. You don't have to concur, because it is fine to agree to disagree, but show your man that you respect what he thinks. Don't belittle what he says, even if it might seem foolish to you, and don't ignore it, even if that would be the easier way. Let him know you have heard and understood his opinion and you respect it.

Smart Heart women understand that love means being considerate of their partners' wishes.

Loving action doesn't mean that you never get to do what you want if it happens to conflict with what your partner wants, but it does mean choosing your battles carefully. It may mean deciding that, on occasion, what you need and want may be more important to you than what he needs and wants.

Smart Heart women understand that love means behaving tenderly.

When you come from a loving space, you can be tender with your partner whenever he is hurt or upset and, hardest of all, when he makes mistakes. Such a response shows him that you accept his humanness and you love him. Sometimes, words aren't necessary to convey such a message. Nonverbal communication can be just as powerful. Simply by holding him

132

during a trying time you can express your acceptance in the most tender way of all.

Smart Heart women understand that love means having frequent, meaningful conversations.

Studies show that husbands and wives spend very little time directly communicating. They spend a few minutes saying "Good morning" before rushing out the door to work and ask a few cursory questions like "How was your day?" before turning on the TV. Loving couples need to talk to each other, for an hour or more at least once a week, because communication is the tie that binds you. Without meaningful conversation, differences multiply as things go unsaid; needs go unmet; joys aren't shared; and the ties that bind begin to fray.

For a relationship to be more than just two people living separate lives in the same house, meaningful communication must occur. Loving action means making the time to be verbal, even when you don't feel like it, and being an eager listener when it's your partner's turn to speak. Honor your partner by making every effort truly to hear what he is trying to tell you, even if he doesn't always say it clearly. Make weekly dates to check in and discuss your life, feelings, hopes, and fears.

The distinctions among the forces of Eros, Sex, and Love and the mature nature of love are important aspects to be consciously aware of in order to develop a long-term partnership. Obviously, there is nothing wrong with enjoying sex without combining it with Eros and Love. To create a deeply satisfying and intimate relationship, however, we need to know that Love is a choice, a skill, and a way of giving to the other, rather than seeking something solely for ourselves. Love generates fulfillment, contentment, and grace for both our partner and ourselves. A Smart Heart woman knows, in being human, that she will occasionally trip and fall. That is part of the journey. If she keeps getting up, moving forward, and maintaining her focus on the commitment to love as an act of will and consciousness, in combining conscious choice with pleasure and the erotic force of sex, she can create an enduring elixir, the effects of which can last a lifetime.

Hormones, Pheromones, and Other Moans

A s a Smart Heart woman, you have started to utilize your conscious awareness to think, as well as feel. If you believe that thinking and feeling are enough to take charge of your love life, however, you're wrong! Welcome to the weird science of your body's biochemistry. Many women are aware of the alien feelings and emotions that overtake them once a month: that time when PMS has friends and family looking for activities outside the home to take them as far away from you as possible until the hormonal storm passes. Most women are unaware, however, that when they fall in love or lust not only are thoughts and feelings stirred up but potent hormones also get into bed with them. Your body's hormones control your sex drive, steering the course of your love life, whether you are aware of it or not.

At some point, what woman hasn't wondered, "What on earth could have possessed me to dump a cute, funny, smart doctor for a loser who has never paid back the money he borrowed, never calls unless he is drunk or horny, and never stays for the entire night after sex?" We have all been there at one time or another. We may be bright women, but once we have had sex with a man, our feelings take over and we lose our ability to judge him wisely. We may know that he isn't right for us; we may know that he's such a lout that he isn't right for *any* woman. Women also need to know, however, the role their body chemistry plays in generating sexual agendas as they go through different stages, from adolescence to old age. Our hormones can generate desire, frustration, bonding, love, and a magical attraction to the wrong guy. When we finally return from the hormone-induced detour on the road to love, we wonder, "What happened to me? What could have come over me to be with such a jerk for so long?"

The research is fascinating and unsettlingly. It is liberating to discover that in controlling our own minds, bodies, and feelings, hormones affect our mates as well. Is it possible to be addicted to someone's scent and touch? Why do I stay with him when I know he is wrong for me? Why can't I let go and move on? Does love at first sight really exist? Why does being in love make me feel nauseated and out of control? When it's over, why do I crash and burn in depression and defeat? Answers to these dilemmas can be found in contemporary research.

Research has been done, both with animals and humans, to expand our understanding of the effect and implications of the formidable ways in which hormonal fluctuations powerfully influence our relationships. Dr. Theresa Crenshaw is a leading expert in the field who asks salient questions in attempting to solve these perplexing hormonal puzzles that affect us so profoundly.

Most of us have a general awareness of the "male" and "female" hormones such as estrogen, testosterone, and progesterone, but we also need to be informed about the lesser known, yet equally important, influences of oxytocin, DHEA, LHRH, and PEA—how as individual substances they potently affect us, in addition to how they interact with one another within the body. Research conducted over the last twenty years overwhelmingly reveals that our biochemistry profoundly affects our lives, loves, and sexuality.

Hormones basically function as dictators, telling other substances what to do and how to operate. Often, they wreak havoc, bullying us with radical mood swings and behavior contrary to our normal patterns. These overpowering chemicals operate with abandon until they are recognized, understood, and treated. What a relief to know that our internal feelings are not precursors of insanity or neurosis but are often merely a result of hormonal activity!

This chapter will further familiarize you with the more commonly known hormones that comprise your body's biochemistry as well as introduce you to some of the lesser-known hormones, so that you can understand how these chemicals shape both your and your prospective partner's perceptions. You will learn why it's not such a great idea to jump into bed immediately with a man with whom you want a long-term partnership, why you like chocolate and how it can affect your love life, why you have a tendency to hold grudges, why you seek touch more than men do, how you can have great pleasure in sex without experiencing orgasm, and why men who act territorially have difficulty talking about their feelings and making a commitment. Feelings and behaviors that previously made you feel crazed or weird will not only make sense but also seem natural, and may even make you laugh.

Customized Love Potions: PEA, Pheromones, and DHEA

Don't forgo the sexy lingerie, wine, candles, soft music, or even painted toenails and an alluring new outfit to entice your mate. Be aware, however, that within your own skin you have natural potions that act as seduction mechanisms.

What is PEA? It's phenylethylamine, an internally produced amphetamine that induces sexual excitement in our bodies. Romantic thoughts and activities raise our PEA levels, acting as a natural aphrodisiac. Not surprisingly, there are significant amounts of PEA in chocolate. No wonder men bring us boxes of chocolate when they court us!

PEA plays a significant role in the weird science of love. It floats around naturally in our systems. The amount varies, depending on our feelings, thoughts, and experiences, with romance spiking the levels upward.

PEA may trigger the visual component of "love at first sight." If you have ever been smitten in this manner, you know the euphoric feeling that comes with the circulatory surge of PEA. PEA combines with the senses of smell and touch, triggering pheromones (a secret scent that magnetically draws someone to you).

Research shows that PEA reaches heightened levels during romantic periods. Synthetic PEA is known as a powerful pharmaceutical antidepressant. This is why after love sickness strikes, when PEA decreases, we experience symptoms similar to amphetamine withdrawal—i.e., sleeping longer than normally, overeating, and going into emotional overdrive.

PEA raises the question "Are we really in love, or are we chemical lunatics under a hormonally induced spell?" Research has shown that, on occasion, high levels of PEA have been found in people with severe mania and schizophrenia. Research in areas related to psychiatry are ongoing, and results are proving to be increasingly interesting.

PEA PROFILE

Most people don't know that PEA:

▶ Rises with romance
▶ Can cause depression, at low levels
▶ Has been associated with psychosis, at high levels

PEA:

▶ Works as an antidepressant in both sexes
▶ Is similar to an amphetamine and works like a diet pill

As for sexual roles, PEA:

▶ Is a stimulant
▶ Spikes at orgasm and ovulation

As for behavior, PEA:

▶ Causes giddiness and excitement
▶ Could be involved in love at first sight
▶ Could be a cause of "love addiction"

Sex Stinks

It's strange, but true, that sexual behavior may initially be dictated by smell. Even before your hormones merge into a chemical cocktail, pungent sexual forces may be working on you below your conscious awareness.

Pheromones affect the olfactory senses, causing specific reactions in the opposite sex of the same species. In the animal kingdom, pheromones have the power to influence procreation by luring mates for the primary purpose of intercourse. When members of the opposite sex detect pheromones, they are powerless to resist their sexual desire and are lured exclusively for sex. Modern science has found pheromones in human sweat and in vaginal secretions.

DHEA, the mother of all hormones, is the basis of many animal pheromones. Humans, instead of frothing at the mouth, mad with sexual desire or irresistible compulsion, seem to be influenced sensually more than sexually by sexual pheromones. We might feel an inexplicable sense of intimacy and well-being with a total stranger. At one time or another, who hasn't exclaimed, "Oh, I feel as if I've known you my whole life. I'm so comfortable with you, and we've only just met"?

Generally, a woman's sense of smell is more acute than a man's as a result of higher levels of estrogen in her body. While a woman's perception of subtle odors is more refined than a man's, men are able to handle pungent, noxious odors better than women. If you have an adolescent son, you may have noticed his ability to delight in gross personal hygiene or having a dirty, stinky room.

We detect pheromones using a special type of cell called the vomero nasal organ. According to Dr. David Berliner, a researcher for the Erox Corporation, which develops commercial pheromones, these cells are unlike any others in their ability to detect pheromones, although they operate less acutely than in animals, whose survival depends on their smelling capability. Research has shown that pheromones in human sweat influence a woman's menstrual cycle. Female roommates or co-workers will often begin to menstruate at the same time, as a result of pheromones.

Dr. Crenshaw believes that, through our pheromones, human beings send out insistent chemical sexual messages that we may be too "civilized" or evolved to consciously detect. She feels that our capacity to detect pheromones will affect with whom we connect and to whom we are attracted.

DHEA (dehydroepiandrosterone) floods our system from the time we are in utero and is the main hormone produced by the fetus. It is the most powerful, versatile, and dynamic of all the sex hormones.

It manipulates sexual selection through our sense of smell, creating our own unique scent. It influences whether or not a woman can become pregnant and how strong her bond is with her baby. It promotes courtship and mating rituals and is present at its highest levels when we are in our twenties, steadily declining thereafter. Active DHEA is significantly higher in the brains of women than men.

As a sexual chemical, it seems to have a direct influence on whom we feel attracted to, as well as the intensity of that attraction. DHEA directly stimulates desire. For many years, it was believed that if a woman had her ovaries removed, her sexual desire would decrease and production of DHEA would cease. A study done at Sloan-Kettering Research Institute, however, revealed that, in a woman whose ovaries were removed due to cancer, sexual desire was retained and DHEA levels remained consistent.

138

As a result of her research, Dr. Crenshaw believes that DHEA serves as a natural aphrodisiac in both men and women. She has successfully treated women with low sexual drive by increasing their levels of DHEA. She has also found that stress decreases DHEA levels and that long-term meditation increases DHEA.

DHEA PROFILE

Most people don't know that DHEA:

▸ Is the most abundant hormone in the body—in both sexes

▸ Can transform into almost any other hormone

▸ Improves cognition, protects the immune system, and protects against certain forms of cancer

▸ Serves as an antidepressant for both sexes

▸ Promotes a "futile fatty acid" cycle causing weight loss without decrease in food intake

▸ Is actively synthesized and broken down in the human skin

▸ Decreases cholesterol

▸ Promotes bone growth

DHEA:

▸ Is a steroid hormone, regulated by ACTH, manufactured mainly in the adrenals, but also by the ovaries, testicles, and brain

▸ Blood levels in adult men are one hundred to five hundred times greater than testosterone levels

As for sexual roles, DHEA:

▸ Is the precursor of pheromones in some animals and most probably in humans, as well

▸ May influence whom we find attractive and who responds in return

▸ Increases sex drive, more so in women than in men

▸ Increases in the brain during orgasm

As for behavior, DHEA:

▸ Is the only hormone that peaks around age twenty-five and declines steadily thereafter

▸ May be a key factor in male menopause

▸ Is beneficial to the quality of life and longevity

▸ May have different effects on males and females

Touch: A Double-edged Sword

The emotions associated with caring, intimacy, relaxation, and nurturing, which we take for granted in our daily lives, may play a much greater role in our well-being and capacity for love and happiness than previously thought.

During the last two decades, research has confirmed what we seemed to know instinctively as babies: that touch nurtures, completes, and inspires us. Touch supports our physical, emotional, and mental health and well-being and contributes greatly to our happiness, as well as promoting a satisfying sex life.

We have a biological need for touch in order to survive. It is a natural, instinctual necessity. The noted family therapist Virginia Satir said that in order to be mentally healthy we need a minimum of eleven hugs a day! We know that babies fail to thrive, and often die, as a result of not being touched and held. The initial research done by Dr. Rene Spitz in the 1930s with orphans showed that if an infant deprived of touch did manage to survive, it had a much greater tendency toward delayed development, both mentally and physically, often resulting in retardation. She also determined that the elderly became senile more rapidly, and even died sooner, without physical contact and the comfort of touch.

Touch feels great! We cannot live a long, full life without it. People who aren't touched regularly and tenderly become unwell. They fall victim to emotional maladies, such as depression, anxiety, aggression, and stress, which taking a pill won't cure.

What does touch have to do with being a Smart Heart woman? Touch causes us to secrete endorphins, which are natural opiates our body releases to protect us from pain. Touch also stimulates secretion of a hormone called oxytocin. Levels of oxytocin soar whenever someone touches us. You can just imagine what happens when we have sex! As a result, oxytocin binds us at an involuntary physical hormonal level whenever we are physically touched.

Sleeping with someone too soon can be particularly "touchy" if you're interested in a long-term relationship. If you have continual physical contact with a man, count on increasing your oxytocin level, as well as the degree to which you are bound to that person, even if he isn't the right guy for you.

Oxytocin: Stronger Than Krazy Glue

Why does a woman bond with a man she sleeps with, not only for an intimate evening but for months or years thereafter? Scientists believe the reason may be a hormone called oxytocin. Oxytocin causes us to experience a feeling of bonding with one's partner, to "chemically commit," and, in conjunction with another hormone called vasopressin, oxytocin affects nipple response, sexual arousal, orgasm, erection, and ejaculation. Oxytocin is also secreted by women when they breast-feed their babies. This is nature's way of solidifying the bond a mother has with her newborn infant.

In addition, oxytocin plays a role in the interaction between a woman and the man with whom she sleeps. Oxytocin is produced in both women and men and serves to stimulate the smooth muscles in the body and to sensitize the nerves. A decade ago, researchers from Stanford University thought oxytocin might be produced during sex, so they began to measure the levels of the hormone released during intimate relations. They found that women produce much more of it. They produce it during foreplay, while men do not, and they secrete much higher levels than men before achieving orgasm. These high levels of oxytocin may play a role in a woman's ability to have multiple and total-body orgasms.

The Stanford researchers also found that oxytocin does more for women than just make sex feel good. Unlike other hormones, oxytocin seems to tie in to emotional, as well as physical, cues. Seeing, hearing, or smelling a lover can cause the oxytocin levels to rise in a woman's body, making her want to be with him again. Oxytocin binds women to their sexual partners. While this may serve an evolutionary purpose, it can be disastrous for a Smart Heart woman attempting to move on from a bad partnering choice.

Though specific research on human bonding behavior has been limited, scientists have used animal models to discover more about oxytocin's role in the link between men and women. Many of these studies involve a species of rodents called a prairie vole. Female voles, unlike their rat cousins, form monogamous partnerships with their mates. Scientists have documented that female voles who have mated with a male later prefer to spend more time with that male than with any other male, and they prefer being with him to being alone. In other studies, the female voles weren't given the chance to mate but had the hormone oxytocin injected into their brains before they spent time with a male vole. When later given a choice, these rodents selected the males they had been with following the oxytocin rush. Even when the male was taken away and not returned until several weeks later, the female still preferred the one with whom she had had the oxytocin experience.

To verify that the oxytocin caused the bonding effect, the hormone was chemically blocked from circulating in the female rodent during sex to see if a preference for her sex partner still developed. Those female voles in whom oxytocin could not circulate did not prefer any specific partner later—even if they had spent hours mating with the male.

"We certainly know that women can become overcommitted to the men that they sleep with," explains oxytocin researcher Rebecca Turner, M.D., associate professor of psychology at the California School of Professional Psychology in Berkeley, California, who recently completed a study on oxytocin's effects on women's personalities. "Given what we know about oxytocin, it certainly seems plausible that the hormone is what is causing these women to bond."

Turner says that when she gives her lecture on oxytocin and female bonding to her graduate students, the women in the class always respond in the same way: "We know that already from our own lives!" they uniformly tell her. They formed lasting attachments to men they had slept with, regardless of whether or not the men were "right" for them.

Oxytocin is one of the biological factors that can work against a woman in her quest to be smart about her relationships. Biology doesn't have to be destiny, but there are physiological differences between women and men that undermine a woman who isn't aware of them.

Sex is a natural biological act that is a positive, healthy activity. It feels wonderful for adult men and women to derive pleasure from making love. Sex feels great! Releasing your energy in this way, by sharing sex and love with another, is a critical part of adult life.

Decisions about sex have long been influenced by rigid cultural and religious notions—e.g., that sex is something "good" girls don't do, or that it is morally wrong or shameful. From Victorian novels to contemporary literature, movies, and television shows, sex has been portrayed as a manipulative tool for women to control men. These ways of perceiving our sexual selves are constricting and unnatural. They are destructive to our psyches and stop the natural flow of pleasure and energy we need to be whole and vibrant human beings, physically, emotionally, and mentally.

A Smart Heart woman does not accept these negative views of sex and knows that sex is as good for her as it is for her partner. A Smart Heart woman understands that sex, love, and touch are necessary and important parts of adult life.

What You Should Know Before You Sleep with Him

If you are a Smart Heart woman who is in touch with your sexuality and sensuality, and you want to exchange adult pleasures with a man, having sex with him can be mutually satisfying and fun, as long as you are clear about your relationship objectives. If you are a younger woman without much sexual history behind you, having sex with a variety of men can help you learn about what feels pleasurable. Each man brings a unique sexual perspective to the bedroom, pleasuring you in a different way. You can also experiment with what feels good for him. If you are a recently divorced or widowed woman, you may not want to settle down again right away. Having free-spirited sex with a variety of willing partners may feel right for you. Like the less experienced, younger woman, you also might benefit from learning about what feels good for your body through experimentation with a variety of partners and their unique techniques.

As Smart Heart women, we take responsibility for our lives and bodies. When we choose to have sex without an emotional attachment, we must take extra care to protect our health and safety. Choosing partners wisely and using protection against both pregnancy and disease are important components of being a sexually mature and responsible woman.

A Smart Heart woman looking for a long-term relationship or marriage, however, will find that jumping into bed too early can be a terrible mistake—not for moral, cultural, or power reasons, but because it is an oxytocin nightmare. The biological reality of oxytocin is that it can prematurely bond you to a man you might not otherwise be interested in if you had been thinking clearly before you hopped into the sack. If you are a Smart Heart woman who is looking for a mate, postpone momentary sexual pleasure so that you can more clearly evaluate the man you are with to determine if he fits into your long-term relationship objectives.

An oxytocin sexual cocktail can definitely cloud your ability to think clearly. We can all think of women, ourselves included, who deemed men passable for the first few platonic dates. Then, after wild, passionate sex, they just can't let go, despite their better judgment. It is almost as if they have a physical addiction to the men. In a sense, they do, because they are bound by the oxytocin hormone released during sexual activity, which acts like emotional Krazy Glue.

In her memoir, Kelly Flinn, the first female B-52 pilot, who resigned from the military after her adulterous affair with Marc Zigo, unknowingly reveals the power of oxytocin over a woman's otherwise well-reasoning brain. "Why did I fall so completely for a man whose own mother says he's a pathological liar? Who knows?" she writes in her book, *Proud to Be: My Life, the Air Force, the Controversy.* Flinn knew Zigo was married but later found out that he had lied to her about numerous things, ranging from where he was born to a fictional career as a professional soccer player. None of that mattered, however. "Once we'd slept together [six weeks after meeting]," Flinn continues, "I let myself fall head over heels in love. Despite a private warning I got from [his wife's] first sergeant to stop seeing Marc, I just couldn't get him out of my mind or out of my heart."

My client Jacqueline also couldn't get her sexual partner out of her mind. He was a man with such a serious jealousy problem that Jacqueline couldn't go anywhere without his approval. (She even had to sneak off from work in midday to see me.) She had slept with Hal when they had barely known each other, at a time when she mistook his attentiveness and concern for sincere indications that he cared about her.

As the weeks went on, Jacqueline began to see Hal as the disturbed person that he was, yet she couldn't let him go. She knew it wasn't logical, but she felt fixated on Hal whenever she was with him or spoke to him on the phone. "When we are apart, I vow that I am not going to see him again, listing all the rational reasons why he is a bad match for me. Then he calls or comes over, and I just melt," she told me, describing, without being aware of it, the effects of oxytocin. Jacqueline used the skills from the Smart Heart Partnering Process to break up with Hal, but two weeks later he showed up at her office and she let herself get hooked again. Whenever Jacqueline saw, heard, touched, or tasted Hal, the oxytocin level rose in her body and reeled her in. Only when she cut off all connection and contact with Hal was she finally able to pursue a more appropriate partner.

If you are not looking for an intimate partner and you have an affair or fling with a man you know is unavailable, even if you consciously make the choice to do that, you still run the danger of getting stuck in the relationship. Your intention may not be to become involved, but if you continue to be sexually intimate with him, you will become bound through the hormonal rush of oxytocin long after you want to move on to create something different for yourself.

The lesson for a Smart Heart woman is clear: *It doesn't matter how smart you are or how carefully you design your relationship objective, if you agree to sex too early in a relationship, you will be detained from reaching your goals for weeks, perhaps years.* If you sleep with a man too soon, you run the risk of being swept away by sexual desire, and oxytocin distortion won't allow you to see clearly who he really is.

Be smart with your heart. If you are looking for a long-term partner or mate, you should make a commitment to avoid sexual intimacy with a man until you are certain that your head and heart are in agreement that he could be the one for you.

OXYTOCIN PROFILE

Most people don't know that oxytocin:

▶ Promotes touching
▶ Promotes bonding between mates and parents and children
▶ Is involved in the birth process, breast-feeding, and orgasm
▶ Decreases cognition and impairs memory

Oxytocin:

▶ Is secreted by the posterior pituitary
▶ Has a synergistic relationship with estrogen
▶ Is pulsatile (i.e., pulsating)
▶ And dopamine modulate each other
▶ Sensitizes skin to touch
▶ Is widely distributed throughout the brain and body
▶ Increases dopamine, estrogen, LHRH prostaglandins, serotonin, testosterone, prolactin, and vasopressin

As for sexual roles, oxytocin:

▶ Spikes at orgasm
▶ Causes uterine contractions during orgasm and during labor
▶ Increases sexual receptivity
▶ Speeds ejaculation
▶ Increases penile sensitivity

As for behavior, oxytocin:

- Rises in response to touch and promotes touching
- Induces parenting behavior
- Promotes affectionate behavior
- Has been linked to obsessive-compulsive disorder

One-night Stands, or Taking a Stand for What You Want

A man can have sex one night and forget about it (and you) by the time he's having his morning coffee. For men, sex is a physical release and pleasure that satisfies, relaxes, and fulfills. Initially, it is not usually about emotional connection. This makes it easier for men to walk away afterward without another thought. Men can't help it—it is how they are made. Alternatively, when a man gets shot by Cupid's arrow and has that "chemical charge" for you, he can't control or explain it, just as you can't control what happens when you sleep with a man too soon.

Men are wired biologically to be hunters. What excites men on a deep and conscious level is pursuit, whether it is pursuit of a woman or a business deal. Men also like to know that when they go after something, there is a good possibility that they will win. For this reason, it is important for you to let them know that you are available and open to them; you don't want to make yourself an impossible challenge. If a man is truly ready for a long-term relationship and he is interested in you, even though he would like to have sex with you the first chance he gets, he will wait, within reason, to be with you.

I am not advocating being prudish or physically cold toward him in order to keep him interested and challenged. While you are getting to know him, be affectionate with him in other ways. Do whatever you feel comfortable with and be creative—just keep your clothes on. Taking your clothes off brings you to the next level of intimacy, a stage where you want to be only when you know the man is right for you. Until you have more facts, stop yourself before you jump into bed with him. (During this time, you can also pleasure yourself sexually to fulfill your physical and emotional needs for release without prematurely bonding yourself to the wrong man.)

If a man is really interested in you, he will not go away. If he is only interested in having sex with you, he will disappear pretty quickly once he knows that you're not planning to have sex with him immediately. If you are really excited by and attracted to a new man, you should determine a minimum amount of time to wait before sleeping with him—e.g., after ten dates. This does not mean ten marathon dates in a week and a half but ten dates over the course of a month or two, in order to experience different moods and a variety of situations. If you both had full lives before you met, (work, friends, and outside interests), you probably won't be able to fit ten dates into a short period of time. If he can, you should consider why he is so available. By spreading dates out and postponing sex you will be able to see if he continues to be interested. If he isn't, he will disappear and you will have saved yourself the effort. Over the course of a month or two, you will be able to get a better sense of who he is. Then you can be more certain you are heading toward your relationship objectives before you open yourself up sexually.

Had Sex Too Soon? Start the No-contact, Three-month Plan

If you're already sexually involved with a bad bet, all is not lost in your quest for the right relationship. To free yourself from a poor relationship choice and be able to attract the right man, you must sever all ties with the man you are now seeing. The oxytocin Krazy Glue requires time to dissolve. You need to put some time and distance between you. Generally, a minimum of three months is necessary to break the chemical spell between you and your intimate partner.

Because oxytocin facilitates bonding with your partner, it doesn't work to see him occasionally, or begin dating other men while still seeing him. When you are with another man, you may decide he is wonderful and you are willing to be open to him as a relationship choice, but, inevitably, you return to Mr. Right Now and find yourself repeatedly in the same predicament. Just hearing his voice on the telephone may be enough to get your oxytocin levels soaring and your connection to him reestablished.

If you truly want to break free of a man, you should not have contact with him. Don't see him; don't go out with him; don't listen to his voice on the telephone; don't smell, taste, or touch his body. I wouldn't recommend looking at his picture! Have nothing to do with him for at least three months. It often takes even more time to get your head straight. Construct and enforce a no-contact plan for that period of time.

Lauren was a twenty-nine-year-old client of mine who knew she was ready for a husband. She spent two years dating Todd, a man with whom she shared few long-term goals or common interests. Although she had utilized the Smart Heart Process tools and techniques to break up with Todd on three separate occasions, he would show up at her house a few nights later with a good story, begging her to take him back. Then, they would have sex. Each time she came in for a session, she would forlornly tell me that they were back together. Even though her head knew she needed to let Todd go, her hormones kept him in the picture, in her bed, and in her heart.

When Lauren was finally able to break up with Todd, she severed all connection to him. She instructed her roommate never to let him past the front door. She changed her phone number. Later she went on a date with Gregg, whom she had recently met. After their second date, he asked if he could come up to her apartment. A little tipsy from the jumbo margarita they had shared at the Mexican café, she agreed. They ended up having sex all night long, possibly the best sex Lauren had ever had.

After that night, Lauren couldn't stop thinking about Gregg. The pair made passionate love several times a week during the next few weeks. Gregg then dropped a bombshell—he was married and had no intention of leaving his wife who had been out of the country on business for the past month. Lauren was crushed. Gregg said he still loved being with her and he hoped to continue seeing her on the side after his wife returned. Although this arrangement was not what Lauren wanted, she agreed to Gregg's conditions. "I know this relationship is a dead end," she said, crying in my office some months later, "but the sex is so terrific I don't want to give it up. Every time I'm with him, I just can't stand the thought of not seeing him again."

Lauren already knew this arrangement was not right for her. After three months, she was able to break up with him. She knew, this time, in order to break the bond, she had to sever all contact immediately. A total break is the only way a woman can hope to escape the effects of oxytocin. If you continue to see the wrong man for a once-a-month quickie, you will not be able to break the chemical spell. You will merely continue to divert yourself from your real relationship objective. If it's love, partnering, and long-term intimacy that you really want, don't short-change yourself by settling for sex.

"Friends" Is a TV Show, Not What Happens After You Stop Having Sex with a Man

The idea that you can be in an intimate, sexual relationship with somebody, then stop having sex and just be friends is ludicrous. Only if you are highly evolved spiritually (which most of us aren't) or if you can see your former partner and truly be glad in your heart, even though he is sleeping with another woman, is a continuing friendship possible.

This means acknowledging (without getting sad, mad, or hysterical) that he is having sex with another woman. You must sincerely hope that his new relationship works out well. A continuing friendship can only happen when he has the same altruistic feelings, which, depending on the nature of your breakup, may not happen simultaneously.

Women often come into therapy asking, "It isn't working romantically, but can't my partner and I still be friends?" The answer, for now at least, is definitely "no." The notion that you can ease into friendship with a man you've recently been in bed with is not realistic. The reason it's called "breaking up" is because you need to have a break from each other. You have not broken up if you are still together "as friends." You are just practicing another version of seeing each other, but this time without sex. Women constantly hope this transformation will occur, but it seldom does. You're deceiving yourself if you think you can break up without disrupting the flow, bringing it to an end, or changing the relationship significantly. It would be like seeking sobriety without abstaining from alcohol or drugs.

Sometimes the hardest part of breaking up with a man who is not right for you romantically is that you may also lose a wonderful friend. Maybe you both enjoy racquetball or dancing at nightclubs. Unfortunately, you must accept this hard truth and move on to other men and other friends, at least until some significant amount of time has passed and you both are romantically involved with other partners.

We cannot turn back the tide, pretending that we have never been lovers. A relationship ends because the participants want it to. One party usually has a stronger desire to remain romantically involved than the other. For that person, a continuing friendship may be the best she can hope for, but it is not what she wants, and her unhappiness will eventually contaminate the friendship.

149

No magical formula exists for how long such a process takes. It is different for every relationship. As a rule, it doesn't happen before one year. I enjoyed a relationship with a man whom I knew I did not want to marry. I was sad to release Michael after we had dated for almost a year, but I felt it was the right thing for both of us, since he was very open about wanting to be married soon. We broke up and stopped seeing each other completely.

Some months later, I heard through a mutual girlfriend that Michael was engaged to another woman. I can honestly say I was thrilled for him, and I knew that I could be friends with him and his new bride. I stayed away, however, because my girlfriend told me that she sensed he was still pining away for me, although he seemed happy with his new partner.

I lost touch with Michael, then ran into him at a local art gallery many years later. He told me that he was happily married to a woman whom he dearly loved but that it had taken him five full years to completely get over me! He had considered calling or sending me a card, but he decided against it, since I held such an emotional charge for him. Both of us are now romantically complete, emotionally sound, and at the point where we can be friends again.

Can you have a friendship with a man with whom you've had a sexual fling? This is another delusion. You need to go "cold turkey" and let him go. Having a weekend sexual partner, a married man or male friend you date on Saturday nights, inhibits the energy available to find a suitable partner. When you release Mr. Wrong, you give yourself the opportunity to attract Mr. Right. Only when you are free and energetically open can your signals to potential suitors hit the mark.

When it comes to ex-lovers:

▶ You cannot switch to being "just friends" immediately following a breakup.

▶ You must cut off all contact (no phone, no dates, no sex!).

▶ You need to abstain from seeing, hearing, or touching him for at least three months.

▶ You can "be friends" only when you are happy knowing he's having sex with another partner, and vice versa, a process that may take a year or more.

Better Choices Through Chemistry— or by Biochemical Default

All women know their body chemistry changes significantly, and often dramatically, when they enter menopause. Night sweats, intensified feelings, reduction of vaginal lubrication, hot flashes, and wild mood swings punctuate this passage. Few women, however, realize that their changing chemistry also contributes to an increased ability to make wiser, less chemically influenced decisions regarding partnering choices. After years of problematic relationships, women in menopause find themselves attracting men who are better for them. After thirty years of being unhappily married, a woman may decide, "I don't want to be with this man any longer." Why does this happen?

Contributing factors are numerous, but research shows that women's capacity to manufacture oxytocin diminishes significantly as they enter menopause. Freed from uncontrollable and inappropriate biochemical bonding, they tend to be smarter with their hearts and able to use their heads without hormonal interference. The hope is that, as we age, we learn from life experience. If we've made poor choices, it becomes too painful not to examine our part in failed relationships. A woman can change life patterns that have not served her well. She needn't play victim, with her head in the sand, blaming the man for everything. Life eventually demands that we understand our part in the situation, make better choices, and move toward a relationship that fulfills our objectives.

If you are a younger woman just beginning your romantic journey, utilizing the Smart Heart Process can offer insight into how to avoid some of life's pitfalls. You can counteract your hormonal influences by choosing to abstain from sex until you have been able to clearly evaluate your man to determine if he is right for you. You can also be more aware of when you are under a chemical "spell" and make your choices accordingly.

Other Moans

Estrogen gives us soft skin, rounded hips, full breasts, and warm, moist vaginas. When your system is flooded with estrogen, you send out chemical signals to a man that says "Take me, I'm yours!"

151

During menopause, estrogen levels decrease, along with a drop in oxytocin. Our ovaries become estrogen factories that have ceased production. With enough estrogen in our system, we are willing and open to sex, although it is male testosterone that creates the chemical desire to initiate sex. Estrogen makes romantic love seem like "a form of temporary insanity that derails and detours us from rational thought." If a woman is well-adjusted sexually, when her system is flooded with estrogen she can enjoy an array of sexual feelings ranging from a feeling of deep intimacy and sensual connection to "I don't care who you are; just take me now, hard and fast." She may experience a need for increased genital contact or she may seek nonsexual, sensual touch and sweet snuggles.

When estrogen is depleted, your libido flies out the window. Other sexual side effects surface as well. If you are menopausal, celebrate the decline of oxytocin and make sure your estrogen is supplemented so that you can remain sexually supple and available. When your estrogen is sufficient, sex is welcome and enjoyable. The desire to be penetrated can be stimulated by estrogen. You long to be held. You feel receptive and inviting.

If you find that you like hot, aggressive sex, you probably have higher levels of testosterone in your system. This hormone is responsible for the proactive pursuit of sexual contact, and you will be more interested in being the seducer. It also promotes the desire to masturbate. Even if you have an available sex partner, there is a tendency to want to masturbate more frequently.

152

ESTROGEN PROFILE

Most people don't know that estrogen:
- Improves cognition
- Improves and stabilizes mood
- Increases performance, reaction, and vigilance
- Protects against schizophrenia
- Protects against Alzheimer's disease

Estrogen:
- Is produced by the ovaries. It is also produced and stored by fat cells and the brain.
- Is an MAO inhibitor (mild antidepressant)
- Potentiates oxytocin

- Maintains skin tone, collagen
- Prevents osteoporosis
- Prevents heart disease

As for sexual roles, estrogen:

- Maintains receptive sexual drive and promotes frequency
- Generates attractive body odor and texture
- Sustains texture and health of vagina and vulva
- Promotes vaginal lubrication
- Improves vaginal, urethral, and genital tissue
- Prevents senile vaginitis
- Promotes lordosis

As for behavior, estrogen:

- Prevents depression
- Prevents or reduces stress
- Improves sense of taste and smell
- Decreases appetite

More Moans

153

Brain research in recent years shows that male and female brains are physically different. Differences exist in the corpus callosum, the nerve cable connecting the right and the left sides of the brain that allows the two hemispheres to communicate with each other. Because of thicker nerve fibers in the female corpus callosum, women's brains are more integrated, whereas information may move more slowly between the right (artistic) side to the left (verbal or analytical) side in men's brains. Scientists theorize that this is why females excel at verbal expression. According to Steve Gaulin, Ph.D., an anthropologist at the University of Pittsburgh, it could also mean that "the two hemispheres [of the brain] in men seem to be more specialized and less willing to switch functions" (Self, March 1992). Another controversial theory is that "the female brain is symmetrical, whereas in the male, the right side is depended on more than the left" (Self, July 1990). Noble Prize–winning scientist Dr. Richard Sperry, of the prestigious California Institute of Technology, was a pioneer in right-versus-left-brain research prior to his death. His studies of the corpus callosum revealed that the chemical makeup of the neurotransmitters of this membrane causes it to function differently in women than in men. This membrane separates a female's left brain from her right brain in such a way that it allows her to integrate thought and feeling at the same time. Because of this physiological structure, a female can, in effect, connect her heart to her head, whereas a man has more difficulty thinking and feeling simultaneously.

If a man thinks that he is not ready to commit himself and be in a serious long-term relationship, even if he feels great love and deep desire in the throes of passion, the structure of his brain limits connection of the opposing ideas at the same time. If he is also in the process of maturing from Knight to Prince, the structure of his brain may make it difficult to envision his lover in the next stage of his development. It's not that he is being malicious or spiteful; it's simply that divergent parts of his brain challenge him to think about a woman simultaneously as someone he has considered "just for pleasure and fun" and yet someone to whom he would want to make a commitment. Once a man has made his developmental transformation to Princehood, he is ready for a committed relationship. Even if he has feelings for the woman in his current relationship, he may not yet have thought about her as a potential partner. He will start to think about the next woman he meets and is attracted to as a potential long-term partner or wife. When a man changes his mind, he will change his feelings. The ability to separate feeling from thought is why a man can have sex with a woman yet maintain that he has no feelings for her.

Pam, thirty-three, a corporate attorney, was stunned by the news that her ex-boyfriend, with whom she had had a loving relationship for six years, was getting married. On the day she heard the news, she burst into my office and blurted out, "He's getting married! Can you believe that?!" Pam and Anthony had been together for seven years. After being introduced by mutual friends, they began dating. When a year and a half had passed, they decided to move into a little bungalow in Santa Monica, not far from the beach. She brought up the topic of marriage, but he brushed it off with "What's the rush?" They were seemingly best friends who would often spend weekends together, not realizing how isolated they were becoming.

Pam assumed that once they were settled professionally (Anthony worked for a record company), they would get married and perhaps have children. After their sixth anniversary came and went without a proposal, Pam broached the subject again one night over dinner. Anthony was surprised that Pam wasn't as happy as he was with the status quo. They loved each other and had a great relationship, so why ruin it? After all, he reasoned, they had agreed not to get married. Pam, however, didn't think marriage would ruin their great relationship. Not long after their breakup, she told me, "The last time we talked about marriage was five years ago! Things were different then. Everything was so right between us for all that time. I can't understand why he wouldn't want to marry me." Since they couldn't reconcile their two conflicting needs, they sadly and reluctantly broke up, even though there was nothing fundamentally wrong with their relationship. Pam was heartbroken for months.

A year after the breakup, Pam heard the shocking news. She couldn't fathom that only a year ago Anthony had chosen to break up with her rather than get married, despite how much he loved her. How could he have met someone else only six months later and proposed so quickly?

Unfortunately, it had nothing to do with how much he loved Pam. Because he initially thought of her as a permanent girlfriend, not a potential wife, he couldn't change how he perceived her. A man's thoughts and feelings live in two different worlds. When Anthony started to date again, he decided that he wanted to get married and he sought that kind of relationship. His feelings matched his thoughts and decisions. He was able to marry quickly when there was no conflict between his thoughts and feelings. It may not be fair, but it's the harsh truth.

On occasion, a man entering a long-term relationship without marriage on his mind might change his perspective, if you force the issue, but most will not. Pam is not alone in her predicament. Many women believe that if they don't broach the subject of marriage, the man they are with will just magically change his mind of his own accord. You needn't waste time by waiting in vain. Don't end up like Pam, with so much of her love and hard work being transferred to the next woman. If he says marriage is not what he wants, then you need to pay attention and listen to him.

If you are in a long-term relationship, eventually hoping for marriage, but your original discussion of the topic ruled out marriage, your man may have a hard time envisioning you as a potential wife, no matter how he feels about you. If that's the case, rather than waiting for five years to broach the subject a second time, you must give him a clear, fair, calm, and loving ultimatum. Nagging, complaining, or whining will not succeed in changing his mind. Tell him that, in order to be with you, he has to alter his thoughts about marriage. Give him a minimum of ten weeks to think about it, during which time you shouldn't see or contact each other. This is very important. If he decides that he still doesn't want to marry, you should let him go because he will never change his mind. If you give him this time on his own

155

without slamming the door between you, you afford him the opportunity to uncover his deeper feelings. If he really wants to be with you, he will come back to you in ten to fifteen weeks. If you really want to be with this man, don't seek another relationship until that time has passed. If he is going to choose you, he will be back.

Another couple, Brian and Julia, had been together for two years, after which time she gave him a loving ultimatum and then cut off all contact with him. At first, he painted the town, celebrating his newfound freedom and telling his friends he narrowly escaped being trapped into marriage. For weeks, he dated up a storm, barely thinking about Julia. Most women experience a time of mourning following a breakup and don't date again until they heal. Men take a longer time to react. After about ten weeks, Brian sank into a major depression, realizing what a huge mistake he had made by letting Julia go. When he finally called her, she told him she was dating someone else and she needed to see where it would lead. If it didn't work, she would call him back. After that relationship ended two months later, she called Brian. After reconciling their issues, Julia and Brian were married.

It is important to use the Smart Heart Partnering Process to discern your relationship objectives at the outset and evaluate whether or not the man you are with wants the same outcome. It is mind-boggling to realize how our natural hormones and gender differences affect us mentally, emotionally, and sexually. How we treat each other, for better and for worse, depends on not only our state of consciousness but also our awareness of how the puzzle pieces fit together. It seems overwhelming, at times, to discover the extent to which our biochemical makeup affects our path toward love and connection, or heartbreak and despair. Awareness of these factors increases our ability to take control and modulate our responses to make more informed decisions using both our heads and our hearts.

Is He a Knight, Prince, or King?
Why It Matters

T he "seasons of a man's life" should suggest more to a woman than whether he still has a full head of hair or, alternatively, has had time to amass a big bank account. Women are generally unaware of the distinct developmental stages a man goes through. Men evolve in a predictable, unconscious, natural progression toward maturation. If you asked a man "What developmental stage are you in?" he probably couldn't articulate a response. Men have a slight sense of where they fall within these stages and will show distinguishable signs to that effect. Women, however, can tell a lot about where a man is developmentally by listening to his responses to certain pointed, direct questions and deduce salient facts. Armed with this information, you can avoid certain detours in the course of moving toward your relationship objectives.

The three developmental stages through which men pass as they mature and evolve are:

❶ Knight

❷ Prince

❸ King

One way to look at these developmental stages is to think about a man as if he were on a quest. Within this framework, a young man begins his romantic life as a Knight. After he has successfully met certain challenges, he moves on to become a Prince. Finally, after a period of time, he can sit back, enjoy the fruits of his labors, and crown himself a King. As women, we evolve through predictable and somewhat parallel developmental stages. For our purposes, I call them Maiden, Princess, and Queen. We move through these stages more quickly, however, and are much more interested in the nesting and the serially monogamous aspects of relating to someone of the opposite sex. For men and women, each period comes with unique tasks, challenges, and specific relationship skills and needs of which every Smart Heart woman needs to be aware—for your own sake, as well as your partner's. If you are unaware of the stage your man is in, you run the risk of misinterpreting certain behaviors as signs that he is ignoring or rejecting you. You could end up resentful, hurt, and angry because you take personally what is simply a part of his growth process.

Many of these developmental signposts are obvious. For example, young men usually have a desire to "play the field," chase adventures, and look for conquests and are not interested in being tied down to one woman; older men, on the other hand, generally look for something more stable, comfortable, and satisfying, which is less risky as a life choice. Other distinctions are more subtle, yet equally critical, and you need to be able to identify them if you are going to utilize the Smart Heart Partnering Process to your own advantage. By understanding the various developmental stages, you can choose a partner more wisely because you will be able to determine whether he is just dating for fun and companionship or is actually looking for a long-term, family-oriented commitment.

It is important to be able to recognize the stage the man you're with is in, but it is equally important to determine which of his stages is conducive to your life and lifestyle. No one stage is better than another. Learning more about who you are, what you want, and the stage your partner is in will help you determine if your union is destined for success, stress, or failure. Certain pairings are more energetically compatible and complementary in terms of life patterns. A Princess, ready for a committed relationship in which she can have children, will not usually find happiness chasing a Knight, because he will be chasing someone else, too. Kings and Queens would obviously make great matches.

The following profiles will help you to determine the stage the man who you are with is in or the one toward which he might be moving.

Knight

A Knight is a young man, generally between the ages of eighteen and thirty, who craves fun, conquest, and adventure. Nothing thrills a Knight more than moving from one woman to the next, in addition to carousing with other Knights. Not interested in commitment, a Knight will generally agree to marry only if his honor is at stake.

Knights love the chase and conquest. They crave the Eros of relationships, that hot surge of energy, passion, and sexuality encountered when the chemistry first clicks. Consequently, they move on if they become bored or fearful of being tied down. When the heat of the relationship fades, they are gone in a flash.

Julie, twenty-seven, was a client of mine who had a serious encounter with a Knight but wasn't able to recognize the signs. She was a cute, sweet, outgoing blonde, the kind of woman who, had she not had a burning love of architecture, could easily have put her bright smile to work in commercials. Wherever she went socially, guys would approach her.

Julie was attracted to men who shared her sense of adventure, who didn't fear the diamond-ranked ski slopes or heading to a bar in a bad part of town just before closing time.

Julie met twenty-nine-year-old Larry on an early-morning fishing excursion. Larry was a friend of one of the boat's regulars. They hit it off right away and spent the day snorkeling in the warm, clear water. By nightfall, when the boat returned, Julie knew that she liked him a lot.

They dated for months, spending their time together in an activity blitz that exhausted even them. Sometimes they would spend quieter times taking long walks by a nearby pond, talking about their lives and common interests. Julie found it curious, though, that on several occasions when she talked of wanting a long-term partner, kids, and a stable home, Larry shifted the conversation to their next adventure. If Julie pressed him about their future together, he always managed to dodge her questions.

"You want kids someday, don't you?" Julie asked him one afternoon.

"I don't know, maybe someday," Larry replied. "I think they would get in the way of a good time. I mean, you can't exactly be spontaneous with a one-year-old in tow."

"That's true," said Julie, "and I love a good time as much as anyone, but I think commitment and a family could eventually offer as much enjoyment as sailing, hiking, or anything else we do now. It would just be of a different kind of pleasure."

"Look," said Larry, changing the subject, "there's the new BMW convertible I would love to get for next summer. That's a good-looking car."

If Julie had been paying attention, she would have been able to see that Larry's need to dodge her questions about the future was a clear indication that he was a Knight, and that he was quite happy being one. Instead, she continued her adventure-filled relationship with Larry for a year, figuring that he would come around in time. As soon as she started pressing him about making a commitment for a future together, he was gone, completely disappearing from her life as if their year together had never happened. Julie later learned that Larry had gone on a snorkeling trip with another woman.

Julie was heartbroken and devastated by Larry's sudden departure, but worse, she had lost a valuable year by spending it with a man who had no intention of ever committing to her. Had she been able to read the Knight signs from the beginning and clearly stated what her relationship objectives were for the future, she would have saved herself heartbreak and a year of waiting.

How to Identify a Knight

Watch his behavior carefully. Does he:

1 Have difficulty making long-range plans?

2 Spend a lot of time with his friends, going out to bars and parties?

3 Like to date different women?

4 Show an interest in high-risk, high-adrenaline activities or business ventures?

5 Boast of having many women conquests when you request information about his past relationships?

If he doesn't seem to know what he wants from your time together, he is probably a Knight. He will openly admit, when asked, that he likes being free and having a good time. He is not interested in committing but just wants to see what happens.

Listen carefully to what he says, because nine times out of ten, he's telling you the truth. Women need to listen *and believe* what a man reveals about himself. If a man is a Knight, meeting a great woman will not necessarily make him graduate to Princehood any faster. Women mistakenly believe that a man will change his thinking about a committed relationship after they have spent quality time together and he discovers how great she is. *Forget it!* It will never happen.

If a man says he isn't interested in getting married now, he is still a Knight. He can bring over his toothbrush, his pajamas, even his prized stereo system, but that doesn't mean that he is thinking about a future with you in it—just that he wants to be more comfortable.

If you are going to spend your time with a Knight, you must accept that Knights are best for having fun, great sex, passion, and adventure. If you're looking for a committed partner or husband, however, the Knight's shining armor will keep out the intimacy and commitment you want.

Warning: It may be possible to trap a Knight into a commitment if you get pregnant. A Knight may commit to defend your maidenly honor, but if you trap him, he will feel robbed of his natural developmental process and will always feel an underlying resentment about having been trapped rather than freely choosing you. He will be hesitant to surrender to you with the deep-connectedness that you want and deserve in order to evolve to a state of love and mutual consent. If commitment, marriage, and/or family is what you're after, a Prince is a better choice for you.

Prince

During their late twenties to mid-thirties, most Knights trade in their armor for the velvet robes of a Prince. There are, of course, exceptions. Some men will make the transition from Knight to Prince earlier than others. There are many men, however, who call themselves confirmed bachelors or who suffer from "Peter Pan syndrome," unwilling to let go of a Knight's life and fantasies, even after such behavior has become inappropriate and unattractive.

Unlike the Knight, who is forever in pursuit of excitement and adventures, a Prince is on his way to "becoming." His sights are set on creating and building a glorious kingdom. In the modern world, this quest includes focusing on his career and finding someone with whom he can have a serious, committed relationship and possibly start a family. Princes spend a lot of time talking about the future, namely their plans and dreams and how things will eventually be. When they talk about the future, they usually include someone else in the description of that scenario. It could be you or some hypothetical woman with whom they wish to build their kingdom and their dreams.

A Prince is not only ready, willing, and able to settle down; he also wants to do that with someone he considers special enough to build a kingdom for and eventually share the results of his many years of hard work. If you are a woman who is interested in a long-term, committed relationship or marriage, you should look for a Prince to date. If you are still in your Maiden stage, be forewarned that if you choose a Prince, he will become very impatient with you because you are looking for fun and adventure while he wants to move on to the stage of commitment.

The tricky thing about Knights and Princes is that they often don't know when or how they'll make the transition from one developmental stage to another. A change comes over a man in ways he cannot articulate. This transition can sometimes happen seemingly overnight. One minute they are content playing the field with different women, and the next they are on their own quest for Ms. Right. The timing and reasons for the shift seem to make no sense, which drives many women crazy.

Thousands of women can relate to Barbara's experience. "I was furious," the thirty-three-year-old striking brunette said to me. "David and I dated for two years, during which time he constantly told me he didn't want to get serious. Then, I finally drop him to find someone who might make a commitment and he turns around and marries practically the first woman who comes along."

Why does a man spend years in a serious, committed relationship with a woman whom he says he loves, but is not yet ready to marry, then lead another woman down the aisle almost immediately? It has nothing to do with whether you are good enough for your man or whether he loves you enough to marry you. Rather, it has to do with the developmental stage he is in, as well as how his brain works (refer to chapter 8, "Hormones, Pheromones, and Other Moans").

Before a man makes the transition from Knight to Prince, he must have a feeling of success and of moving forward in his life. Once a man's career starts visibly to shift, he becomes more of who he is, moving from trainee to trainer, from employee to manager, or from associate to junior partner. He starts to feel like a Prince. At this point, he wants someone with whom he can share this progress and his newfound success. Although Princehood is indicative of men moving into a secure, expanded sense of themselves, financially and professionally, for some men it may just be gaining the expertise or experience they need in order to be better artists, musicians, or creative people. It may not always be attached to tangible business successes. In many men, the psychological change may precede the tangible external business success. At other times, it may lag behind the career achievement, especially if a man is successful in business at an early age; for example, a young trader who has been very sharp during the bull market or a young high-tech entrepreneur who had a great idea and sold it for big bucks. Be advised that an early Prince may not feel he has fully played out his romantic Knightly adventures.

Although it can be frustrating that a man can change on a dime from one stage to the next, you may discover you're Ms. Right if you meet a guy immediately after he has moved into his next stage. Timing, as they say, is everything.

163

How to Identify a Prince

Watch his behavior carefully. Does he:

❶ Know where he sees himself five years from now?

❷ Have a long-term game plan?

❸ Describe his game plan, with someone else in it besides himself?

❹ Clearly express his own ambitions professionally, spiritually, and emotionally?

❺ Seek your opinions, feedback, support, and encouragement about his ideas and process? (If he asks "What do you think about this idea?" you should respond with "I think it is wonderful and I have no doubt that if you put it into action, you will succeed.")

A Prince will usually do whatever it takes to court and convince the object of his affection that he is a worthy choice. If you're dating a man in the

Prince stage, know that it might not be as exciting as hooking up with a Knight, but the courtship stage should be pure pleasure. Bolstered by his own achievements and his commitment to finding and winning his own Guinevere, a Prince will often outdo himself in order to attract a Princess to his castle to reign over his growing kingdom.

Warning: Once a Prince is secure in knowing you're there to help him build his kingdom, you can count on him to turn his attention elsewhere. It's seldom to another woman, though; rather, it's back to his work and career. Because they are unaware of princely motivations, many long-term girlfriends or wives mistakenly fear that their Princes may have moved on to other women.

Rachel, a thirty-two-year old client of mine, thought she'd won the lottery when she first met Tom, an ambitious thirty-one-year-old who had just opened his own clothing store. Tom was attractive, with a real sense of how to treat a woman, in contrast to many other men whom Rachel had dated. From the very beginning, each time they saw each other, Tom brought her thoughtful little gifts, like flowers or five pounds of her favorite gourmet coffee. He took her to the newest, most fashionable restaurants in town, even though she knew money was tight.

After eight months of heated pursuit and attention, he proposed and she happily accepted. She agreed to move into his house while they planned their wedding. That's when he started working fourteen-hour days. The string of romantic presents abruptly stopped, except for the perfunctory birthday or holiday gifts. Not only did Tom and Rachel seldom go out for dinner anymore; they rarely had dinner together at all, since he often came home after Rachel was already in bed. He constantly reassured her there was not another woman in his life, that he just needed to devote his attention to the store if it was to succeed.

Rachel felt angry and betrayed by what she perceived as Tom's deception. "How dare he put on one face to lure me in, only to reveal another one once I took the bait," she said to me one day, crying. She had no idea about men's developmental stages. She loved the security and lifestyle her Prince had to offer, but she couldn't understand why she couldn't also have the adventure and fun she had experienced with the Knights whom she had dated previously. When a man is a Prince, he does whatever it takes to win his Princess, but once you're in his castle, he wants you to take care of it, and him, while he shifts his focus to securing your future together.

As a Smart Heart woman, Rachel learned not to see Tom's shift as a betrayal—a reaction that is common among women who don't understand the developmental stages of men's lives. She was able to reframe her experience by understanding Tom's developmental stage and see that his working long hours was, in essence, his commitment to creating stability and future security for her and the family they'd have together. She was able to understand how much Tom loved her and that he was expressing that love through his hard work. She restructured her responsibilities within the household and ran the kingdom as a positive gift. She was also able to go back to work herself so that she wasn't spending her days and evenings waiting for him to come home and entertain her. By returning to work, she was able to stimulate and support her own creative and personal growth.

She was also able to encourage him to balance work time with the pleasure and downtime of enjoying each other's company. She quickly came to see that when she encouraged Tom and supported his efforts, she received security and a stability that allowed her to move forward and plan on having children, knowing they would be well taken care of. She understood how much Tom truly loved her and that his efforts to work so hard honored her in a greater way than going out on exciting dates and participating in high-adrenaline activities would have, by putting her in charge of his kingdom to provide for their happiness, comfort, and security.

In today's tough economy, it is very difficult to have both money in the bank and a partner or mate who is home for dinner every night at 5:30. Building a successful career is a time-intensive pursuit. You must not take it personally when your formerly attentive Prince stops giving you little gifts or taking you out on the town every weekend. A Smart Heart woman understands that he is expressing his affection in a different and, to him, more substantial, way by working night and day for the two of you. Understanding this stage more clearly and accepting that it benefited and supported their dreams together for the future, Rachel learned to show Tom how much she appreciated him by supporting him emotionally and psychologically rather than feeling resentful or insecure.

If you are with a Prince, you must understand the power of your love and the importance of support and encouragement. If you don't, your relationship with him will begin to unravel. It is very common and, unfortunately, disastrous, for a woman to turn her misunderstanding of this developmental stage into resentment by withholding her love, support, and affection from her Prince. If you want to become a Smart Heart woman, you should know that these are the things a Prince needs most from his partner. Even if you are working hard yourself at a job outside the home or raising your children, you still need to give your Prince acknowledgment, appreciation, and love to keep him moving forward. This doesn't mean that you don't need the same acknowledgment, love, and appreciation, as well. If you request them from your Prince with an open heart, he will be more than happy to give them to you. In so doing, you will align yourself more strongly with your partner to create a more secure foundation for your future together.

King

A man becomes a King when he shifts from "becoming" to "being." In his own mind, he will crown himself because he knows that he has arrived. A King knows who he is, is confident and secure in what he does, and has nothing to prove to anyone. Being a King may mean that a man has finally reached the corner office or has decided that being a VP is enough. Maybe he sold his small hardware store and is living off the modest proceeds for his retirement. Though related to his career, this stage is also related to his maturation and age. Kingship is much more a state of mind than an external circumstance. A CEO may need several years before he feels comfortable moving mentally and spiritually from being a Prince to becoming a King, whereas a mailman, having been in the same job for decades, might suddenly feel deeply contented with his role. Men generally anoint themselves King somewhere between their late forties to mid-fifties, or even early sixties. A man older than that who isn't secure about himself and his place in life or doesn't know who he is probably will never be a King and is best avoided.

You can tell if a man has moved from becoming a Prince to a King by watching him in business. A King takes fewer risks and becomes more conservative. He may open another store or buy out a competitor as he did when a Prince, but, as a King, he will probably only do it if it is a sure thing. Like a retiree moving money from the riskier stock market into safer CDs, a King doesn't want big losses that might take years to reverse. He no longer has the energy level needed to recoup his losses, nor is he interested in the same kinds of challenges.

A King, unlike a Prince, is not in the process of building his kingdom. He has already created it. Rather, he is looking for someone with whom to share it. In addition to looking for appreciation and admiration, a King loves to share his expertise, whether it's his talent in the kitchen to his savvy business sense. A King never makes excuses for who he is. He does not want much advice. He does not want a makeover or to be told what to do—to change his clothes, or even his attitude.

Unlike a Prince who will seek his partner's opinions and wants to know what he can do to improve what he does and who he is, a King wants a woman who will listen to his stories; enjoy his company, knowledge, and expertise; and share his kingdom.

How to Identify a King

Watch his behavior carefully. Is he:

1 Very well established, both personally, professionally, and often spiritually?

2 Emotionally and financially secure?

3 Aware of who he is, what he wants, and what he likes?

4 Divorced, i.e. previously married at least once, perhaps with grown children with whom he may or may not still be involved?

5 Appreciative of the pleasure of a woman's company and looking to her to stand by his side?

6 Looking for a woman to look up to him?

7 Generous and a gift giver? Does he share his time and life experiences?

8 Not interested in changing?

9 Not receptive to nagging or criticism and seldom looking for your suggestions about how he can improve?

Warning: If you choose to be with a King, you stand alongside him as a Queen. Remember, he is your King and you need to feel comfortable about "giving over to him"; i.e., allowing him to contribute to you in a loving, benevolent way. If you are a woman who likes to receive and be indulged, who can enjoy watching your King as he holds court, telling you why he is the greatest lord in the land, a King is the man for you. In return for your devotion, your King will give you his kingdom and all that is in it.

Women who don't understand Kings could find themselves in a very difficult predicament. A client of mine named Lynn landed in such a situation.

A twenty-something woman who fell in love with a wealthy King, Lynn learned the hard way that Kings are not the same as the Princes she had been used to dating. It was such a traumatic experience for her that she wrote about it in an article for *Cosmopolitan* magazine.

At fifty-four, Hank was a successful investment banker who owned a thriving firm. Having reached near-legendary status, he sold his business to travel around the world. He returned several years later and was just beginning another investment company when he noticed Lynn. A striking, thin woman with beautiful hair, Lynn was the perfect complement to his elegant existence. He bought her glamorous, form-fitting clothes; jetted her to South Beach for exotic weekends; took her to the fabulous parties to which he was constantly invited; and entertained her and her friends in his Manhattan penthouse. Lynn fell in love with the romance, glamour, lifestyle, and, by extension, Hank.

After a year, they were married in an intimate ceremony in Lynn's parents' Iowa hometown, but Lynn felt upstaged when Hank asked a celebrity friend to be best man. That was only the start of their troubles. Lynn, who was only now moving from Maiden to Princess, was busy thinking about how to become a more successful reporter and writer. She didn't have a clue about what makes a King tick or what it meant to be his Queen.

Because his new company was just starting out, she would sometimes ask him why he wasn't putting in more hours at the office. Not knowing that a King doesn't want to be told what to do, she was startled when he responded by lashing back at her, saying that he knew perfectly well how to run a business and hadn't asked for her advice.

He expected her to oversee the maintenance of their fancy penthouse, to see that it was beautifully decorated, and to manage their social calendar, all the while wearing a tight leather miniskirt. "I hated being the woman behind the great man, keeping him company while my own career dissolved before my very eyes. I was afraid that I was becoming a numb housewife without direction, the kind of woman I had ridiculed in my early feminist days."

Lynn attempted to try to break out of her gilded cage by enrolling in a local Master's program. This enraged Hank because he wanted her to be reachable at home. Soon the power struggles between them got in the way of their good times. The relationship quickly degenerated into constant bickering and battles for power.

Although Lynn loved accepting Hank's money and all the privileges that came with it, she wasn't willing to accommodate to his needs and demands. She didn't understand that this is often typical of a King. She did not know that her "job" was to preside over his castle and that he was not interested in having her tell him what to do or how to live his life. To Lynn, her suggestions were offered with love. In turn, she felt completely unsupported by him in her own endeavors. The unhappiness and anger between them escalated, she moved out, and they divorced.

If Lynn had really understood her King, Hank would have been more than happy to help her get her Master's degree had she requested his help and understanding. If she had let him know that she wanted to be available to him but that other things were also important to her, and if she had been able to ask for his help, she would have found that Hank would have been more than happy to compromise. Lynn could have continued to enjoy that lifestyle, his money, and his support, while she expanded her career, if she had been willing to move more slowly and had asked him to support her in the process.

For a woman to be in a successful relationship with a King, she must feel comfortable with who she is, be secure within herself, and not be competitive with him. She must be able to graciously and gratefully accept his gifts, time, lessons, and attention and not try to remake him or his desires. A woman needs to realize that if she is involved with a King, her contribution comes from being completely receptive to her King's needs and wants while supporting his Kingly ego.

As a Smart Heart woman, you may want to choose a King rather than a Prince because Kings bring with them many benefits. A King is generally more financially successful, emotionally stable, and often more generous because he can afford to be. Women who are consciously seeking Kings are happy to admire and appreciate them in return for the rich rewards that generally follow.

A woman who has been married to a Prince for many years must also be aware of when he suddenly becomes a King. If she continues to hold him in her mind as her Prince, she may be contributing to the demise of the relationship. More than one King has come to my practice complaining that he's looked up to at work and treated like a small child at home. This is why some Kings leave their wives of thirty years for young Maidens or Princesses. A King wants respect, admiration, and appreciation. If his wife does not give this to him, he will look elsewhere. Men who leave their wives for someone else often say that a lack of appreciation and understanding ultimately broke their relationship apart.

If you are a Maiden looking for a King, be advised that these May-December relationships have their problems. Maidens usually want their own fun, adventure, and perhaps children. A King can obviously afford to support these desires, but he may not want these things for himself at this stage of his life.

The reverse of the May-December Maiden/King combination is the Queen/Knight or Queen/Prince pairing. A Knight who is involved with a Queen and then becomes a Prince while he is still with her may decide that he now needs to be with a Princess or Maiden instead.

If you are presently in or are thinking about such pairings, you need to know that they are time limited and chances are they won't be ongoing because of the different needs of men and women at different developmental stages. When the pairing is reversed, i.e., the King/Maiden or King/Princess, if it is a conscious decision accepted by both parties, the chances are better that the relationship will succeed in the long run.

Essentially, a Queen who knows who she is and understands the needs of a King is generally the best partner for a King. Rather than competing with him (the way Lynn did), a Queen is equally secure in her sense of self and doesn't need the approval and emotional support from her partner in the same way she did when she was a Maiden or Princess.

All this is not to say that a Princess can never succeed with a graying King. It's just that she must transcend some of her own desires and consciously choose to meet his very different ones. Shelly, a client of mine, was able to do just that. She is an actress who, until last year, was still hoping to break into the big time. At thirty-four years old, she had many bit parts, and just as many two-bit boyfriends. Then she met Harold, a famous movie producer who, at fifty-five, no longer needed to work much anymore.

"Early in our relationship, I thought that, by knowing Harold, I would be introduced to someone who could make me a star," Shelly now says, laughing, "but he had other ideas." Harold wanted Shelly out of Hollywood as much as possible to spend time with him on his yacht in the Pacific, in his beachfront condo on the coast of Mexico, and on the ski slopes at his favorite resort. Shelly really can't devote much time to her own career, which means that she probably will never see her name in lights.

Like other Princesses who have successfully joined with Kings, though,

Shelly has no regrets about what she has given up. "I love my life with Harold, and I know where he is in life. I can't have him and also devote time to a demanding career. There is no guarantee, even if I had continued with my acting, that I would have made it. Instead, I'm returning to school so that I can teach children the craft that has brought me so much pleasure." For Shelly, the security, stability, and constancy that are a part of their life together have more than compensated for the sacrifices she has had to make.

Warning: Some Kings are less generous and more dictatorial, believing that it's their money and they'll choose how to spend it. Be sure your prospective King is beneficent and loving, not eager to make you a captive Queen whom he will behead at the first sign of insurrection. Tyrannical Kings (or, for that matter, tyrannical Knights and Princes) make terrible relationship partners. Although a less than beneficent King can certainly provide security and financial comfort, what you must give up psychologically and spiritually can never be worth it.

Understand, too, that a King is not likely to support or encourage your dreams, if they conflict with his lifestyle, unless you are a very good negotiator. Don't get into a relationship with a King unless you are confident about who you are and are happy to enjoy the spoils of his success.

171

Knight, Prince, King: Who Is Right for You?

It is impossible categorically to state whether a Knight, Prince, or King is the best man for you. All stages of life have their benefits and drawbacks. Most women looking for a spouse with whom they can have a family find that their best bet is with a Prince. A King could also fulfill this role because many Kings happen to be better fathers the second time around. They are more mature than when they were Princes, and they usually have more leisure time to spend with their children. Conversely, if you are looking for fun, you will probably be happier with a Knight.

How do you determine which stage is right for you?

❶ Ask yourself what you want from a relationship. Is it fun, family, stability, and/or financial security? This, along with examining your own aspirations and experience, will help you figure out if you are a Maiden, Princess, or Queen.

❷ Evaluate the man you are with to determine if he is a Knight, Prince, or King.

If you are a Maiden, you are interested in erotic adventures and experimenting with dating different men. If you are a Princess, you are aware of your need and desire to settle down, nest, and create your family. If you are a Queen, you've completed the first two stages. You've had your fun, been with various men, and had pivotal life experiences. You've raised your family and/or completed your career. You have a sense of who you are.

There is no stage that is better than another. The important thing is to know which stage you are in. These stages are not necessarily dictated by a specific age or in chronological terms, but rather by being aware of what is needed to complete your life experience for that period of time. For example, you may have skipped over your Maiden stage and immediately created a family and raised your children. Now divorced and on your own, you are interested in adventure and experimentation with different partners. We usually go through the Maiden stage in high school or college, followed by the Princess stage. As our children grow up and our careers become established, we move into our Queenly nature. We begin to feel comfortable in our own skin, and we know who we are and the value of the gifts we possess.

Women usually spend less time as Maidens than men do as Knights. By nature, women are more interested in partnering and being serially monogamous, which is one of the primary distinctions between men and women. By and large, women are interested in sampling different men for short periods of time, but they would rather find one person to be with and are able to move more quickly out of the Maiden stage into becoming Princesses.

As women have moved into the workforce, however, there has been a shift. Women are choosing to be Maidens longer, partly out of necessity because they must spend more time and energy focusing on building their careers. Many women want to continue being Maidens throughout their twenties and into their early thirties so they can freely explore sex and fun within the context of casual relationships.

If you are a Queen, your profile will be similar to your male equivalent, the King: you are a woman who is established and relatively successful both financially and professionally. Perhaps you've raised a family and have grown children and *you don't necessarily need to be in a relationship.* A Queen knows who she is, is successful in other endeavors of her life, and has a clear and well-defined sense of self. A Queen can afford to have a young Knight in her life to entertain and pleasure her. She may prefer a Prince, whom she can support in his goals, or she may opt to stand by the side of a King.

Only when you know what you want and where your man is developmentally can you determine if your individual stages will complement or conflict with each other. Armed with this information, you'll gain an important sense of whether he is a man with whom you can create the kind of relationship you desire and deserve, or if he's more suitable for a short-term, delicious affair.

Bad Boys Are Bad Bets

D o you ever remember your mom telling you that it's just as easy to love a rich man as a poor one? Mother's advice is often wise and worth listening to. A bad boy isn't a guy who happened to be broke because he built a business and recently lost it, or one who's attending law school and on his way to a lucrative career. Bad boys are different, and there are warning signs and signals a Smart Heart woman needs to be aware of. Whether you are looking for a long-term partner or a playmate, bad boys are guaranteed to lead you down disastrous, often dangerous, avenues on the way to your relationship objectives. The operative word here is *boy* as compared to *man*.

Bad bets are often more charming. They initially appear attractive, but you need to identify their modus operandi so you can protect yourself before it's too late. Every minute of every day, smart, successful women are duped by these con men. Before they got taken in, these women had self-esteem and felt empowered in their lives. Blinded by hope, hormones, and feelings, they permit the confidence they had about themselves to be destroyed by a continuing relationship with a bad bet. Often their physical, mental, and emotional health, as well as financial well-being, suffer from such an involvement.

As you review this list of bad bets, it may seem as if there are no good men left. That is far from the truth. There are many loving, honest, and aware men available. The operative word is *men*. Bad boys, regardless of their particular character flaws, have not matured and grown up.

"My Love Will Change Him"

Most women are die-hard romantics. In our attraction to these kinds of men, we feel we will be the ones who are going to nurture and support them and make up for their history, pain, and unfortunate life experiences. These men pull at our heartstrings and we feel their pain. We futilely believe that, through the power of our love, we can turn an emotionally crippled, wart-covered frog into our dream prince. Deep in our hearts, we feel that this man is the way he is because no one has ever really loved him or cared for him. We erroneously believe that our love is the only missing ingredient needed to heal his sordid past. Forget that idea forever! Bad boys are always bad bets.

Love is not a panacea for another person's problems, especially when it comes to a man who is a problem partner. If you love a dud, you will not alter him. He's simply a dud who is loved. By his own volition, he needs to make difficult changes, indicated by his past and present problems. Neither your love nor anything you do will change him if he doesn't want to change. Don't fall victim to your own magical thinking.

"So what if he doesn't have a job or an apartment and he lives in his car. If I let him move in with me, at least he'll be good company. That's better than being alone." *Wrong!* A problem partner is far from a benign influence on your life. On the contrary, he will take your energy, money, self-esteem, dignity, freedom, and joy, while returning nothing positive. Ask any woman who has been involved with a man like this and she will undoubtedly tell you that being with no one would have been a better choice.

As a Smart Heart woman, look for and pay attention to the danger signs flashing around a bad bet. Learn how to run, not walk, away from them and stop wasting your valuable time, energy, and emotions on these roadblocks to happiness. You can't build a lasting, meaningful relationship on pity and potential. These men don't deserve your heart and affection, let alone your credit cards or the keys to your apartment or car. Your hope, help, and concern will never motivate them to get their lives together. The odds of successful, long-term relationships with these men are definitely not in your favor.

175

It is within the realm of possibility that a man like this could have a spiritual epiphany and turn his life around, although the epiphany is not going to manifest itself as a result of your love; it will be the result of no longer being able to tolerate the pain and consequences of his own abhorrent behavior. A few may be able to improve because they want to hold on to you, but bad behavior is the hallmark of a bad boy and his history is dedicated to it.

Run, Don't Walk, Away from a Dangerous Man

These troublesome types don't attract only women who are themselves down and out. If they did, it would be easy for smart, successful women to avoid them. They can turn on and tune in to even the most savvy woman's heart. Some of the brightest, most successful women I've seen in my practice have fallen under the spell of dangerous bad boys.

Emotional and Physical Abusers and Ragers

Ragers and their more extreme counterparts, abusers, are men who are unable to control their anger. Often provoked by nothing more than a minor inconvenience, they magnify a slight provocation until it totally consumes them and those around them. A woman who remains with a Rager is acquiescent in a life on the edge. She places herself in danger, not knowing what will next enrage him. Worse still, his outbreaks of rage are not infrequent. You can count on men with this emotional affliction to be angry at least 5 percent of the time.

Very often, a rage-oholic or an abuser will not show that side of himself during the initial courtship. My client Carla was involved with a man named Stan whom she encountered frequently in social situations with other friends. He always seemed smart, polite, charming, and down-to-earth. After they had been dating for two months, she started to evaluate him as a possible long-term partner. During dinner one evening, a waiter returned after taking Stan's order to report that the kitchen no longer had the prime rib he requested. Stan reacted with an irrational explosion that embarrassed and stunned her. She immediately decided to stop dating him.

Even if irrational behavior is not directed at you, it is only a matter of time before you will be the target. Fortunately, Carla had a strong sense of self-worth and was able to make a smart choice. Women often rationalize abusive behavior by saying "Well, he only gets angry at them, not at me."

There's a small percentage of men in this category who won't ever be directly abusive toward you, but even if you are never physically in their line of fire, living around this destructive energy is spiritually toxic for you and your children, if you have them.

Life is downright dangerous with a man who is an emotional, spiritual, or physical abuser. Men who are abusive physically, verbally, or psychologically generally won't stop until forced to by the courts. After they have thrown you to the ground and broken your collarbone, they exhibit extreme remorse by bringing you flowers, chocolates, and promises that they will never repeat that behavior again. For these men, however, this behavior is recurrent. They can't stop it without some kind of professional help. Frequently, even court-ordered treatment programs don't stop these types of men from acting out, and they turn their abusiveness on their children as well.

It's hard to believe that smart women stay involved with men who display this serious affliction, but they do. Women trapped in an abusive environment and constantly exposed to its toxicity develop their own affliction, a learned helplessness from which they are powerless to escape without professional help.

177

The Warning Signs of Ragers and Physical Abusers

- ▶ He has sudden explosions of anger completely out of proportion to the situation (e.g., if he has trouble opening up a jar of mayonnaise, he'll start screaming and cursing and throw down the jar on the kitchen floor).

- ▶ His anger goes from zero to sixty in three seconds.

- ▶ His expresses his anger by yelling, throwing things, hitting, name-calling, and cursing.

- ▶ He is emotionally overwrought and angry more than 5 percent of the time.

- ▶ He throws objects across the room (or at you) when he's frustrated.

- ▶ He is constantly critical and gets pleasure out of belittling you in front of others.

- ▶ He is often racist, bigoted, and close minded.

- ▶ He hits or kicks animals and children.

- ▶ He hits you.

Substance Abusers and Addicts
(Alcohol, Drugs, Sex, Food, and Gambling)

An addict is someone who can't give up whatever he is addicted to, no matter what the consequences. There are many types of addictions, not only substance addictions like drugs and alcohol but also sex, food, gambling, and other things. An addict may not necessarily indulge in his addiction on a daily basis. Some alcoholics can go for months or years without a drink before they finally succumb, with negative consequences; they may go on a bender, experience blackouts, or exhibit poor judgment. If a man can't stop himself, take responsibility for his actions, or predict the consequences of his compulsive behavior, he has an addiction problem and he's a bad bet as a relationship partner. An addict will have not only personal relationship problems at home but also professional problems and difficulties in every other area of his life, which could entail serious health or legal problems.

Sheryl was an expert when it came to computers, but she was rather awkward with men. She was statuesque, blond, and beautiful, but she felt too tall and was afraid men wouldn't be interested in her. She was shy and aloof around most men she met, except Henry. Henry was six three, charming, and outgoing. He gravitated to Sheryl immediately when she came to program software for his new business. Before she left his office, he took out a stash of cocaine and asked her if she wanted a snort. She was surprised that he was so open about his drug use, but she had never experimented with drugs before and thought perhaps it was something he did infrequently. When she declined the cocaine, he asked her to dinner instead. Thrilled that someone (who was taller, no less!) had taken an interest in her, she agreed.

They started seeing each other soon after that. Henry didn't have much money, but he attributed that to the start-up cost of his new business. Although he occasionally snorted a line in front of Sheryl, his behavior and demeanor appeared normal. He was wonderful to be around, sweet, funny, and adoring. When he started sleeping in his office because he didn't have enough money to pay both office and house rents, Sheryl invited him to live in her spacious home. She even gave him money when he was short on cash. It wasn't until three months later, when she caught him stealing her jewelry, that the warning bells went off in her head. She nervously wondered, "He seems normal, but is he a drug addict?" Unequivocally, the answer is "yes."

178

Despite the widespread notion that someone who is addicted to drugs or alcohol lies in the gutter and can't hold a job, the truth is that many people with serious addictions are highly adept at functioning at work and in other areas of their lives. A drug addict or alcoholic isn't just a transient holding up a "help me" card near the freeway on-ramp. He can just as easily be a cute, smart doctor or college professor indulging in his chosen substance on nights and weekends, yet somehow managing his addiction while on the job. Each kind of addiction has different warning signs, but the following lists should help you in your evaluation. If you have suspicions that the man you are with falls into one of these categories, you can contact a twelve-step program such as Alcoholics Anonymous, Sex Addicts Anonymous, Overeaters Anonymous, Gamblers Anonymous, and Narcotics Anonymous to get their guidelines for evaluating addictive behavior.

The Warning Signs of an Alcohol or Drug Addict

▶ He denies he has a problem, becoming angry if you suggest that he might.

▶ He is obsessed with the substance over everything else, including you.

▶ He needs the substance to feel good or have a good time.

▶ He has trouble being without the substance and will even go out in the middle of the night to get more.

▶ He tries to hide his use of the substance.

▶ He has been arrested for possession of an illegal substance or for driving under the influence.

▶ He never has enough money, even if he earns a good living.

▶ He has radical mood swings, difficulty holding down a job, and may disappear for a period of time while bingeing.

▶ He has legal, health, or work-related problems.

The Warning Signs of a Sex Addict

▶ He has an unhealthy obsession with sexually arousing material, e.g., X-rated videos, pornographic magazines, or sex phone lines.

▶ He is obsessed with sex, constantly wanting to experiment in a variety of ways.

▶ He masturbates excessively, even if you are having regular sex.

- He spends a lot of time surfing the Web with the door locked.
- He isn't interested in anything unless it has sexual content.
- He makes frequent, inappropriate sexual remarks and innuendos.
- He is uninterested and distant after sex.
- He frequently turns conversations into sexual discourse.
- His sexual activity is often dangerous or threatening to you and your well-being.

The Warning Signs of a Gambling Addict

- He sees winning at gambling as a viable way to improve his life.
- He has sold or risked something secure to finance his gambling.
- He gambles until his last dollar is gone.
- He gambles when he gets frustrated or is disappointed about other things.
- He can never walk away with his winnings without relinquishing some of them.
- He gambles more than he can comfortably afford to lose.
- He will risk everything for the Big Win.

The Warning Signs of a Food Addict

- He is obsessed with what, how much, and where he is going to consume meals.
- He eats when he is not hungry, especially as a way to escape worries or trouble.
- He binges on food, both secretly as well as openly.
- His thoughts about food take priority over everything—including you.
- He often eats meals in the car.
- He may be overweight, but food addicts are frequently thin—even anorexic.
- He is physically unhealthy.
- He is prone to fits of rage and depression.

The Warning Signs of an Exercise Addict

▶ He craves the endorphin high released by his brain when he exercises.

▶ He has no flexibility about when and how he exercises.

▶ He must work out every day, no matter what, and flips out if he misses a day.

Law Breakers and Benders

A Law Breaker is someone who is either involved in unlawful activity or very good at bending the law to fit shady, borderline pursuits. He could be involved in white-collar crime or petty theft. A contemporary outlaw doesn't look like an outlaw of the past. The modern-day Law Breaker often dresses in expensive, tailored suits and lives in a beautiful house in a fashionable neighborhood. He may travel first class and drive an expensive car, often with a driver or bodyguard. If he is a petty criminal who is not in charge of the operation, he may not have an exorbitant income, but he has money, jewelry, and wheels exceeding his station in life.

The thrill of being with such a man and of reaping the rewards of his ill-gotten gains may be initially appealing. He might take you places you've only dreamed about. Due to his irregular hours, he might have lots of free time to spend with you. Because he thrives on risk, he'll be fun and exciting to be around.

In the end, though, the government and their attorneys get the proceeds, and the Law Breaker goes to jail. With a Law Breaker, you live in fear of his arrest or death. When you can't handle the risk anymore, he might promise to quit "after one more deal." That last deal will keep turning into another and another, because men who live in this fast lane can't voluntarily walk away from it. Also, his associates may not let him leave, even if he wants to. You, on the other hand, have a choice. If you have a sense that his business affairs aren't legitimate, leave before you're in too deep.

The Warning Signs of a Law Breaker or Bender

▶ He has a lot of money to spend, especially after having gone on a trip.

▶ He won't let you see where he works and is vague about his job.

▶ He doesn't introduce you to his colleagues and is evasive when pressed for details about his business.

▶ He always wears a beeper and has secret phone calls.

▶ He has lots of free time that can't be accounted for.

▶ He carries a gun or has one in his house or car.

▶ He moves frequently without leaving a forwarding number or address.

Con Men

A Con Man is someone who dates to get what he wants, never for intimacy or marriage. This man goes after a woman for what she can give him that he can't provide for himself. This could mean sex, money, prestige, or access to people who can help him. It could even be your entire family fortune. An expert Con Man makes the news by swindling his multiple wives out of all their money. Often, he can use his powers of persuasion to enlist a woman's help in his shady endeavors. Regardless of his aim, once he gets it, a Con Man will be gone.

A smart woman is too clever to be taken in by a Con Man, right? *Wrong.* Ask a woman like Clarissa. Jeremy dressed well, drove a slick sports car, and had a charming English accent. Clarissa was involved with another man when Jeremy snared her. He was persistent and persuasive, and she finally agreed to have dinner with him. That's when he really turned on the charm. He told Clarissa she was the most beautiful, intelligent woman he had ever met. Despite her upper-class background, her degree from Sarah Lawrence, and a successful career as a high-profile Hollywood producer, she perceived herself as below average in terms of looks and intelligence. Because she had a distorted self-image, Jeremy's attention and acknowledgment swept her off her feet.

Clarissa was thrilled to be with someone with whom she could spend some quality time, and, after only two months, she invited him to move into her hilltop Hollywood home. They dated for four months, during which time Jeremy was on his best behavior. When he asked her if she could cosign a loan for his new luxury car because he was having some credit troubles "related to past business problems," she agreed. A month later, he requested a "small personal loan" of $10,000, to tide him over "until a big commission came in." Again Clarissa agreed, thinking they would have a future together.

After the check had cleared, she came home to discover he had moved out. She never heard from him again, although she did hear from the car dealership which notified her that, if she wanted to keep her good credit, she should keep paying off the car loan. It seems that Jeremy (who took the car with him) was no longer making payments.

A Con Man is someone with no moral compass, conscience, or heart. He feels no remorse for his behavior and will berate his victims for allowing themselves to be so gullible. ("She gave me the money as a gift, after all. I can't help it if she stupidly thought she would be getting something back for it.") Don't allow yourself to be taken in by a suave swindler. He'll rob you of your heart and anything else he can get.

The Warning Signs of a Con Man

▶ He is overly charming and persuasive.

▶ He lies with ease and has no conscience.

▶ He rationalizes improper behavior.

▶ He is secretive about his past relationships, work, and family.

▶ He asks you to do him large favors early in your relationship, e.g., requesting money, credit cards, and personal loans.

▶ He shows no guilt or remorse for causing others harm.

▶ He often blames others for getting talked into negative situations created by him.

183

Extremely Controlling and Dominating Men

Some men take control and domination to the most extreme level. A woman involved with this type of man will eventually become a prisoner in the relationship—not merely a "kept woman," but someone whose every move and thought is watched and controlled by a partner who supposedly shows his "love" this way. This kind of tight control is *NOT* love but a warning sign of a severe personality disorder.

This man's desire to control every aspect of a woman's life overrides any opportunity to have a healthful, happy relationship. An atmosphere of distrust poisons any love that might once have grown between you. Choosing to be with a controlling, dominant man has numerous consequences for a woman. In an extreme case, such a man may kill his girlfriend or wife in a horrifying attempt to prevent her from involvement with others. Being able to disengage from a man with this kind of deep-seated sickness will probably require professional help or police protection.

Cindy was consistently attracted to men she thought were protective but who, in reality, were domineering, controlling, and suspicious of her every move. She mistook their jealousy for love and their possessiveness for concern. She repeatedly chose men who grew increasingly controlling.

Then she got involved with Tony. He was in a whole new category. In a matter of months, life with Tony shifted from being a mere annoyance, because he continuously asked her where she was going, to an absolute nightmare. He followed her and watched her every move. He forbade her to see her family and friends. At first, Cindy thought she could convince Tony that she was wild about him, that there was nothing for him to be jealous about. But he began to exert control over her every action, how she dressed, when she could leave the house, where she could go, to whom she could talk. He planted doubt in her mind that she could make these decisions herself. After several months of this behavior, one day when she put on a dress to mail a letter he accused her of secretly having an affair with the postal clerk.

This behavior is not to be confused with that of an insecure man with a slight jealousy problem. Cindy finally realized that Tony was very disturbed. He became more and more oppressive. She couldn't reason with him to curb his insane jealousy and desire to control her every move. After she made the decision to leave him, Tony was not willing to let Cindy go. Her rejection of him confirmed to him that she must be involved with another man. He proceeded to stalk her for six horrifying months trying to verify his suspicions, and Cindy sought a restraining order and protection. She believes that Tony finally stopped stalking only because he found another woman to terrorize instead.

The Warning Signs of an Extremely Controlling and Dominating Man

- He won't let you see your family or friends.
- He questions your every move.
- He constantly demands to know what you are doing and with whom.
- He doesn't want you to leave the house without him, ever.
- He constantly accuses you of seeing other men. He flies into fits of rage over imagined indiscretions.
- He doesn't respect your privacy; he goes through your mail and purse.
- He surveys your every move. He may tap your telephone, follow you, or show up uninvited to check up on you at work or when you are out socially.

▶ He questions your ability to make decisions independent of him and instills feelings of fear and hopelessness that you can ever break free of him.

Energy Vampires

This category of men is a drain on a woman's spirit and emotions more than an actual physical or mental threat. In extreme cases, physical violence is a real risk, but these men, for the most part, will wound you in less obvious but no less harmful or lasting ways. You will need to evaluate each man individually, as these personalities manifest themselves in various forms, but generally, the following are negative personality traits that are best avoided.

Jealous Men

A man who is jealous is different from a man who is extremely controlling and domineering in that jealousy alone is not indicative of a person who suffers from a deep-seated wound. Usually jealousy is based on a man's insecurity and lack of self-worth. It appears in varying degrees. If a man is mildly jealous, he might show those feelings at the inception of the relationship and then get over them as he becomes more confident and secure. There are many men, however, who never get over those feelings. No matter how much women reassure them, they are suspicious because, at a deep level, they don't believe in their own value. There may be a family history of infidelity that creates suspicion and discord in a relationship. These men are distrustful, and the jealousy inevitably destroys the possibility of deep intimacy.

Women often confuse initial interest and concern with a man's desire to protect them. They may misread this behavior by believing his "love" is what makes him so upset. These actions have nothing to do with love. They have to do with control, insecurity, self-doubt, and inability to trust. If you are involved with a jealous man, ask yourself how long you can have a relationship with someone who does not trust you.

The Warning Signs of an Extremely Jealous Man

▶ He demands to know what you are doing and with whom.

▶ He looks through your purse and personal belongings to check up on you.

▶ He interrogates you about your activities.

185

▶ In milder cases, he will try to keep you from your family and friends; in extreme cases, he will tell you whom to see and when.

▶ He threatens you and is always suspicious of your motives.

▶ He tells you how to dress, shop, clean, cook, etc.

▶ He doesn't want you to leave the house without him.

▶ He accuses you, for no reason, of seeing other men.

Men Who Are Emotionally Frozen and Unavailable

Women who are easily seduced by money or sex are sometimes willing to initially forego affection, love, and intimacy. These are crucial aspects of healthy relationships. These women hope, over time, that their love and caring will thaw out a man who is emotionally frozen. If you choose a man like this, you will be waiting until Hell freezes over to get what you want.

Tara came to my practice because she felt that she was living in an emotional wasteland, desperate for affection. Tara's husband, Fred, was cold and distant, never expressing his own emotions and never wanting to hear about Tara's. "Feelings," he once declared to her matter-of-factly, "are for poets, not for regular people." Being a warm, vivacious woman, Tara was very much in touch with her emotional nature, and she felt isolated from Fred.

Fred was a great provider and their sex life was fairly decent, but she couldn't get Fred to share more deeply and intimately with her. A true heart connection will never be available to her with a man like Fred who is stuck in his head. Such men live from the neck up, overcompensating for their lack of passion with their intellects. As children, they were often ridiculed for revealing their feelings. As men, they have learned to detach themselves from all emotion. They have difficulty expressing tender affection or profound feelings. They withhold their feelings from themselves, as well as from you, and have learned to forget the importance of emotions in their lives. If you get involved with a man like Fred, you are asking for a lifetime of emotional detachment and loneliness.

The Warning Signs of a Man who Is Emotionally Frozen and Unavailable

▶ He is always reasonable, reacting from his head, not his heart.

▶ He never shows his emotions and seldom raises his voice or laughs spontaneously.

- He cannot remember the last time he cried.

- He thinks feelings are weak, appropriate only for girls or sissies.

- He becomes impatient, uncomfortable, or angry when you express your feelings.

- He will ridicule you if you share your feelings and emotions.

Workaholics

It can be difficult to spot the problem if you are in a relationship with a man who is addicted to his work. Our culture praises and supports this kind of addiction. Work consumes many Americans' entire existence, not just those people with legitimate work requirements, such as starting a business or dealing with a crisis, but in workaday life. What are we working for? When work goes beyond taking care of our financial needs and creative expression, it no longer enhances our lives; it *becomes* our lives, leaving no room for healthy relationships. Healthy individuals balance work with other parts of their lives.

Ellie is a client of mine who was dating Tim, a handsome entertainment business executive. He was a great guy but a total workaholic. They barely got to spend time together. He worked seven days a week. For three nights, he would sleep at the house of a colleague who lived just a few blocks from the office, so he wouldn't have to worry about making a midnight drive home. The other four nights, he got home after eleven. After they had dated for several months, Ellie accepted Tim's offer to move in with him in hopes of allowing them more time together. Knowing she was conveniently at his house, however, simply made Tim stop trying to find time for her. Tim couldn't excuse or rationalize his behavior by claiming a big salary or a need for recognition at the office. He really didn't make much money, considering the amount of hours he worked. No one at the office was aware of how long he worked because they all left the office by 7 P.M. Tim didn't work those hours for his boss or for career advancement. He did it because he was addicted to work.

A man who cancels dates repeatedly because of business is a man who is going to cancel your life together if you marry him. If you're involved with a work addict, you must be prepared to go to social events alone, take care of the house by yourself, and raise your children alone. Friends and relatives may be more understanding that your man can't make another holiday celebration because he has to work, rather than because he has gone on a drinking binge, but the reality for you won't be much better. In either event, you will be alone. Many workaholics use their work as the excuse for not forming intimate relationships, but that merely masks their emotional and psychological inability to do so. Work becomes a way of hiding from the kind of commitment, even if they had the time, that they are incapable of giving.

The Warning Signs of a Workaholic

▶ He doesn't have time for family, friends, hobbies, relaxation, or you.

▶ He always works late into the night and on weekends even when his work doesn't require it.

▶ He works on Christmas and major national holidays.

▶ He never takes a vacation (or if he does, he is constantly phoning or faxing the office). He is uncomfortable being away from work for longer than a three-day weekend.

▶ He constantly cancels plans with you because of "pressing" business situations.

▶ He never commits to plans in advance, even for nights or weekends.

▶ He works longer hours than his salary or career advancement would dictate.

▶ He is unable or unwilling to cut back on his work, even if you ask him to.

Loners and Isolationists

Beware of a man who has no friends. This type of man may live alone and only go to work and back day after day. There are two types of these loners. The first are men who are socially backward and have no real human interaction or contact other than what is absolutely necessary. Such men may spend an inordinate amount of time surfing the Web, visiting chat rooms with strangers, because they are more comfortable spending their time with their computers than with women. Shy around people in all social situations, with the possible exception of work, these men are never going to be comfortable bonding intimately with any women. They often live at home with their parents well beyond the age when their peers strike out on their own. This enables them to hide from interacting with people in the world at large on a mature level.

There are also loners who just don't like people and don't want to be around anyone but you. They don't rely on 900 numbers or chat groups for human contact because the less human interaction they have to endure, the better. The only person they might let into their net of isolation is you.

Both of these types find limited ways of connecting with women, for example, through their mothers, relatives, work associates, or on line. Sometimes they meet women by happenstance simply because they are forced to interact, to some degree, with human beings in society. The problem in being with a loner is that your life will become equally isolated. He will tend to be uncomfortable with your bringing people into either his world or your shared world. All of the responsibility for any social life or interesting activities outside of the relationship will be yours because, if the decision were left to these men, they would be content with only you. At first this may seem romantic, but eventually it just becomes a huge energy drain on you.

The Warning Signs of a Loner or Isolationist

▶ He avoids and dislikes most social situations.

▶ He is extremely awkward or agitated around other people.

▶ He spends hours on the computer, watching television, tinkering in the garage, or pursuing other solo activities or hobbies.

▶ He has had very little experience dating or with relationships.

▶ He still lives with his parents.

▶ He prefers fantasy to reality.

▶ He has a history of calling 900 numbers, using prostitutes, or frequenting massage parlors.

Married (or Attached) Men

If your goal is marriage, getting involved with someone who is already married or committed to someone else will not help you achieve your relationship objective. Seemingly smart women get involved with married men all the time, even when they are fully aware of their marital status. In the past, most cheating married men used to try to hide their marriage, but today many of them don't even bother to take off their rings. They make up stories about how their wives don't love or understand them, or they are only staying together for the children. If you pay attention, you can easily read between the lines to discover the truth.

It doesn't matter if a man says he is planning to divorce his wife. Until

189

he actually leaves, such a man is a bad risk for a marriage-minded woman, not to mention the toll it takes on you to play the role of home wrecker, especially if the man has children. Men who haven't already filed divorce papers might make a million promises. If you agree to date them before they've left their spouses or significant others, there is no guarantee they will ever end their relationships. Even if such a man does leave his wife, odds are he won't do it for a relationship with you. Studies show that once men actually leave their marriages, they want to start fresh; they tend to sever their ties with the women they have been dating on the side.

Bear in mind that a married man has already have proven he is capable of infidelity. If a man has cheated on his first wife and you succeed in becoming the second, the odds are high that he will cheat on you, too.

The Warning Signs of a Married Man

▶ He won't tell you the legal status of his marriage, or he's vague about it.

▶ He will not bring you to any family or holiday gatherings.

▶ He tells you not to call him at home, giving you only his beeper or work number.

▶ He tells you that the woman you've spotted him with is his sister or cousin.

▶ If you do know he's married, he promises he will leave his wife "when the time is right," yet he perpetually postpones severing his first-family ties.

▶ He says his wife doesn't understand him.

▶ He says he never really loved his wife and she has never truly loved him.

Emotional and Resource Vampires

These men unendingly drain a woman's energy, emotions, and resources. They are incapable of a reciprocal energetic exchange. They are the takers and you are the giver, without exception. You can never receive sustained satisfaction from the following categories of men:

Overly Needy, Dependent Men

Brandi has always considered herself the mothering type. She looks forward to the day when she has her own children because she knows how much she enjoys being needed. Her desire to fulfill someone else's needs, unfortunately, attracted her to Peter.

From the moment they met, he made it clear that he couldn't live without her. He wanted to be with her all the time, go everywhere with her, even to her dentist appointment or to the hair salon. He wanted to share her every thought and desire. "Peter must really love me because he never wants us to be apart," she confided to me a few weeks after the pair had met. "He makes me feel so wanted and loved."

What starts out as flattery quickly becomes suffocation. It isn't necessarily you he needs to be with all the time. It doesn't really matter if it's you or someone else. He just needs to be with someone, period. While it's true that Brandi wanted a child to take care of, a thirty-four-year-old son isn't exactly what she had in mind. Like a baby who demands to suck at your breast long after he's been fed, a man like Peter just takes and takes, without concern for how much you feel comfortable giving. He is like a giant vacuum sucking up all your energy, leaving you physically, emotionally, and spiritually exhausted. This clinging man has no respect for your boundaries and is eager to make you his entire life. If she rejects him, this type of man may even passively stalk a woman—for example, sit in his car and watch her with binoculars from across the street—in order to be near her.

The Warning Signs of an Overly Needy, Dependent Man

- He doesn't ever want to be without you, even if you only recently met.
- He is available to you every hour of every day, with no plans of his own.
- He calls you dozens of times daily.
- He doesn't respect boundaries or the word *no*.
- He turns up where you are, even if you didn't tell him where you were going.
- He drops his plans, if he has any, just to be with you.
- He always wants to know what is on your mind and in your day planner.
- He leaves you feeling constricted and smothered.

"Mr. Excitement": The Life of the Party

On the surface, this kind of man is very seductive. It might seem as though he has great joie de vivre, but, in reality, he lacks an internal life, and the only way he feels alive is through creating melodrama and larger-than-life situations. For example, "Mr. Excitement" may pick you up for a second date in a helicopter and fly you up the coast for dinner. Such a man suffers from severe mood swings and is constantly on an emotional roller coaster. He is prone to impulsive spending sprees, wild sex, and dancing at a night-club with a lampshade on his head. He may initially seem like the free-spirited life of the party, but his showiness eventually ceases to be spirited and instead becomes excessive. His behavior may actually be indicative of a severe personality disorder.

Underlying his extreme activity are his severe mood swings. He might be ecstatic one day and depressed the next. His need for action and his un-healthy impulsiveness and unpredictability often mask an intense feeling of emptiness. There is an element of mania to his actions, and he will shift be-tween positives and negatives. One day he could be singing your praises to the moon and stars, saying you are the greatest woman on Planet Earth. The following day, he might lash out at you for no apparent reason, calling you harsh names and accusing you of being selfish or controlling.

You won't be able to convince him that he is out of touch with reality. He compulsively needs to create ongoing excitement and incidents to fill his own internal blank space; he often laughs hysterically when something isn't even funny or seethes in anger when no one has done anything wrong. Calm sex, normal conversations, or real intimacy are seldom a part of his life. He is emotionally reactive because he seeks only outside stimuli to feel alive.

A woman involved with a man like this will never find the relationship fulfilling; she will feel overly stimulated, emotionally and spiritually, to the point of exhaustion. This kind of man has a demand for intensity that is nearly impossible for any woman to keep up with. You will always be the tar-get of his self-destructive acts, frequent arguing, and inability to make and keep long-range plans.

"I was willing to put up with a lot of Jack's craziness because I really loved him. He was always creating exciting, glamorous events I had never previously experienced," Carolyn said to me, crying, one day before she got up the courage to finally break off her relationship with him. "Over time, I just couldn't live with his mood swings and misperceptions, even though I hadn't changed or done anything wrong. One day, I am the love of his life, the greatest, most perfect woman in the world; the next day, I am an idiot or a bitch." It is an emotional energy drain to be involved with a manic man who is futilely trying to avoid his own emptiness. He is incapable of loving you over the long haul, and he will only destroy your self-esteem.

The Warning Signs of an Overly Emotional Man

- He needs constant excitement in his life.
- He engages in numerous spur-of-the-moment activities.
- He manufactures incidents (both positive and negative) to fill in slow or boring moments.
- He rationalizes bizarre or inappropriate behavior in nonsensical ways.
- He has severe mood swings.
- He has difficulty being open and intimate with you.
- His perception of you constantly wavers.

Mama's Boys

It's true that you can judge a man by how well he treats his mother. If he is sweet, loving, and respectful of her, he will probably treat you the same way. It's equally true that you should diligently avoid a man who is controlled by or is overly enmeshed with his mother. If you are in a relationship with this type of man, you will always be second in line.

A Mama's Boy is different from a devoted son. He hasn't given up his role as a little boy. Part of what it means to be a mature individual is to separate from one's mother. Most cultures have rites of passage that mark the age at which an adolescent boy leaves his mother and enters the adult male world. Numerous men, however, pass beyond their twenties, thirties, even into their forties and fifties, without ever letting go of their moms.

A Mama's Boy, in essence, still lives at home with his mother. Even if he has moved away, it won't be too far—most likely to a house or condo she purchased for him. He still hasn't gained any psychological distance from her. He will check with her before making a decision, will seek her approval of his relationships (if she doesn't approve of you, you're dropped, even if you are perfect together), and will tell her everything that's going on in his life, even matters better left private.

If the choice is between changing a burned-out lightbulb for his mother or keeping a dinner date with you, Mom is always going to win. There can be only one woman in this man's heart, and if Mom already occupies the space, forget trying to squeeze yourself in there, too.

The Warning Signs of a Mama's Boy

▶ He phones his mother several times a day.

▶ He consults his mother before making any decision.

▶ He either lives with Mom or very nearby.

▶ He frequently has dinner with Mom.

▶ He is financially supported by his mother.

▶ He can't reject his mother's requests, no matter how unreasonable they are.

Paupers

He lives in a shed behind the neighbor's garage. He walks two miles to your house because he can't spare the bus fare. When he finally asks you to dinner, he takes you to a hot-dog vendor in a local park. What's wrong with this picture? If the guy under discussion is eighteen years old or struggling to finish graduate school, nothing. If, however, he is a thirty-five-year-old man who works at odd jobs only when the mood strikes him, if he has no education and no plans to obtain one, or if he has no future plans whatsoever, it's a problem, because this is a man destined to be a Pauper for the remainder of his adult life.

A Pauper is a man with no interest in making money, who may even have a childish disdain for it. He is unwilling to understand the role money plays in the life of a healthy adult. He doesn't realize it can assist one in living a freer lifestyle, contribute to peace of mind and security, promote self-esteem and self-sufficiency, as well as confer a sense of personal wealth and value. Like a young child, this man will always need someone to support him. If you get into a relationship with him, that "someone" will be you.

Couples who have money problems at the onset of their relationship often look back fondly on their struggling "salad days." When you link up with a Pauper, you are destined to be eating that lettuce and celery forever, unless you plan on being the sole breadwinner. A Pauper may be a nice guy, but he is still a bad bet. With his irresponsible attitude toward work and money, he is likely to be careless or thoughtless with your hard-earned cash. Having a Pauper for a mate is like having a teenage son, an angry one at that, who never goes out of the house without asking for some cash and the keys to your car.

The Warning Signs of a Pauper

▶ He is over thirty and has money only from menial odd jobs.

▶ He has no car, checking account, or credit cards.

▶ He has never had a consistent job and has no plans to get one.

▶ He doesn't live in a decent house or apartment and has no intention of doing so.

▶ He has a low-level education and no plans to go back to school.

▶ He has a negative, distorted view of money as evil and unnecessary.

Dreamers, Drifters, and Losers

A relationship with a Dreamer, Drifter, or Loser is similar to one with a Pauper, only with different motivations and attitudes. In our materialistic society, the term is often misused to denote someone who hasn't struck it big. A real Loser, however, is someone who can't even strike it small. Unlike a Pauper, a Loser may desire money, but he can never get himself together long enough to acquire any, for any number of reasons. He might have addictions, keep getting into fights with his boss, or have an attitude problem at work. He may have a tendency to blame others for his fate or be unwilling to take responsibility for making changes. Perhaps he can't get over his dream of becoming a professional boxer, dashed years ago when he shattered his arm. He may have delusional dreams of being an astronaut, although he has never taken any concrete steps to move himself toward that goal. This type of man sees himself as a hapless victim of bad luck, who says he has tried to be successful, but every attempt he has made has never worked out.

Often experts at charming their way into a woman's heart by garnering her pity, most Losers, Dreamers, and Drifters don't have money of their own and have had to rely on others to get them through life. If your heart has succumbed to one of these men, give him a little charity, but don't begin a relationship with him.

The Warning Signs of a Dreamer, Drifter, or Loser

▶ He never has enough money to take you out on a date.

▶ He always has some hard-luck story about why his life isn't working out.

195

- His bad luck is always somebody else's fault.
- He is always waiting for a "big break" that never seems to come.
- He has no credit cards, bank account, or car.
- He has no goals or plans for the future.

Rebounders and Widowers

A relationship with a man on the mend from a broken relationship or death of a loved one is generally not a good idea. This doesn't mean you can never get involved with someone who is on the rebound, but you shouldn't do so until he has had ample time to heal and deal with his grief. This could take months, or even years, depending on the length and intensity of his lost love. Otherwise, you are guaranteed of having your mate try to squeeze you into the spot occupied by his previous lover or partner. He won't be involved with you out of genuine love for you but rather because you fill the void left by his lost loved one, whether it's a parent, sibling, friend, or romantic partner. Someone on the rebound may try to short-circuit the process of grieving by distracting himself with a replacement, even one who is not quite right for him. The problem is that, when he heals, the relationship may not stand on its own rocky legs.

The Warning Signs of a Man on the Rebound or Widower

- He got out of a serious relationship less than a year ago.
- He is mourning the loss of a parent, a close friend, or even a pet.
- He tries to accelerate the relationship after the first date.
- He doesn't make a genuine effort to get to know you as a person.
- He deludes himself that he's over his grief, when he really hasn't dealt with it yet.
- He constantly compares you with his former girlfriend or wife.
- He tries to make you dress, talk, or act like "her."
- He constantly talks about the person he lost.

Playboys and Perennial Bachelors

Some men are trapped in the constant pursuit of Eros and are always interested in conquest (particularly of hard-to-get women). Their charm and pursuit is seductive and intoxicating for many women. The first few weeks or months of a relationship with a Playboy can be very exciting and romantic. Once he's captured his prey and the erotic force starts to wear off, however, his interest dwindles. Once the thrill of the hunt settles down to the day-to-day hard work and energy necessary to build and maintain a loving, committed relationship, a playboy doesn't want the responsibility. His need to seek fresh excitement overtakes his best intentions. He must move on to conquer another woman. A man who has had many relationships and has never settled down for any significant time is not likely to do so with you. A Playboy, as his name implies, is a juvenile, only interested in the play of relationships—unlike a man, of whom work is required.

In contrast, a Perennial Bachelor is a man who has been single for most of his adult life. He's at least forty and has never been married or in a truly committed, long-term relationship. It is unlikely that this devoted bachelor will be able to incorporate you into his life in a meaningful way. He is set in his ways and extremely inflexible about how he lives his life. The chances are slim to none that there is room for you. Of course, a man may have remained single because he was a Prince who was very involved in building his business, perhaps traveling frequently, or simply hadn't found anyone with whom he wished to share his life. This man might be able to overcome lifelong habits with effort and commitment on his part, as well as considerable understanding and patience on yours. It will be a difficult process, though, and one you need to consider seriously before taking him on.

The Warning Signs of a Playboy

▶ He has never had a long-term, serious relationship.

▶ He is smooth and experienced when he woos you.

▶ He is more interested in erotic pleasure and conquest than in intimacy and longevity in a relationship.

▶ He lives for the pursuit more than the prize.

▶ He has left a string of brokenhearted women behind him.

The Warning Signs of a Perennial Bachelor

▶ He has never had a long-term, serious relationship.

▶ His sole interest in dating is for common interests, not intimacy (e.g., he needs a golf or skiing partner).

▶ He is inflexible and wants things his way.

▶ He has never shared his home or his life with a woman.

▶ He does not seem interested in finding out who you are or what you want.

▶ He always maintains his own separate residence.

▶ He isn't interested in substantively integrating himself into your life.

▶ He bristles if he thinks you are encroaching on his personal space.

If you have previously made bad choices, forgive yourself and resolve simply to be more alert and aware the next time around. We have all made bad decisions about the men in our lives, but we needn't berate ourselves or assume we are doomed to repeat those mistakes the next time around. As you become a Smart Heart woman, your goal is progress, not perfection.

A Smart Heart woman heeds the warning signs for these troubled types. She will observe, ask questions, and pay attention to her romantic prospects, rather than allow her smitten heart to lull her mind into a romantic blackout. She will remain aware during dates, and if she finds her boyfriend, partner, or mate is one of these bad-boy bets, she will listen to her head when it tells her to let go and move on. Only then can she open the door to someone infinitely better suited to her needs and wants.

Before we move on to finding Mr. Right, I have one additional caution regarding involvement with a man who already has children. These are not necessarily men to stay away from, but they are men with whom women need to be cautious before proceeding. Getting involved with a man with children complicates a relationship. A Smart Heart woman needs to enter such a relationship knowing what she can and cannot expect.

Yellow Light: Look Both Ways If He Has Kids

The following scenario is not uncommon: A young woman who has not had the experience of being a mother becomes involved with a man who has children from a previous relationship. Because she has not experienced the unique emotional bond and commitment that occur between a mother and her child, she might feel resentful or jealous when a man spends time with his children. If this is a familiar experience, you need to reevaluate it because it is virtually impossible to successfully form a new family unit if you are unable to appreciate a man's children as a valuable asset to you and to your life with him. You must be able to see that his dedication to these children will allow him to be equally dedicated to the children he may have with you. As a mature adult, you need to be aware that these children have already been emotionally torn apart. They need you to welcome them in a loving way, although they may be incapable of reciprocating in the beginning. Though their hearts may be shut to you, as an adult you must be committed to being open, loving, understanding, and reassuring.

You must also be aware that a child may blame you for the breakup of her parents' marriage, even if you weren't in the picture then. The children will always view you as a threat to reuniting their parents, so you must be willing to participate in a long-term process to help them overcome this perception. Rather than giving up the commitment to befriend children, you can choose to be the mature adult, helping the children work through their anger and hurt until they are able to accept the love you are offering.

How You Can Be a Source of Love for the Children of a Partner

- ▶ Acknowledge how hard their parents' separation must be for them.

- ▶ Explain that you understand the negative feelings they may harbor toward you.

- ▶ Be mature enough to give love to the children unconditionally until they are able to reciprocate.

- ▶ Have no expectations of the children in the beginning.

- ▶ Help the children reframe their experience to see how lucky they are to have many adults, not only a mother and father, to love and contribute to their lives.

- ▶ Make it clear that you are not trying to replace their real mother.

If you are with a man who has sacrificed his relationship with his children for his own pursuits or career, it is important for you to help him recognize his children's need to have a relationship with their father. Children whose father is not involved in their life will feel that there must be something wrong with them or their father would be there. It is important that you become the catalyst for reconnecting an estranged father with his children, if he has not reached out to them for a number of years. You also need to help your partner be aware that, at first, his children may be angry and/or hurt, not open and forgiving, after the initial contact. As a Smart Heart

199

woman, you need to be supportive of a partner in the process of reestablishing a relationship with his children.

When you enter into a relationship with a man who has children, your guiding force should be what is in the best interests of the children. Often, you will need to put aside what might be preferable to you and your partner personally, and make your decisions accordingly.

You need to be proactive regarding his ex-spouse, as well. Even if your boyfriend's or mate's former spouse seems like the Wicked Witch of the West, she is still the mother of his children. A Smart Heart woman would never slander or contribute to negative drama. It does not serve a child, or your partner, to have the birth mother vilified. You need to remain neutral in order to be a source of love and confidence in the child's life. Not only will you and the child benefit from this course of action, but your partner will also be eternally grateful for your assistance.

Tiffany had a similar challenge when she became involved with Bob, whose ex-wife, Krista, was very unstable. Krista would forget to pick up her daughter at dance class more often than she would remember. She frequently stayed out late, leaving the ten-year-old girl by herself. When the daughter complained about her mother, it would have been easy for Tiffany to agree with the litany of shortcomings and add a few herself. As a Smart Heart woman, however, Tiffany made a conscious choice to resist contributing to the problem. She knew that negativity, combined with the child's fear and neglect, would not improve anything but would only make a bad situation worse. Tiffany chose consistency and stability in order to become a calming and safe force in the child's life. When Krista forgets to pick up her daughter, the young girl simply beeps Tiffany with the beeper she gave her. Tiffany can then pick her up right away. What a relief for the child to have an adult in her life who is able to respond to her! Tiffany calls her every evening to ensure her care. If her mother isn't home, Tiffany can bring her back to spend time with her and the child's father. They all have developed a loving, special relationship with one another, and the added bonus for Tiffany is that her boyfriend cherishes her for her loving concern for the daughter he adores. Tiffany accepts the reality that as long as she is involved with Bob, and she hopes she always will be, Krista's miserable mothering will remain a part of her life, as well. Krista isn't going to change, but Tiffany can give this child the experience of a loving woman who can nurture her even though Tiffany is not her birth mother.

What to Be Aware of with a Man Who Has Children

▶ Watch and pay attention to how he parents. You will see exactly how he nurtures his children and how he may parent children that you may have with him in the future.

▶ Does he believe in hitting children?

▶ Does he believe children should be seen and not heard?

▶ Is he overabsorbed in or obsessed with his children?

▶ Is he disengaged from and uninvolved with them?

▶ Does he think young children should be in bed at 7 P.M. every night, or does he think it's okay for them to stay up at night and be around the adults?

▶ Does he believe that they should be sleeping in bed with the two of you?

▶ Does he try to pawn his children off on you or on baby-sitters?

▶ Does he consistently abide by his custody agreements?

▶ Is he willingly involved with his children?

▶ Is he able to be openly affectionate with his children?

▶ Are his children a major priority in his life?

You Can't Exit the Ex, but You Can Draw the Line

When children are involved, a man is tied to his ex-wife forever. He must see her and talk to her, and he will have to send her money for child support. Some men, however, have trouble setting appropriate boundaries with their ex-wives. An ex-husband may still run the woman's errands, allow her to put charges on his credit card when she is low on cash, even let her borrow his car when hers is in the shop. He may even allow her access to their former shared home, answering machine, and mail.

A Smart Heart woman involved with such a man must draw the line and insist that he set appropriate boundaries with his previous partner. It is not okay for an ex-spouse to know everything that is going on in her former partner's life or to make any decisions for him that do not involve the children. If the two ex-partners do need to meet to talk about the children, it should be done in the light of day.

Sometimes, a man keeps his ex-wife in his life simply because it is convenient, safe, and comfortable for him, not because he cares more for his ex-wife than for you. If you ask him to draw the line, he may immediately choose to honor your wishes. If, despite your pleas, a man cannot strike a balance in his involvement with his ex-spouse, you need to walk away from him. He may be divorced on paper, but clearly he is not yet separated in his head or heart. His actions are signaling that he is still in a relationship with her, and honoring her wishes may supersede honoring yours.

What's more, the energy your man puts into that relationship is energy he doesn't have for you, especially when everyone's lives are hectic and their schedules are busy. Relationships take tremendous effort, and a man who won't give you his best effort is not someone to whom a Smart Heart woman should devote her time and energy.

When He Won't Introduce You

It is not appropriate for a man who has children to introduce you to them on the first date. It is too confusing for them. Once you become an integral part of a man's life, however, you will want to become involved with his children. If he takes them to the zoo on Sunday, perhaps you can go along. If his daughter has a Saturday soccer game, you might come to cheer and go out for pizza afterward. This gives you an opportunity to observe the father's parenting style and get to know the children. They can then get to know you in the event that the relationship proceeds to long-term partnership or marriage.

It's a danger signal, however, if he never introduces you or never broaches the subject of his children, even after having dated you for several months. If he insists on keeping you separate from them and has no intention of including you in activities with them, you will probably need to let him go. A Smart Heart woman would never consider asking a man to give up a relationship with his children in favor of a relationship with her.

Why do some men insist on keeping their girlfriends and children as far apart as possible? Divorced men often like to generate the illusion that they are free and single, guys with a limitless future and no discernible past. Another reason is that men may want to have complete control of their parenting decisions. In this way, they can respond to their children however they choose without worrying about another person's input, even if that person is someone they love and admire. Incorporating another person's wishes is a complexity many men would like to avoid as long as possible.

Some men are simply overly protective of their children. Aware of the pain brought on by the divorce, they don't want to exacerbate the situation by bringing another woman into their lives. While this is understandable, and even appropriate with casual acquaintances, when part of a more serious relationship, the father needs to balance his desire for protection with his new life. He has to come to terms with his needs as a man, in addition to his role as a father. A Smart Heart woman is looking for a man who can keep these roles balanced and not sacrifice one to the other. If he is unable to do so, you might have problems with your relationship.

If You Are the One Who Has Children

The reality is that combining families is extremely difficult, whether they are his children or yours. When they are your children you will obviously feel that more is at stake for you. You will want to discuss family issues carefully, in advance, rather than just operating with blind faith, hoping things work out for the best.

Men and women usually have diverse reasons for getting involved with someone who already has kids. A woman's motivations may range from her desire to mother, to recognition of the need for the child to have a female figure in the house, to her need to support the man she loves by assisting with his child. A man's motivation is usually more straightforward—he takes the children because that is the price he must pay to get the woman he loves.

Any man with whom you want to have a serious relationship should be a man who not only loves you but loves your children as well. Simply tolerating your children is not sufficient. He must want to be a parent to them. When you look at your prospective partner, ask yourself, "If something were to happen to me, could I trust that he would take good care of them?" If, in your heart, you know that he would not care for them as his own, it is best for you to move on.

You need to consider the ramifications of involvement with a man who does not have children of his own, or with a King who has grown children.

203

Such a man is often happy to support your children with his wallet but is not interested in supporting them with his heart or in parenting them. This could be a detriment to both you and the children if they do not already have a father who is involved in their lives and contributes to their parenting.

If you have children of your own or will be having children together, you need to try to solve parenting issues beforehand. A child must be clear as to what is expected of him or her from a new adult playing a role in his or her life. The new adults—i.e., you, your ex, his ex, and all the grandparents—must agree to try to work harmoniously for the sake of the children.

Falling in love and living together are enormous challenges in themselves. Blending families is an additional challenge, but it can be successful and provide tremendous satisfaction and fulfillment. Careful planning and deliberation, however, are needed before you move forward with such an arrangement. As a Smart Heart woman, you must engage your head, along with your heart, before leading yourself and your children into such a relationship. You would never want to needlessly hurt yourself or your children. We have so much at stake when our children are involved. When designing a new life for yourself and your children, heed this advice by addressing potential problems before they happen.

The Myth of the "Man with Potential"

A man with "potential"—i.e., one you hope to change—isn't an obvious bad bet or loser but one who, in your opinion, merely needs a few improvements to make him a decent find. You deem him a diamond in the rough. As a Smart Heart woman who uses her head and her heart, you need to walk away from these guys, too.

One of the cruelest things a woman can do is to love a man for his potential. Everyone has both faults as well as character traits of which you are proud, but if you love a man for who he "could be" rather than for who he is, you are setting the stage for future disaster.

If you feel your man is "great, but," you should release him. Let him be great with no drawbacks for somebody else. A man needs to feel that he is a hero in his woman's eyes, that she loves him just the way he is. Men who think you see them as failures will be hesitant to give fully of themselves. They will always hold a part of themselves in reserve because they feel you don't totally accept them. These men often fear showing you the intimate, hidden sides of themselves out of concern that you would criticize those aspects, too. To be in a happy, loving relationship, a man needs to feel that his woman accepts him as he is, in his entirety.

"It's not that Johnny is a bad catch," Stephanie, a client of mine, recently explained to me. "He is a sweet guy. He treats me wonderfully and I adore him, but he should leave that low-paying, dead-end artsy job for something better. He would look more presentable and professional if he would cut his hair and wear a suit. If he sticks with me, I'll help him get ahead." Stephanie is not being fair, either to herself or to Johnny.

To become a Smart Heart woman, you must resolve to stop "potentializing" dates and future mates. If you can't love a man exactly as he is now, you will never find happiness with him. By seeing him as a project, you are loving someone who may—or may not—exist in the future. Being in a relationship predicated on future actions prevents you from having a loving relationship in the present.

Kelly was in love with Michael, who, she felt, was a gifted novelist. He worked hard at his craft every day and didn't want, or need, a regular job. Kelly was convinced that he would procure a publisher and a spot on the best-seller list. Michael, on the other hand, didn't care about who read his work, just that he was able to write it.

Kelly worked diligently and happily at her consulting job to support the two of them. After four years, she found herself becoming impatient with his lack of initiative in earning a "regular" living. "When are you going to finish that book and try to get it published?" she finally demanded. "Whenever it's ready, and it isn't ready yet," Michael earnestly replied. Kelly found herself checking Michael's computer to see how many words he wrote each day. When he discovered this, be became angry. Within a few months, he packed up his computer and moved out. By that time, Kelly was happy to close the door behind him.

During the first few years of their relationship, Michael had been under the misconception that Kelly encouraged his personal fulfillment as a writer. Had Kelly been more aware of her motives, she would have realized that what she was attracted to was Michael's potential to make a lot of money as a famous, best-selling author. It was only after his "potential" never seemed to manifest itself that she realized it might never happen, at least not according to her timetable or without her financial support. Even if

Michael stayed with Kelly and eventually sold his book, their relationship was irreparably damaged when he realized she didn't believe in him as a writer and was no longer willing to support his work.

It is easier for a woman to rationalize falling for a man's potential when the man is just starting out and full of dreams. She falls in love with him because of what he is going to be when he graduates from law school or gets the promotion for which he has been working so hard. What happens if a man decides to change course and do something else with his life, something that may not be as promising financially, such as leaving medical school to paint, or quitting his job as a stockbroker to open a bed-and-breakfast? A woman in a loving, healthy, mature relationship need not view her partner as a failure for not pursuing her goals and dreams for him, or of not actualizing his "potential." If she loves him for who he is, she will support his endeavors no matter what career or educational path he chooses.

A Smart Heart woman asks herself, "Can I still love him if he never loses those fifty pounds? Can I still love him if his catering business never takes off? Can I still love him if he is content with his mid-level job and never strives for more?" Even if your partner seeks to better himself (he vows he'll start that diet tomorrow), you have to be willing to love him even if he does not succeed.

You Can't Change Him, But You Can Change Yourself

You might think that he would want to better himself solely because of his love for you. This supposition leads to trouble. A person will change only if he wants to. No amount of cajoling, dreaming, or nagging can force a person to alter something about himself unless he personally sees the value in doing so. The notion that you can change someone else is a delusion; it simply can't be done.

Some men are good at "talking the talk," promising you they will stay sober, get a permanent job, or stop staying out all night. As a Smart Heart woman, you deserve a man who honors you enough to be honest about his intentions. Don't keep listening to empty promises, hoping this time he will finally take action. You might believe an unemployed thirty year-old still living at home when he says that this arrangement is temporary, but a forty-five-year-old in the same situation isn't going anywhere else before his cemetery plot. Waiting around wishing this man will get himself together drains energy from you and your relationship with him.

A minority of men may realize they must alter certain things if they hope to keep you and use that as a motivation to finally change. There is a critical distinction, however, between a man who loves you enough to be inspired to change and your mistaken belief that your love is enough to move the immovable. Remember also that the process isn't easy. It can be slow and difficult with two steps forward and one step back. If you aren't willing to support him through this arduous process, it is better to let him go it alone.

Rather than trying to transform your man, you should concentrate on self-change, so that you can attain for yourself what you're hoping to get from him. If you want a wealthy man so that you can reside in a penthouse, leave your own dead-end job for one with a career track that will eventually lead you to riches. If you want to associate with high society, volunteer to work at fund-raisers for charitable organizations where you can meet illustrious people.

When you change, your partner's response to you will change. Perhaps he will adore the "new you" and want to do whatever it takes to remain with you. Alternatively, he may feel you now dance to a different drummer, and he'll opt to leave. A Smart Heart woman who feels her current relationship isn't serving her well and lets go of it won't then attract a lesser man. Often, she attracts exactly the man she had hoped for in the first place.

Putting the Smart Heart Partnering Process to Work

At this stage in the Smart Heart process, you have begun to clarify your relationship objectives, as well as expand your awareness and understanding of unconscious motivations and distorted images. I hope you've also chosen to abstain from sex, at least in the beginning of the relationship, so you can get to know your partner better and your hormones don't sabotage your efforts. If you've already found a man who is a relationship possibility or you're on the verge of meeting someone who will support your emotional and spiritual well-being, what else do you need to know, as a Smart Heart woman?

Part 3 will give you additional guidance as well as some practical tools (such as the Personal/Partner Profiler [PPP]) to systematically determine if your prospective partner is right for you, whether your relationship is at its inception or if it's a long-term commitment. If you're dating for fun and frolic, it's not as crucial to know his family history or in what faith he would raise his children as it is to know his personal inclinations (e.g., is he a perfectionist, laid-back, or adventurous?). This knowledge would increase your capacity to understand him and enable you to derive more pleasure from your involvement with him.

To further increase your odds of success, you need to consider the following:

1. Personal compatibility. *You will discover how to determine both your and your man's personality numbers with the Personal/Partner Profiler (PPP) to determine your diverse personality styles.*

2. Life-stage questions. *Do you both want the same things for your lives right now, based on your age, experience, background, and values?*

3. Overall compatibility. *Can you discuss touchy topics like money, sex, goals, and interests to learn more about yourself and your partner?*

If you are mutually compatible in these areas, he just may be the man for you. As you enter into this next stage, remember:

1. *A Smart Heart woman is always learning from past relationships so she can make wiser choices for her future.*

2. *She forgives herself and her former partners for mistakes and transgressions.*

3. *She doesn't judge her future prospects from her past experiences.*

4. *She knows that by utilizing the Smart Heart Partnering Process she can improve her relationships.*

5. *She is committed to her growth and development and enjoys the journey.*

6. *No matter what happens, she remains open to the outcome.*

The Personal/Partner Profiler (PPP)

ompatibility in the key areas of life forms the foundation for all successful relationships. No one area is critical to happiness. Rather, it is the integration of these factors that increases your prospects for a successful relationship. For example, you might be in love with a man with whom you share goals and interests, maintaining a good assessment of each other's personalities. If you are older and don't want children, however, whereas he is younger with a desire to start a family, your life stages could prevent the partnership from succeeding. Similarly, if your values don't mesh—for example, you want to save the rain forest, whereas the only thing he wants to save is money for his Ferrari— your personalities and life stages might be complementary, but your lifestyles might clash.

How the PPP Can Help You Understand Both Your Personality and His

In my practice, I use a PPP with 175 questions. I requested that the creators of the PPP adapt it to 72 questions for this book so that women may obtain a quick, succinct profile of their own and their partner's personality styles. It will take approximately twenty minutes to answer the questions in the PPP. You will come up with a number, from 1 to 9, that best describes your particular personality style. You can also copy the PPP and have your partner take it so that he can determine his own number. Knowing your numbers will help you to recognize and better understand certain aspects of your personality. Whether or not you are presently in a relationship, the PPP can provide insight into your personality for further development and serve to illuminate ideas about your compatibility with a prospective mate. If you are currently involved with someone, it can also help you assess potential problem areas and assist you in how to deal with them.

The Personal/Partner Profiler is based on the Enneagram (pronounced *Any-a-gram*), an ancient method used by the Sufis and Jewish mystics for self-discovery. It was brought to the West, originally to South America, during the last century. In the United States, it began to appear in the 1970s, primarily among Jesuit priests, before the general public gained access to it. Although the Enneagram was handed down from the ancient mystical schools, its uncanny accuracy in categorizing personality styles is relevant in today's world. As a testing mechanism, the PPP parallels modern psychological tests, such as the Myers-Briggs Personality Inventory and the Minnesota Multiphasic Personality Inventory (MMPI), commonly used by many corporations to assess and evaluate potential employees.

214

I first became aware of the usefulness of the Enneagram as a tool for self-knowledge when I was searching for a simple system to help my clients more readily understand complex personality issues (both positive and negative) that were affecting them and their relationships. I found an easy-to-use test developed by psychologist Mona Coates, Ph.D., and her husband, Ed Jacobs, M.Ed. My clients could take this simple test to determine quickly which of the nine personality types they and their partners were, and how this might be affecting their relationships.

The PPP offers insight into human nature by providing an understanding of how we perceive ourselves and others, as well as direction for our personal growth and development. The PPP can assist you in evaluating whether or not your personality is compatible with someone whom you are currently seeing, as well as serve as a guide for what to look for in the future. When you are able to understand another person's perspective, you develop greater tolerance and compassion in situations that might otherwise anger or upset you. When you possess greater understanding and awareness, another person's "illogical" behavior makes more sense to you. Even if you choose not to behave in such a manner yourself, you can at least understand why your partner might be doing so and avoid being personally offended.

Taking the PPP is not an esoteric indulgence. You can use this information in practical ways to enhance, strengthen, and deepen your relationship. Mona and Ed, the designers of the PPP, have found it very helpful over the course of their marriage. Ed and Mona met when she moved into his rural Pennsylvania town in the fourth grade. They were "sweethearts" until the eighth grade. When Mona's father unexpectedly died, she and her mother moved to the West Coast. Mona and Ed soon lost touch with each other and later went on to marry other people.

A shy homebody, Ed was enticed to go to his high school class's twenty-fifth reunion because he was hoping to hear news about Mona, whom he thought of frequently. Ed had been divorced by that time and so had Mona, as it turned out. Although no one at the reunion knew of her whereabouts, two years later one of the attendees found Mona and told her that Ed had been looking for her. "I had incorrectly heard years earlier that Ed had been killed in Vietnam, so I was overjoyed when I heard that he was still alive. The woman gave me Ed's phone number, and I couldn't get to the phone fast enough." Still living on the East Coast at that time, Ed immediately flew out to California. They began a bicoastal romance and subsequently married.

Not long after they were married, personality differences surfaced and became troublesome. Mona was a Number Seven (indicative of an Adventurer, the life of the party), and she wanted to socialize frequently. Mona loved action, the more the better. Ed, conversely, was a Number Five (an Observer) who enjoyed spending quiet evenings at home, avoiding groups of people as much as possible. "I got upset because, with dinner parties and people over all the time, there was no time for resting, reading, or relaxing with Mona—things that I love to do," Ed says. "Meanwhile, Mona was embarrassed by my lack of social graces. I wasn't fun to be with at these parties because I felt like the walls were closing in on me. I don't like sharing my personal life with strange people. I'm sure Mona was afraid that she'd married a dud."

The two soon realized that these differences were putting their relationship and marriage in jeopardy. Because Mona and Ed were both students of the Enneagram and aware of the nine personality numbers, they decided to put that information to work in their own relationship. "I came to understand that Mona just needed to keep moving. Her Number Seven

215

orientation meant she was like a pinball, bouncing around just to remain in motion. Sevens have a tremendous fear of pain and boredom. They constantly seek fun and excitement to avoid slowing down and possibly experiencing unhappiness," Ed explained. Meanwhile, Mona could see the fear of people and intimacy underlying a Number Five's personality. By understanding their personality types through the Enneagram, Mona and Ed could acknowledge and accept each other's perspective, and their respect for the differences between them deepened.

Mona and Ed were equally committed to evolving within their own personality styles so that they could live together more harmoniously. While Mona made an effort to slow down and spend more quiet nights at home with Ed (which, to her amazement, she started to enjoy), Ed worked on relaxing and having fun in the company of others.

"Understanding how our numbers were influencing us and our relationship has changed our lives," Mona concludes. "It is such a simple system, but it has dramatically enhanced our marriage, as well as the marriages of many of my counseling clients."

216

Determining Your Number

It's easy to find out what number you are, then to use the information to strengthen or enhance a current relationship or be better prepared for a new one. Just take the simple short quiz at the end of this chapter, plot your answers on the graph that follows, and find your number on the wheel.

If you think your present partner might be right for you, ask him if he would take the test, too. If he doesn't want to take it now, *don't force him.* Don't decide for him and tell him what *you* think his number is. Each of us is solely responsible for our own personal understanding and growth. Once you take the test, tell him how interesting it has been for you and how you have benefited from this self-knowledge. He may eventually want to take it to learn more about himself, as well. Regardless of whether or not your partner takes the test, you can still use the knowledge you have gained about the various numbers to improve your relationship, regardless of what your man chooses to do.

There is no number that is better than any other. Similarly, no relationship pairings are inherently better or worse than any others. On the one hand, the PPP will assist you in using your head, along with your heart, to enhance your personal growth, expand your understanding, and meet the unique challenges your particular number presents. On the other hand, some pairings offer greater challenges than others, but if you are both aware, any number pairing can work with positive results. Within each of the numerical types, a wide range of possibilities exists as to how a person expresses his or her core traits; we are all unique individuals, even though many of us have the same PPP number.

This is not merely an interesting exercise. If you want to become a Smart Heart woman, you need to be responsible for your own maturation and evolution. The PPP can provide an understanding of how your characteristics and personality traits facilitate growth and development in your life, as well as how they inhibit your progress. You can decide which traits you like about yourself, which you need to improve upon, and which ones you might want to tone down or amplify. Knowing your number and personality orientation will help you in all aspects of your life, as well as with a prospective partner.

The Personal/Partner Profiler Personality Test

Find a quiet time when you can fully concentrate on this brief test. The entire process of answering the questions and finding your number should only take about twenty minutes.

Before taking the PPP, be aware that:

▶ There is no right or wrong number to be.

▶ Not every part of your number description will apply to you.

▶ Your number does not change throughout your life.

▶ Your number isn't the only thing that defines you; we are more than our personalities.

▶ You must be willing to be honest in your assessment.

▶ Don't answer the questions based on how you wish you were.

▶ These numbers are not based on intelligence, achievement, or education.

▶ These numbers describe your orientation to life, not whether you are good or bad, smart or stupid, desirable or undesirable.

▶ Even if you skipped ahead and have scanned the number profiles, don't choose a number until after you have taken the PPP quiz. (At first glance, I thought I was a Number Eight, and it wasn't until I took the quiz that I discovered I was a Seven.)

Part I

Directions

1 As you read each statement, respond according to how you have generally felt, thought, or behaved. Your responses should be based upon your deepest desires and tendencies—the real you, not how you wish you were.

2 The statements are organized into groups of three. Within each grouping, circle the number of the *one* statement that fully and best describes you. In cases where two or all three statements describe you, decide which *one* best identifies you. *Circle only one statement per group.*

3 If only part of a statement describes you, do not circle it at all. There may be some groups in which none applies to you. In that case, *do not circle any in that group.*

4 Remember that *all statements are of equal value; there are no right or wrong answers.*

The Test

1 People lean on me for protection because they know that when "the going gets tough," I get tougher.

2 Because it is extremely important for me to excel, I'm usually prepared to "do what it takes."

3 I enjoy being on the go, having a full calendar, and refuse to "miss out" on life.

4 I'll do almost anything to prevent conflicts and arguments.

5 I'm emotionally sensitive and get drawn into the drama of relationships.

6 In social situations, I prefer to find out about others rather than tell them about myself.

7 I am dedicated to people and to the groups I am part of, and I want others to be this way.

8 I am diligent and idealistic, correcting wrongs when I can.

9 I am people oriented, nurturing, and long to feel close to others.

10 I'm an independent person who prefers privacy and having my own quiet time.

11 It is important for me to feel in unison with others and to avoid conflict.

12 I feel different from others and often express myself in unusual ways.

13 I strive for precision and correctness and to be above criticism from others.

14 I have a strong desire to assist others and to be important in their lives.

15 I value loyalty and people doing their duty the way I do.

16 I am free with money and spend more on fun "binges" and impulses than I really should.

17 I know how to say no, and I don't back down or get intimidated by authorities.

18 Even though I may get depressed or upset, it's extremely important for me to present a self-assured, confident image.

219

19 I can get too involved in others' problems and make myself too emotionally available.

20 I often need to consult others when I feel insecure about making important decisions.

21 I know what's right and wish everyone else worked as hard as I do to achieve it.

22 I want to project the right kind of image to avoid failure or lose to the competition.

23 I don't really mind going to extremes or bending a few rules to create an exciting adventure for myself and others.

24 I am more comfortable being in charge and in control than I am with having someone else in control.

25 I very much want to be treated as an individual, someone who is special and different from others.

26 I am not a "joiner" and do not belong to, nor seek membership, in many organizations.

27 I don't let things "get to me" or disturb my internal equilibrium.

28 I tend to be self-sacrificing and feel good when I'm helping others.

29 I enjoy receiving recognition and acknowledgment (awards, rewards) for my efforts.

30 I have highly refined tastes and often feel others lead rather drab lives.

31 When making a significant purchase, I base it on well-researched data and need, rather than on impulse.

32 I feel a responsibility for making the groups I'm in function effectively.

33 I often plan new adventures and excursions before the current one is over.

34 I trust my own strength and courage; when it comes to taking a stand, I won't compromise.

35 My presence is not threatening to others because I'm basically calm, diplomatic, and reassuring.

36 I have very high standards, and I am often frustrated when people and things don't live up to them.

37 I'm an excellent troubleshooter and contribute to the safety and well-being of others.

38 I need lots of friends and excitement; I don't want to miss out on experiences that could be fun or interesting.

39 Other people might describe me as earthy, blunt, and street-smart.

40 I tend to remain calm in a crisis; I don't get upset as others do.

41 I know how things should be done and don't like to accept imperfections, especially in myself.

42 I make sacrifices for others and let them know when they take me for granted.

43 I am a "go-getter" who is more concerned with success than many people are.

220

44 I spend a considerable amount of time searching for authenticity, the "real" me, and comparing myself to others. 3 3

45 I prefer to sit back and observe others rather than getting involved in small talk or their emotional issues and problems.

46 I work differently from the average person, requiring freedom from convention; I need to follow my own style. 3 3

47 I can get so involved in my projects that I forget to eat or sleep properly.

48 To feel secure, I work hard to maintain my commitments and responsibilities.

49 When I want something, I go for it; I see no reason to be deprived of things I enjoy.

50 I am strong willed and don't hesitate to protect my loved ones and friends. 3 3

51 I appreciate all sides of an argument and consider pros and cons equally.

221

52 I feel a moral responsibility to set things right when I think people are clearly in the wrong.

53 I feel compelled to help others and sometimes overdo my giving with few rewards coming back. 2 3

54 I am usually very good at "keeping the troops" on track so that we win in the end.

55 Other people see me as orderly, precise, and maybe a bit formal.

56 I am ambitious and push myself to "hit the mark" regardless of the competition. 1

57 Some people see me as aloof, detached, and not very sociable.

58 I spend time fantasizing and "reviewing" past conversations and events. 3 3

59 I'm more skeptical and better suited than other people to sense danger or threatening circumstances.

60 I am a powerful survivor and protector of those who are weaker than myself.

61 I stay busy, juggling activities and keeping up with the latest developments.

62 I find myself acting as a "go-between" because I have a calming influence on others.

3 | **63** I like to have a special place in others' lives; knowing what's going on with them helps me feel close to them. _____

3 **64** I have trouble saying "no" because I dislike getting into disagreements with others. _____

65 I often get approval from my superiors for preparing well and following the organization's policies.

2— **66** I know that projecting a successful image is important for my career and lifestyle.

67 I "push the limits" and create adventure rather than wasting time doing nothing or being passive.

68 I am constantly trying to improve myself and the world around me.

222

3 3 **69** I'm a sensitive person, and I turn to my own feelings and intuition to resolve my problems. _____

3 **70** I spend much of my time helping others because it feels good to be needed. _____

71 I value rugged individualism and my ability to control my environment.

3 **72** My ability to concentrate and focus on specific tasks, without direction from others, is one of my assets.

Part II

Directions
Now that you have completed the Profiler, go back over the items you circled and weigh how much each item describes you. Write 1, 2, or 3 in the left margin beside the circled items.

    1 = Generally descriptive of me

    2 = Strongly descriptive of me in most situations

    3 = Absolutely descriptive of me almost all the time

SCORING YOUR PERSONAL/PARTNER PROFILER

1. Once you have completed the PPP, including both parts I and II, transfer your weighted ratings for each statement you selected in the corresponding spaces below. In other words, write 1, 2, or 3 next to the numbers of the statements you selected. Transfer the numbers carefully, because most of the statements are out of order.

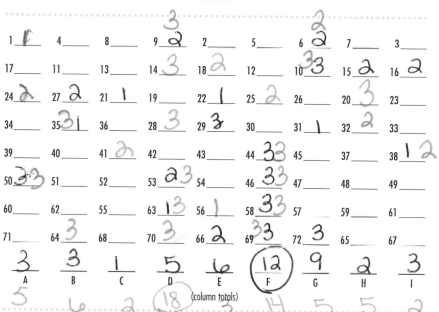

2. Now add each column (A through I) vertically, writing the total for each on the "Column Total" line provided at the bottom. Note the letter that has the highest total. Find the number that corresponds to that letter below. This number is your PPP Number.

A= Number Eight, Leader

B= Number Nine, Mediator

C= Number One, Perfectionist

D= Number Two, Helper/Giver

E= Number Three, Motivator

F= Number Four, Individualist/Artist

G= Number Five, Observer/Thinker

H= Number Six, Belonger/Loyalist

I= Number Seven, Adventurer

Now That You Know Your Enneagram Number

You now know your Enneagram number. Remember, there are no good or bad numbers. You were born with a personality style and number, just as you were born with a zodiac sign. Each number has its own unique attributes and challenges and is special in its own way. Traits overlap from number to number, and there are no absolutes in describing each number. Each human being uniquely and distinctly embodies his or her personality traits. In compiling these profiles, the foremost experts in the field have distilled a lifetime of research and study into a quick, easily used format that is both entertaining and informative. This country's leading Enneagram expert, Don Riso, has evaluated the numerical overviews. Although the description of each number is very concise, it allows a fairly comprehensive and accurate summary of each type. If you are interested in furthering your knowledge on the subject, I highly recommend further study through Don's fascinating books.

224

Before you peruse your number profile, it may helpful to know that these nine numbers comprise three distinct core categories of life tasks and challenges. Each triad, as well as each individual number, has its own set of life tasks and challenges.

Heart, Head, or Instinct: How Do You Lead?

If you are a Two, Three, or Four, you are a heart-centered number. Throughout life, people falling under these three numbers will be challenged by various emotional issues that will require them to discern and express what their true feelings are. Twos (Helpers) have a tendency to overstate the importance of the feelings of others yet stay distant and disconnected from their own emotions, playing the role of loving nurturer to everyone else. Threes (Motivators) disconnect from their feelings and inner life to focus on connecting to others through their successes. In contrast, Fours (Individualists) are excruciatingly aware of the depth of their feelings but have trouble conveying them to others.

If you are a Five, Six, or Seven, you are a head-centered number. Those whose score added up to these numbers are concerned with using—or not using—their heads and intellect to contain and control their feelings and fears. Fives (Observers) rely on their intellect and thought processes to deal with their fears and feelings, rationalizing and knowing rather than feeling. Sixes (Belongers) don't trust their own thinking but choose to rely on other "authority" figures to tell them what they feel and why. Sevens (Adventurers) try to stay busy so they won't have to think about their fears or feel their heartache or deeper feelings. They could be described as human "doers" rather than human "beings."

If you are an Eight, Nine, or One, you are an instinct-centered number. You experience life through your gut reaction and instincts. People characterized by these numbers tend to be fearful and often express their fear through anger at the world or others. They often feel the world is an unfair, dangerous, and harmful place. Eights (Leaders) express this fear by a need to control and seek to dominate problems (and others) by sheer force of will. Number Nines (Mediators) are disconnected from their fear and anger (along with their other emotions) because they work so hard in an desperate effort to keep everything harmonious and peaceful. Number Ones (Perfectionists) are often disconnected from their instinct and intuition, relying instead on order and rigid rules to help them feel safe.

As you locate your number on the nine-pointed wheel on the following page, take note of the numbers adjacent to yours. These are known as your wing numbers, which will also be an influence on your personality. This is analogous to being on the cusp in an astrological sign or how cultural influences along with genetics shape your worldview. Also note the number across the lines from yours, which is known as your arrow number, from which you may also exhibit traits. Wings, arrows, and how they work are discussed in greater depth in further reading suggestions listed in the bibliography.

Why does knowing your number (or his number) matter to a woman wanting to make better choices in her relationships? A Smart Heart woman realizes that knowledge is power. Understanding what makes you who you are and what your unique personality challenges are will help you become a more integrated, expansive human being. Knowing your number can be a helpful communication tool for you and your partner, enabling you to better articulate why you do the things you do and how his orientation toward life is different from yours. Neither way of approaching things is right or wrong, just different. The more we can eliminate differences through knowledge and understanding, the more we can empathize with each other to find commonality. Understanding your partner's number and being aware of what motivates him creates a more compassionate, tolerant relationship. Now that you know your PPP number, you can read and discover more about your primary motivations and perceptions in the next chapter.

Please note that the information presented in this PPP offers an accessible approach to intricate personality issues. I have deliberately limited its complexity. The following chapter provides enough additional information to begin your quest for self-knowledge and personal growth through the Enneagram. If you desire additional information, however, please call 1-888-LIMIT99 (1-888-546-4899) for more in-depth, personalized analysis of the information, or refer to the Enneagram Institute in the bibliography and other resources listed at the end of this book. In addition, there is a Web site where you can surf for further information (www.nolimit-zlove.com).

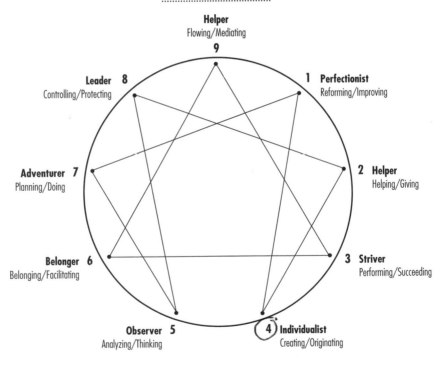

Personal Partner Profiler

Helper
Flowing/Mediating
9

Leader 8
Controlling/Protecting

1 Perfectionist
Reforming/Improving

Adventurer 7
Planning/Doing

2 Helper
Helping/Giving

Belonger 6
Belonging/Facilitating

3 Striver
Performing/Succeeding

Observer 5
Analyzing/Thinking

4 Individualist
Creating/Originating

What's Your Number?

Y our next step is to read the profile corresponding to your num ber to further the process of learning about how your person- ality affects your life. Understanding who you are and how you are oriented toward the world will help you move forward on your evolutionary path.

An important note before you begin: The nine PPP numbers represent the different ways in which each personality sees and reacts to the world, both internally and externally. In each number description, you will be pro- vided with information that will enlighten, entertain, and, if you choose, help you transform yourself within your personality style.

What follows are sections relative to each of the nine numbers repre- senting those personality styles. There is a great deal of useful and inter- esting information for each category, including "famous number" key traits, basic issues, and childhood messages. You will undoubtedly recognize your- self in the traits of several different numbers. After taking the PPP, however, you will see that the information on your specific number will be the most accurate reflection of you.

The descriptions of the personality qualities include one part specifi- cally designed for the Smart Heart woman, the section on personality trans- formation. This section can assist you if you choose to transform and develop your personality traits. Although you are born into a certain number, much like a zodiac sign, there exists within that number's parameters the opportunity to improve yourself. As you read about your number, many aspects will ring true. Other traits and qualities may trigger embarrassment or annoyance, as you may judge them to be undesirable aspects of your personality. My experience is that awareness is the first step toward enlightenment, followed by acceptance of the truth we have come to realize, and finally the willingness to take action to transform. When you shine a light on your weak spots, those attributes will, over time, become your greatest gifts. For example, you might be quick to criticize, without consideration of another person's feelings because you "know" what's right for him or her. If you are aware and lovingly observant, waiting for the right time to make a contribution, your perceptiveness, as opposed to your eagerness to criticize, will be much more readily received. Through specific examples, I'll reveal how negative traits and tendencies have an impact on you and others around you and how, through self-awareness, you can transform those behaviors into positive qualities.

Committing to self-transformation takes motivation and courage. Pain, anxiety, and fear often come to the surface when we try to let go of negative, unconscious defense mechanisms and bad habits. The road to self-discovery is not an easy journey. Many choose just to exist, become old, and die, without taking a single step toward expanding their conscious awareness of themselves and how they affect others. When you make this commitment to yourself, however, you will find great freedom and infinite blessings, not only for yourself but also for your loved ones and the world we live in. Of course, by transforming yourself, you render yourself more desirable to any potential partner.

Practice and commitment are necessary to create results. You can expect that negative habits and thoughts will resurface on occasion. Our spiritual and personal growth is a step-by-step process. Acknowledge each step forward and congratulate yourself for each accomplishment and for being open to the possibility of growth. The first step is always the most difficult, but the path toward enlightened relationships is infinitely rewarding.

Warning: This information can be hazardous to your relationships if you use it to force your partner to change! It is tempting to think you'll improve your partner by making him take the PPP test to learn about his number. Be advised: You can improve only yourself. Your partner will improve himself only if he is personally motivated to do so. Prodding and pressure from you will merely create resentment on his part.

Number One: *Perfectionist*

OTHER NAMES THIS NUMBER GOES BY

Reformer

Judge

Inspector

Idealist

Principled

Planner

Orderly

Hard Worker

Rationalist

Purist

Visionary

MOTTO OF A ONE

Do the Right Thing

FAMOUS ONES*

Pope John Paul II

Margaret Thatcher

Elie Wiesel

Bill Moyers

Harrison Ford

Sandra Day O'Connor

Noam Chomsky

Joan of Arc

Mahatma Gandhi

Al Gore

Barbara Jordan

Katharine Hepburn

Ralph Nader

William F. Buckley

George Bernard Shaw

"Mr. Spock" on *Star Trek*

Ones at a Glance

ONES CAN BE GREAT IN RELATIONSHIPS BECAUSE THEY

- ▶ are dependable
- ▶ are loyal
- ▶ plan well
- ▶ are always prompt
- ▶ strive for self-improvement
- ▶ can be great humorists

- ▶ motivate those around them
- ▶ want to improve the world
- ▶ value their family
- ▶ do their fair share at home
- ▶ value being good providers
- ▶ accomplish a lot

*Excerpted from Don Riso, *Personality Types: Using the Enneagram for Self-Discovery* (Boston: Houghton Mifflin, 1996).

ONES CAN BE TROUBLE IN RELATIONSHIPS BECAUSE THEY CAN BE

- worriers
- inflexible
- nitpickers
- rigid
- critical of others
- workaholics
- moralistic
- too serious
- obsessed with neatness
- unable to relax and have fun
- stressed out from their high expectations
- out of touch with their anger

KEY TRAITS OF ONES

- conscientious
- idealistic
- honest
- well organized
- moral
- objective
- principled
- perfectionist
- self-disciplined
- prudent
- proficient
- judicious
- fair
- rules oriented
- judgmental
- stubborn
- self-righteous
- uncompromising
- critical
- rigid
- intolerant

BASIC ISSUES

- tries to deal with the dangers of the world by imposing strict order and adhering rigidly to rules and conscious goals
- easily angered by own and others' imperfections but represses feelings because anger is a sign of imperfection

PRIMAL NEED

- to be perfect

MOST AFRAID OF

- making mistakes

TYPICAL PHYSICAL APPEARANCE

- clothes neat and well fitting
- posture tall and, often, rigid
- not a hair out of place

WHAT APPEALS TO ONES

- order
- self-improvement
- punctuality
- dedication
- community involvement
- improving the world

ONES AT THE OFFICE

- detail oriented
- great mentors
- perfectionists
- unable to suffer fools gladly
- tireless workers
- strive to improve things

HIGHEST ATTRIBUTE FOR ONES TO AIM FOR

- discernment

MOST DESTRUCTIVE TRAIT TO WORK TO AVOID

- being judgmental

WHAT TEMPERS ONES' TROUBLES

- a sense of reason and a grounding in reality

WHAT DOESN'T APPEAL TO ONES

- messiness
- mistakes
- lateness
- bad manners
- lackadaisical attitudes
- decisions made by the seat of one's pants

Is This You? Is This Him? Checklist for Ones

- I like that other people can count on me.

- People think I am fanatically organized, but I still notice a lot of things that are out of their proper place.

- I am willing to spend a long time on a project to ensure that it gets done right.

- It annoys me that others don't have the same high standards that I do.

- I show people I care about them by being dependable and working hard for them.

- When I have an opinion about something, it is usually the right opinion.

- Others can feel put down when I criticize them, but I find it hard to hold my tongue.

- Almost nothing bothers me more than to be rebuked.

- I enjoy getting involved with such noble causes as saving the environment.

- People value the fact that I am fair-minded.

- I may appear stiff and prim to others, but I don't feel that way inside.

▶ People would benefit if they did things my way more often.

▶ I work very hard, so there's not much time left for relaxation.

▶ I do a lot of research on an item before making a purchase.

▶ I believe that God is in the details—so I focus on getting all of them perfect.

Ones in More Detail

What Motivates Ones

There is no doubt in Ones' minds that there is a right way and a wrong way, and Ones are determined always to follow the way that is proper. Conscientious people with high principles, Ones want to improve themselves and their environment, and they can become angry when others around them aren't willing to do the same. (Since it is imperfect to be angry, however, Ones are generally out of touch with this feeling.) "What's wrong with trying to reach an ideal?" Ones believe. "Making mistakes is a sign that a person simply hasn't put in the effort needed." Hard workers, Ones may already have accomplished much in life and will undoubtedly accomplish more in the years ahead.

For many Ones, perfection begins at home, which is why a One's CDs may be in alphabetical order on the shelf and his socks arranged by color in the underwear drawer. The obsessively clean and tidy Felix Unger from Neil Simon's "The Odd Couple," was the prototypical One, although he was certainly more extreme than most. (Some Ones aren't as concerned with their physical environment as they are with the rightness of their political or social worlds or their relationships.)

Because Ones can see the ideal version of what is before them, they are often visionaries. Whatever the task, predicament, or person, Ones have a clear picture of how it can be improved and perfected—a trait that can cause trouble when Ones impose their vision on people who aren't as happy to see it.

Possible Messages Ones Received as Children

Perfection is the goal, and it is possible to achieve it. Parents may have praised and rewarded Ones for following the rules and rebuked them critically for making mistakes. ("What, only an A–? What did you miss?") What Ones learned from these situations is that anything less than an A+ constitutes failure.

Since a person's feelings and individual needs don't mesh so neatly with the external guidelines Ones vowed early in life to follow, they often repress their own emotions and desires. Because of this, Ones may disown the frequent anger they feel when people (including themselves) or things are not as perfect as they require.

Ones' Basic Fears

Nothing terrifies Ones more than being wrong, whether the mistakes are made in front of others or not. Being criticized doesn't make anyone feel good, but for Ones, even a small verbal rebuke can sting as badly as a torturous whipping. Being judged inadequate or, even worse, negligent, is a catastrophe.

Ones often worry obsessively that they might make a mistake, a mindset that can take an incredible amount of energy away from more positive pursuits. Ones fear that their own anger and other emotions make them less than perfect. Because following the rules is so important to them, they can feel lost in situations where clear-cut guidelines do not exist.

A One's Possibilities for Personality Transformation

233

When Ones Live Unconsciously

❶ Inflexible and rigid, they see the world in black and white, right and wrong. They believe their position is always right and leave no room for compromise with others.

❷ They always tell people what they should do because they know what is best for them.

❸ They immediately reject relationship partners who don't measure up to their ideal standards.

❹ They never allow themselves time to relax because there is always something that needs more work to be perfected. Pleasure is a distraction from their pursuit of correcting the world.

❺ They may be obsessive and compulsive, for example, washing their hands dozens of times before they feel clean or organizing pencils according to size on the desk.

❻ They often have a self-righteous attitude, unable to allow themselves to see their own flaws yet eagerly seeking them out in others. Nothing makes them happier than cutting an imperfect person down to size.

7 Because they cannot face their own anger, when they do lash out at others they may deny that anger is involved. In the extreme, their inability to recognize their own needs and act on them can lead to ulcers, depression, or even cruelty against others.

8 They strive to be perfect and are painfully cognizant that they are not.

The Evolutionary Process for Ones of Average Awareness

1 They may congratulate themselves on taking high-minded positions on various issues, from women's rights to saving the whales. They allow others to have a different opinion, even if they feel it is erroneous.

2 Although they can resist the urge to say "I know what's best" or, worse, "I told you so" some of the time, they are still impatient when others don't do things the way Ones believe they should be done.

3 They remain in relationships with people who aren't ideal, although they can't stop trying to make their partners better.

4 They let themselves go on an occasional vacation or take the weekend off, but their cell phone and computer are never left behind.

5 An "anal" type of personality, they are meticulous when it comes to personal appearance. They constantly worry about controlling their environment.

6 They are easily upset when others do wrong. They frequently make sarcastic and cutting remarks to those around them.

7 They occasionally write letters or obliquely tell others how they feel, but they are mostly uncomfortable expressing emotions.

8 They fear making mistakes, especially in front of others, and spend a great deal of energy preparing themselves for every contingency.

Evolved Ones with Heightened Inner Awareness

1 They are principled but respect dissent and have a tolerance for people and things that are less than perfect. They have no need for rigid rules because they understand that reality is often complex.

2 They know that people need to arrive at their own decisions, even if their choices are not what seems best for them. While others seek Ones' guidance because of their discernment, they can assess to what degree the advice is warranted before offering it.

234

3 They realize that relationship partners, like everyone else, never attain a predetermined ideal. They are content to enjoy their partners as they are, warts and all.

4 They understand that people need rest to rejuvenate themselves. They allow themselves vacation and relaxation time and enjoy it immensely.

5 They no longer fear loss of control and therefore don't compulsively waste time cleaning or organizing beyond what is necessary.

6 They recognize that other people are perfect just the way they are. If they find it necessary to criticize someone else's actions, they do it gently and with a keen eye toward not hurting anyone's feelings.

7 They are comfortable expressing anger and other emotions in a full and open manner. They have integrated their needs and emotions into a healthy life.

8 They understand that *perfection* is simply a word in the dictionary—a process, not a dictum. They accept themselves and others for what they are.

If You're a One, What You Can Do to Become Your Best

1 Remember that you are human; look for progress, not perfection.

2 Know that your best is good enough.

3 Learn to view mistakes as gifts from the universe and that we grow more from our errors than from our successes.

4 Purposefully make a mistake on occasion, acknowledging that the world doesn't come to an end. You're still alive, and you might even have fun in the process.

5 Calm the fears of your "inner critic." Learn to make friends with the self-critical part of yourself.

6 Practice forgiving others for being imperfect.

7 Work on not being judgmental. Practice lovingly accepting the opinions of those you consider less than perfect.

8 Be aware of your unrealistic expectations of others, remembering that life is not the ideal but is inherently complex and often messy.

9 Practice discovering the middle ground or "gray areas" in situations that appear blatantly right or wrong. See if you can accept another point of view.

235

⑩ If you are anxious to tell someone what to do, let him do what he thinks is best—even if you are certain it is wrong.

⑪ Take up meditation, yoga, or other activities to calm your mind and relax your body.

⑫ Take mini-vacations, such as a three-day weekend every few months. When planning your regular yearly vacation, make sure you do something fun that brings you pleasure, rather than using the time to catch up on work.

⑬ Reward yourself for any job you complete, even if it falls short of your expectations. Treat yourself to something special—take a nap or a leisurely walk, watch your favorite TV show, eat chocolates—or do whatever appeals to you.

⑭ Make a small mess in your bedroom or office and try not to clean it up for at least one day! Congratulate yourself on surviving the disorder.

⑮ Remember, just being yourself is more than enough—for you, for your life, and for those who love you.

236

Number Two: *Helper*

OTHER NAMES THIS NUMBER GOES BY

Caretaker

Giver

Guardian Angel

Assistant

People Pleaser

Nurturer

Server

Right Hand

Aide

Supporter

MOTTO OF A TWO

Please Need Me

FAMOUS TWOS*

Mother Teresa

Eleanor Roosevelt

Robert Fulghum

Luciano Pavarotti

Archbishop Desmond Tutu

Barbara Bush

Leo Buscaglia

Barry Manilow

*Excerpted from Don Riso, *Personality Types: Using the Enneagram for Self-Discovery* (Boston: Houghton Mifflin, 1996).

Richard Simmons
Pat Boone
Ann Landers
Doug Henning
Sammy Davis, Jr.

Melanie Hamilton Wilkes in
Gone With the Wind
The Tin Woodman in *The*
Wizard of Oz
The Jewish mother stereotype

Twos at a Glance

TWOS CAN BE GREAT IN RELATIONSHIPS BECAUSE THEY

- are supportive
- are loving
- are great listeners
- have great enthusiasm
- are optimistic
- exude warmth
- give generously
- make others feel special
- appreciate others
- value their families
- love to have fun
- are always there for you

TWOS CAN BE TROUBLE IN RELATIONSHIPS BECAUSE THEY CAN BE

- clinging
- overwhelmingly needy
- overly demonstrative
- ultrasensitive to criticism
- jealous
- insecure
- intrusive
- martyrlike
- easily hurt
- insincere in their praise
- out of touch with their needs
- manipulative

KEY TRAITS OF TWOS

- loving
- warm
- compassionate
- sympathetic
- generous
- caring
- nonjudgmental
- perceptive
- supportive
- appreciative
- selfless
- thoughtful
- tactful
- fun loving
- proud
- manipulative
- victimized
- dependent
- intrusive
- possessive
- clinging

BASIC ISSUES

- overexpress feelings for others with the goal of being loved and appreciated in return

237

PRIMAL NEED
- to be needed

MOST AFRAID OF
- being abandoned by loved ones

TYPICAL PHYSICAL APPEARANCE
- pretty and alluring
- sweet and not shocking
- molded to appeal to the audience and occasion

WHAT APPEALS TO TWOS
- being needed
- being close to people
- being appreciated
- assisting others
- expressing affection
- romantic actions

TWOS AT THE OFFICE
- supportive
- reliable
- the power behind the boss
- customer focused
- solve problems, credit others
- office nurturers

HIGHEST ATTRIBUTE FOR TWOS TO AIM FOR
- service to others

238

MOST DESTRUCTIVE TRAIT TO WORK TO AVOID
- conceit

WHAT TEMPERS TWOS' TROUBLES
- a deep empathy for others

WHAT DOESN'T APPEAL TO TWOS
- being ignored
- being taken for granted
- not helping others
- being cold and distant
- not complimenting others
- apathy toward people

Is This You? Is This Him? Checklist for Twos

- Nothing makes me happier than giving my time or services to those around me.

- I am devastated when a relationship partner leaves me, and I pray that the person will soon come back to me.

- I beam when someone tells others what a help I have been.

- I love it when people ask me for assistance or advice.

- Sometimes I help others to the point of my own illness or exhaustion.

- It feels selfish to ask other people to do things for me.

- I know how to flatter people and make them feel good about themselves.

- I am upbeat and enthusiastic, and people enjoy being with me.

- I have many close friends, but I am always looking for more.

- When I'm not around people, I can feel terribly lonely.

- I hate it when others see my vulnerability and neediness.

- I like to assist and be around people who are powerful.

- When someone tries to get to know me too intimately, I am tempted to flee.

- I can be a very tactile person, hugging and holding friends, even acquaintances.

- I would never ask anyone else to take care of me, but I wish that they would decide on their own to do so.

239

Twos in More Detail

What Motivates Twos

The phrase "I couldn't have done it without you" is music to every Two's ears. Eager to assist and adept at uncovering the emotional needs of others, Twos are eager to assist in meeting those needs. They are terrific at soothing wounded egos, lifting low spirits, and making other people feel special. Those around them, even total strangers, quickly come to feel welcome and adored.

This need to be needed comes at a price, however. Twos are often unable to ask others to satisfy their own desires and frequently out of touch with what exactly those desires are. Consequently, they might use guilt or manipulation to get what they want. Twos may go to extreme lengths to keep others dependent on them.

Helping people is a strong focus in the lives of Twos. They often work for nonprofit organizations or are healers, teachers, and in other service-oriented professions. The world would be a colder place without Twos. Although they may feel more comfortable out of the spotlight, Twos are often the unseen powers behind the scenes.

Possible Messages Twos Received as Children

As children, Twos were often rewarded by their parents for helping. Twos usually loved doing things for members of their families, such as cooking, cleaning, or getting Dad's slippers. They beamed when others delighted in their thoughtfulness.

This message became internalized, however, causing Twos to feel loved due to their helpfulness. Twos may come to feel that their primary reason for being is because others need them. Meeting their own needs is equated with selfishness, a trait Twos seek desperately to avoid. As a result, Twos are often out of touch with their own desires and gain self-worth through others requiring their assistance. Because their desirability is linked to their actions, not their intrinsic value, Twos easily suffer from a low sense of self-esteem.

Twos' Basic Fears

If nobody needs you, does your purpose in life cease to exist? Twos think so. Twos fear being cast out from the inner circle, rejected by the people they are so desperate to serve. They worry that, although they may do a wonderful job, their efforts won't be noticed or appreciated.

Twos also fear what might happen if they suddenly stopped helping others and asked others to help them. Maybe those people wouldn't love them or want to be with them anymore. This a fate worse than death for many Twos!

Twos' Possibilities for Personality Transformation

When Twos Live Unconsciously

1 They view helping other people as an investment, something they do in order to get something in return.

2 They resent others' lack of appreciation and frequently complain about it.

3 They coerce or manipulate "ingrates" into doing things for them. After all, they are entitled by virtue of their past assistance.

4 They frequently get sick and are secretly pleased that their illness means others will be forced to take care of them.

5 They instill guilt in others when they won't do something for them, yet they proudly wear a mantle of martyrdom.

6 They are out of touch with their "negative" emotions, especially anger and aggression, and the suppressed feelings surface in substance abuse or eating disorders.

7 They confuse genuine love with co-dependency and befriend unworthy people regardless of the consequences.

8 They feel indispensable to the lives of others. Without their advice, others would flounder.

The Evolutionary Process of Twos of Average Awareness

1 They enjoy doing for others but mostly enjoy their feeling of pride when praised.

2 They need to have a lot of friends to feel loved and appreciated.

3 They are basically ashamed of their own needs and try to get them met indirectly. Uncomfortable in expressing themselves to others, they hide their fears under the guise of wanting to talk about the problems of others.

4 They work so hard helping and giving to others that sometimes their health suffers.

5 Their constant hovering and doing for others can be annoying and intrusive.

6 They attempt to repress their anger, but it surfaces inappropriately, for example, in lashing out at someone.

7 They strive for equal, available partners who are not overly needy, but they aren't always successful.

8 They can't help feeling that the answer to everyone's problems is their love and concern.

Evolved Twos with Heightened Inner Awareness

1 They are joyfully altruistic, giving and doing without the expectation or thought of getting anything in return.

2 They are self-confident and don't need the approval of others.

3 They are aware of their own needs and can comfortably ask things of others. They trust that the universe will provide.

241

❹ They take care of their own bodies, minds, and spirits. Healthy and strong, they retain the energy to serve others without harming themselves.

❺ Their needs are taken care of directly, therefore there is no need for guilt.

❻ They recognize that all emotions are healthy. They eat and drink only as much as their bodies require.

❼ They seek relationships with healthy, equal partners. They lovingly release a partner who wants to move on.

❽ They give love to and share their talents freely with those who wish them, but they don't require their acceptance by another.

If You're a Two, What You Can Do to Become Your Best

❶ Know that you are worthy and lovable just by being you, not by what you give or do for others.

❷ Direct your inherent compassion to yourself sometimes.

❸ Tend to your own health and well-being. Don't be an exhausted martyr to the service of others.

❹ Devote time to yourself to discern your own needs.

❺ Meditate or do other mind-centering techniques to contact your inner core.

❻ As you discover your own needs, express them to others so they can be met without manipulation.

❼ Serve others only when they explicitly ask for your help.

❽ When you do help, resist the urge to tell the world about your wonderful deeds.

❾ Often assistance is best rendered without recognition or the other party's even being aware of it. On occasion, give anonymously and never reveal your identity.

❿ If someone wants to give to you, generously receive his or her offer.

⓫ Be grateful for the friends and lovers already in your life. Don't worry about getting new ones.

⓬ If someone asks for your help and it's not convenient for you, tell him or her you will do it later. Practice doing this a few times even when you aren't busy, just to see how it feels.

⓭ If you feel taken advantage of, tell the person and, if necessary, end the relationship.

⓮ Once in a while, just say "no" to someone's request. You will live to tell the tale!

⓯ Resist the urge to rescue the downtrodden with your love and affection.

Number Three: *Striver*

OTHER NAMES THIS NUMBER GOES BY

Producer

Performer

Achiever

Motivator

Pragmatist

Manager

Self-Marketer

Succeeder

Doer

Aspirer

MOTTO OF A THREE

Winning Is Everything

FAMOUS THREES*

Bill Clinton

Michael Landon

Shirley MacLaine

Paul McCartney

Tom Cruise

Tony Robbins

Dick Clark

Brooke Shields

Denzel Washington

Arnold Schwarzenegger

O. J. Simpson

Christopher Reeve

Richard Gere

Jane Pauley

Sting

Sharon Stone

Bryant Gumbel

Vanna White

Kathie Lee Gifford

Sylvester Stallone

Truman Capote

243

Threes at a Glance

THREES CAN BE GREAT IN RELATIONSHIPS BECAUSE THEY

▶ are energetic

▶ are optimistic

▶ value their families

▶ strive to look attractive

*Excerpted from Don Riso, *Personality Types: Using the Enneagram for Self-Discovery* (Boston: Houghton Mifflin, 1996).

- exude charisma
- get things done
- are self-starters
- are playful

- enjoy socializing
- work hard for you
- are sexy
- are financially successful

THREES CAN BE TROUBLE IN RELATIONSHIPS BECAUSE THEY

- can be narcissistic
- fear intimacy
- have trouble with feelings
- are overly competitive
- overfocus on image
- hog the spotlight

- aren't good listeners
- are chameleons
- put work before family
- are workaholics
- withdraw from problems
- don't spend time relaxing

KEY TRAITS OF THREES

- ambitious
- self-directed
- energetic
- practical
- inspiring
- hardworking
- image conscious
- confident
- outgoing
- popular
- spirited

- charming
- adaptable
- productive
- ruthless
- opportunistic
- competitive
- grandiose
- arrogant
- vain
- superficial

BASIC ISSUES

- out of touch with true feelings

- focuses on becoming and con-
  vincing others you are a success

PRIMAL NEED

- success

MOST AFRAID OF

- failure

TYPICAL PHYSICAL APPEARANCE

- fit and trim
- dressed for success

- exhausted from many late nights
  at the office

244

WHAT APPEALS TO THREES
- productivity
- success
- image
- beating the competition
- the bottom line
- efficiency

THREES AT THE OFFICE
- entrepreneurial
- solution oriented
- hardworking
- flexible
- want to win
- inspire others

HIGHEST ATTRIBUTE FOR THREES TO AIM FOR
- unpretentiousness

MOST DESTRUCTIVE TRAIT TO WORK TO AVOID
- self-deceit

WHAT TEMPERS THREES' TROUBLES
- a genuine desire to be accepted by others

WHAT DOESN'T APPEAL TO THREES
- laziness
- caution
- feelings
- sitting still
- appearing defeated
- getting lost in the crowd

245

Is This You? Is This Him? Checklist for Threes

- I make schedules for myself and then try to exceed them.
- Working ten-hour days doesn't bother me because I know that's what it takes to get ahead.
- I know that first impressions are crucial, and I do everything I can not to blow them.
- Others are amazed at how much energy I have.
- I love it when I get awards or rewards for my achievements.
- If people want to succeed, I believe they can.
- I care a lot about what others think of me, and I will change to gain acceptance.
- People look to me to lead them, and I am happy to do it.
- If a relationship doesn't work out, I take it in stride. I can't understand it when people fall apart over things like that.

▶ I'm a great persuader and can easily convince a friend, co-worker, or relationship partner to do what I want.

▶ Feelings get in the way of people's successes, so I try not to get caught up in mine.

▶ I get along well with a lot of people, and others love to be around me.

▶ I don't like confrontation, but if you humiliate me, I'll get even.

▶ My personal life is my own business; I don't share that kind of information with others.

▶ I secretly tend to feel superior to other people.

Threes in More Detail

What Motivates Threes

Threes always expect to do great things and they do them. Excellent leaders, role models, coaches, and committed workers, Threes perform well under pressure. They are confident, dedicated, ambitious, and adaptable. In nearly every endeavor, Threes' motivation is to receive approval, excel, and be the stars.

The world could not survive without success-oriented Threes. Natural leaders with high self-esteem, Threes are terrific at seeing the big picture. They are optimistic, yet pragmatic, and are great problem solvers. Threes are often managers and organizers in both work and leisure pursuits. Their contagious enthusiasm wins them a cadre of friends.

Threes are not content just to excel in the world. They need reassurance that others recognize their accomplishments as well. The consummate self-sellers, they put tremendous energy into promoting their worth to others, a task that is ultimately exhausting. Because Threes are so tied up in their successes, even the smallest failure feels overwhelming.

Possible Messages Threes Received as Children

Undoubtedly encouraged to "be a winner" as children, Threes have internalized that message at the core of their beings. Their parents may have applauded their accomplishments instead of valuing their intrinsic nature, causing them to improve and highlight those accomplishments as a way of gaining love. (The overachieving child who staffs the lemonade stand on weekends, baby-sits during the week, and sweeps the neighbor's walkway for money is almost always a Three.)

Because Threes realize that others admire them for their accomplishments, they focus more on their images than on development of their true inner selves. These false personae can lead to a sense of emptiness and a fear that if they reveal their true selves, they won't be liked anymore.

Threes' Basic Fears

The fear of success-oriented Threes is, of course, that they will not be able to achieve enough. No matter what their stature in life or how much money they have, someone else is out there with more—a point of great upset for typical Threes. Threes are also terrified that if they lose all that they have acquired, they will be rejected and regarded as worthless people.

Failure may be the worst thing Threes fear most, but smaller insults like looking bad or stupid in front of others are almost as terrifying. That's why Threes work so hard to keep up appearances, even if reality doesn't support the picture.

Threes' Possibilities for Personality Transformation

When Threes Live Unconsciously

1 Their self-worth is so intricately linked to being perceived as "winners" that they will go to great lengths, sometimes through illegal or immoral means, to conceal evidence of failure (for example, a stockbroker who covers up trading losses until they number in the millions of dollars).

2 They see people for what they can do for them, not for who they truly are.

3 They don't care if others get hurt in their quest to get what they want.

4 They are always envious of someone who has more than they do. They fantasize about sabotaging others who stand in their way or are seeking similar success. Sometimes, they even act on these impulses.

5 In a relationship, they feel they are the more important half of the couple.

6 They expect constant praise and are angered if they don't get it.

7 They feel contempt for people who have not accomplished what they have.

8 They are obsessed by image. They would never openly admit that business wasn't booming or relinquish that luxury car because they could no longer afford it.

The Evolutionary Process for Threes of Average Awareness

1 They frequently feel that their best isn't good enough if someone else is better.

2 They strive to impress everyone around them. They want to be seen as "winners."

3 They'd rather not hurt people, but if that's what's required to succeed, they'll do it.

4 Extremely competitive, they are willing to work nights and weekends to ensure that nobody climbs higher than they.

5 They have an exaggerated sense of self-importance and lack empathy in relationships. They fear deep intimacy because of their inability to reveal themselves.

6 They continually boast of their accomplishments and grow tiresome with their "show biz" personalities.

7 They focus only on those who can contribute to their success and ignore everyone else.

8 They dress flashily and live as high as their income allows because they want others to think they are successful.

Evolved Threes with Heightened Inner Awareness

1 They are deeply content with themselves and their accomplishments.

2 They enjoy being with people because everyone is intrinsically valuable.

3 Getting what they want is not important; rather, they strive to be useful to others and to society.

4 They don't worry about whether others have more than they do, and they are quite willing to share their talents and insights so that others can get ahead, too.

5 They lovingly recognize all the wonderful gifts their partners bring to their relationships.

6 They focus on working steadily to the best of their potential, rather than on recognition by others.

7 They are genuinely benevolent and loving.

8 They are ambitious, not necessarily for money or fame, but because of the satisfaction that comes from living up to one's potential.

If You're a Three, What You Can Do to Be Your Best

1 Learn to release your compulsion to be the best. Your personal best is more than good enough.

2 When in a group, step back and let others take the helm, at least on a few occasions. When you no longer feel superior to others, you'll know you've made terrific strides.

3 Temper your tendency to brag and embellish the truth about yourself.

4 Cultivate feeling humble and grateful, whenever possible.

5 Resist the urge to tell people what you do for a living (especially what your title and status are—for example, the top salesperson at your company). Focus instead on other traits that define you.

6 Analyze your true interests and abilities and begin working with them, regardless of whether you look good or not.

7 Go on vacation someplace far away, where no one will have heard of you, your title, or your company, even if you tell them.

8 Recognize that life is lived one day at a time. Appreciate every day for what it is, not for where it is taking you.

9 The next time someone comes to you with a problem, be empathetic. Resist the urge to offer fix-it suggestions.

10 Tell the truth to your friends and relationship partner, no matter what. It may be difficult at first, but eventually you will see how freeing it is not keeping up false appearances.

11 Pick a worthy charity and give generously—not just your money but also your energy, skills, and time.

12 Tell two people in your office tomorrow what terrific work you think they did.

13 Become aware of how angry you sometimes feel when others cross you. Be aware of how your inflated ego might contribute to negative reactions.

14 If you feel hurt or frightened, take the bold step of sharing this with a close confidant.

15 If deep intimacy scares you, begin slowly by revealing yourself a little at a time. Know that you are much more than the professional role or title you've been hiding behind—that you are intrinsically valuable and wonderful just because you're you.

Number Four: *Individualist*

OTHER NAMES THIS NUMBER GOES BY

Artist

Connoisseur

Unique

Creative

Introvert

Romantic

Original

Atypical

Creator

Intuitive

Auteur

MOTTO OF A FOUR

Feelings Are Everything

FAMOUS FOURS*

Tennessee Williams

Rudolf Nureyev

J. D. Salinger

Bob Dylan

Martha Graham

Maria Callas

Judy Garland

Yukio Mishima

Leonard Cohen

Marcel Proust

Virginia Woolf

Jeremy Irons

Ingmar Bergman

Johnny Depp

Joni Mitchell

D. H. Lawrence

Edgar Allan Poe

Michael Jackson

Ann Rice

Roy Orbison

Blanche Dubois from *A Streetcar
    Named Desire*

Laura Wingfield from *The Glass
    Menagerie*

Fours at a Glance

FOURS CAN BE GREAT IN RELATIONSHIPS BECAUSE THEY

- love deeply
- are honest
- are fun to be with
- are authentic
- easily bond with others
- are original
- have an eye for the beautiful
- provide inspiration for others

*Excerpted from Don Riso, *Personality Types: Using the Enneagram for Self-Discovery* (Boston: Houghton Mifflin, 1996).

- care so much
- are emphatic
- are emotionally strong
- see the irony in life

FOURS CAN BE TROUBLE IN RELATIONSHIPS BECAUSE THEY

- long for an ideal partner
- want what they don't have
- easily get depressed
- can be melodramatic
- are often self-absorbed
- can be hypersensitive
- are emotionally needy
- are easily jealous
- are quick to blame others
- are prone to self-pity
- feel unlovable
- don't easily let go

KEY TRAITS OF FOURS

- individualistic
- passionate
- inspired
- caring
- creative
- unique
- witty
- compassionate
- perceptive
- empathic
- original
- attuned to beauty
- sensitive
- expressive
- melancholy
- temperamental
- long for what's missing
- self-absorbed
- feel misunderstood
- easily hurt
- depressive

BASIC ISSUES

- deep need to express feelings and be seen by others as unique and special
- frequently feel misunderstood by others

PRIMAL NEED

- to be understood (and to understand themselves)

MOST AFRAID OF

- being inadequate

TYPICAL PHYSICAL APPEARANCE

- trendy and a bit offbeat
- occasionally outrageous
- often wear one-of-a-kind finds or costumes they design themselves

251

WHAT APPEALS TO FOURS
- self-expression
- looking for meaning in life
- deep emotions
- connecting with others
- sense of uniqueness
- searching for beauty

FOURS AT THE OFFICE
- original
- artistic
- want soulful co-workers
- high standards
- desire work with meaning
- self-expressive

HIGHEST ATTRIBUTE FOR A FOUR TO AIM FOR
- being even-tempered

MOST DESTRUCTIVE TRAIT TO WORK TO AVOID
- jealousy

WHAT TEMPERS FOURS' TROUBLES
- their brutal honesty about themselves

WHAT DOESN'T APPEAL TO FOURS
- going with the flow
- mundane items
- lack of passion
- superficiality
- anything easily gotten
- keeping your feelings hidden

Is This You? Is This Him? Checklist for Fours

✔ I often find myself thinking the grass is greener someplace I am not.

✔ Sometimes I think I expect more from life than is realistic or possible.

✔ Occasionally I find myself making up a fantasy world and even having conversations with people in my mind.

▶ I love creating new things, be they large works of art or small ways of putting together an unusual outfit.

✔ I am a great listener and can spend hours comforting someone in emotional need.

▶ I feel completely misunderstood by others.

✔ I am terrified of being humiliated and rejected, and sometimes I get rid of my relationship partners before they can get rid of me.

▶ Even if I want something very badly, I often feel disappointed when I actually get it.

▶ When I get depressed, I can retreat to my bed for days on end.

✓ If someone says something bad to me, I obsess over it without being able to let it go.

▶ I relish finding unusual items that others do not have.

✓ I dream of being rescued by my ideal soul mate.

▶ My sense of intuition is wonderful and, when I listen to it, it doesn't fail me.

✓ I love to surround myself with the most beautiful things.

✓ It is hard for me to feel that others truly love me.

Fours in More Detail

What Motivates Fours

"You just don't understand," Fours are apt to say, partly because they feel misunderstood and partly because they derive psychological benefit from being unique and special. For Fours, nothing is worse than being a cog in a wheel, a mass-marketed item created on a factory floor. Preserving their individuality in the face of a commodity culture is crucial to Fours. Part of the way they manage this is by clinging to the belief that they feel emotions more deeply and see beauty more profoundly than others do. This is why so many Fours become artists, writers, and actors, although many excel in other fields when they can feel passionate about their work.

Their unique identity is part of Fours' attempt to find and express their inner self, a self that a Four always feels is somehow missing. They use their art, be it their work as a sculptor or simply their flair for decorating their own houses, as a means of finding out what is significant about themselves. Because Fours are attached to the search, however, it can be hard for them to comfortably settle on an identity and sense of self. Fours are also addicted to longing to the point where, if they meet Prince Charming, get a large house, and achieve the career success they thought they desired, they are still somehow dissatisfied. In fact, Fours derive great pleasure out of feeling that they have more disappointments, more deeply felt, than other people.

Fours appreciate great beauty. Were it not for Fours, the world would be dull and lifeless. They want their environment to reflect their souls' search for the best, most original items. Fours' houses or offices tend to be

253

lush and gorgeous. They often inspire others to surround themselves with what is unique and authentic.

Possible Messages Fours Received as Children

Frequently during childhood, Fours suffered a major loss that turned their paradise found into a paradise lost and left them searching for something for the rest of their melodramatic lives. Perhaps a parent died or divorced; perhaps a father's business went bust; perhaps exotic Aunt Sadie moved out of their home. The pain of this loss hit sensitive Fours particularly hard, leading to the belief that loss inevitably follows happiness or intimacy with others. Fours desire what they do not have, although once they get what they want, they aren't satisfied. In some cases, when no identifiable loss has occurred Fours may still have felt abandoned by perfectly competent parents who didn't understand them.

Because they are sensitive, fantasy-oriented children, Fours look internally to find meaning for their original, grand loss and often come to blame some internal flaw such as their mediocrity or vulnerability. Fours carry a sense of having a special wound with them throughout life and consequently feel uniquely unworthy or defective. Fours' artistic flair and creative expression are often an attempt to find and communicate their true self, from which they feel completely disconnected.

Fours' Basic Fears

Fours deeply believe that no one is like them, that God surely broke the mold after they were created. They fear that, unlike others on whom they keep a keen eye, they have no real self but instead project an illusion of who they are. Fours are terrified that, despite an extensive, intense, lifelong search, they will still come up empty in their quest to know their Soul. They worry that if others get to know them they will be found somehow wanting and will be rejected or abandoned.

Moreover, Fours fear the anger they feel at their parents for letting them down, but their deep sense of emotion makes it difficult for them to let go of the anger. Unable to express that and other negative emotions outright, Fours can retreat to isolation, depression, and even despair.

Fours' Possibilities for Personality Transformation

When Fours Live Unconsciously

1 Under the impression that others are happy and successful, while they themselves are not, they are jealous of everyone.

2 Gratifying themselves through self-indulgent behavior, such as substance abuse or eating disorders, becomes a consolation prize for not finding their true sense of self.

3 They cut themselves off from all feelings and desires, except the self-pity they feel for their sense of personal failure. Occasionally, they feel so worthless that they retreat to bed and are barely able to function.

4 Fearful of being rejected, they often terminate relationships before they are abandoned.

5 They don't want any obligations, except the freedom to be themselves; others can't always count on them.

6 Their rich fantasy life is a large part of their existence and helps infuse their barren emotional life with drama.

7 They can't stand to be surrounded by people and push away even those they once put on a pedestal.

8 They can visualize the most imaginative work of art or music, yet they can't seem to actually sit down at the easel or piano to create it.

The Evolutionary Process for Fours of Average Awareness

1 They don't want the "mundane" existence of others, but they are envious nonetheless.

2 Their search for their sense of self leaves them frustrated and unhappy, resulting in melancholy and moodiness.

3 Hypersensitive to the comments of others, they can become terribly upset by even a mildly negative remark. Such comments can not only ruin their day but also fester for months.

4 They sometimes play hard to get, using the intensity of other people's efforts as an indication of how much they are desired.

5 Taking care of their responsibilities can be difficult, unless they are in the mood. Sometimes, that mood never comes.

255

6 They fantasize, at least occasionally, and are increasingly drawn to the dramatic worlds their minds conjure up.

7 They reveal themselves to only a few trustworthy people because they fear others will see their flaws and reject them.

8 They consider themselves wonderful artistically but don't actually devote much time to creating original works.

Evolved Fours with Heightened Inner Awareness

1 They are happy for others however they choose to live, and others find their life inspirational.

2 Being open to all that life has to offer leads them to an inner truth that helps transcend their ego limitations and facilitates their growth and development.

3 Easygoing toward others, they are respectful in honoring other people's truths and are direct and authentic in return.

4 They welcome others into their lives, cherishing the experience each unique person can provide.

5 They face life head-on, finding inspiration and creativity for everything they need or want to do.

6 They have a keen sense of intuition and a healthy ability to daydream, but they mostly live in the here and now.

7 They are wonderful company for others because they are great empathetic listeners and friends.

8 Their creativity flows freely. They not only express their own personal truths but also touch others on a universal level.

If You're a Four, What You Can Do to Become Your Best

1 Experience your feelings instead of allowing yourself to be defined by them.

2 Realize that others have also suffered tragedy. Release your desire to be unique in your pain.

3 Recognize that everyone is special and different just by being him- or herself.

4 Live in the moment, not in your fantasy world.

5 Know that your true self will be revealed to you as you unearth your inner talents and resources.

6 Have gratitude for the blessings in your life.

7 Embrace the fact that you are a loving, empathetic, generous person who has much to offer other people.

8 Reach out to others, even those who seem different or crass. Be aware of how you use your refined tastes as a way of distancing yourself from people.

9 Embrace your relationship partners for who they are, letting go of any idealized notions you may have.

10 Seek to detach yourself from overwhelming emotions. Meditation may help you witness them without *becoming* them. Your experiences are yours; you are not your experience.

11 Take up yoga, dance, or other movement as a way of grounding you in the body and keeping your depression at bay.

12 Accept whatever limitations your parents may have had. Forgiving them will help you release much pent-up anger.

13 Resist the urge to talk endlessly about your feelings; they are one part of your existence but not its entirety.

14 Exercise any creative outlet that appeals to you. Even if you are not an artist, it can feel wonderful to let your creativity flow. Work on not judging your creation.

15 Be proud of all that you have accomplished.

257

Number Five: *Observer*

OTHER NAMES THIS NUMBER GOES BY

Thinker	Sage
Investigator	Analyst
Eccentric	Detached Skeptic
Wise One	Pundit
Philosopher	Sophisticate

MOTTO OF A FIVE

Mind Over Matter—and Over Everything Else, Too

FAMOUS FIVES*

Stephen Hawking
Friedrich Nietzsche
Georgia O'Keeffe
Simone Weil
Jean-Paul Sartre
James Joyce
David Lynch
Tim Burton
Laurie Anderson
John Cage
Charles Ives

Albert Einstein
Stanley Kubrick
Emily Dickinson
Bill Gates
Jacob Bronowski
Gary Larson
Stephen King
Clive Barker
Vincent van Gogh
Glenn Gould
Bobby Fischer

Fives at a Glance

FIVES CAN BE GREAT IN RELATIONSHIPS BECAUSE THEY

- are self-sufficient
- are trustworthy
- are usually intelligent
- give you lots of room
- can have a great, dry humor
- are happy with a simple life
- remain calm in crises
- don't assault you with problems
- save money well
- don't kiss and tell
- can be very sensual
- have great insights

FIVES CAN BE TROUBLE IN RELATIONSHIPS BECAUSE THEY

- need lots of time alone
- feel they don't need people
- aren't spontaneous
- can be rude when feeling cornered
- can be overly cautious
- are easily suspicious

KEY TRAITS OF FIVES

- observer
- objective
- curious
- open-minded
- insightful
- intelligent
- inventive
- perceptive
- sensitive
- cynical
- judgmental
- withdrawn

258

*Excerpted from Don Riso, *Personality Types: Using the Enneagram for Self-Discovery* (Boston: Houghton Mifflin, 1996).

- love learning
- hard worker
- logical
- realistic
- alert

- rude
- socially inept
- alienated
- arrogant

BASIC ISSUES

- Overly analytical, especially as a way to mask discomfort and fear around people and emotions

PRIMAL NEED

- to be right

MOST AFRAID OF

- looking stupid

TYPICAL PHYSICAL APPEARANCE

- unassuming clothes
- outfits they haven't agonized over or worked too hard to put together
- unkempt if caught up in reading or thinking, since those take priority over personal grooming

WHAT APPEALS TO FIVES

- intelligence
- privacy
- scientific facts

- independence
- quiet time
- small groups

FIVES AT THE OFFICE

- loners
- visionaries
- thinkers

- problem solvers
- hard workers
- discoverers

HIGHEST ATTRIBUTE FOR FIVES TO AIM FOR

- tolerance

MOST DESTRUCTIVE TRAIT TO WORK TO AVOID

- wanting to know it all

WHAT TEMPERS FIVES' TROUBLES

- their perceptiveness in observing reality

259

WHAT DOESN'T APPEAL TO FIVES

- loud parties
- large gatherings
- clinging people
- elaborate emoting
- fast-paced situations
- overly gregarious or showy people

Is This You? Is This Him? Checklist for Fives

- I can concentrate deeply for hours on a single activity that interests me.
- I love going to concerts and lectures but would hate having to perform or present something at one.
- Nothing thrills me more than spending time alone with a great book.
- I tolerate small dinner parties if I have to, but large gatherings make me very nervous.
- When I feel overwhelmed, I shut myself down and withdraw as quickly as possible.
- I am very perceptive about people and the world, and my predictions of how things will turn out are usually accurate.
- Often I am so busy thinking about something that I have trouble relaxing or falling asleep.
- It's much easier for me to talk about my thoughts than my feelings.
- I am a very private person and like to keep it that way.
- People think that I have no feelings, but inside I know that I am very sensitive.
- Sometimes I wonder why I try to have relationships at all; getting involved with others often makes me feel invaded.
- I can be rude to people if I'm not careful and have been accused of being cynical and suspicious.
- It can be hard for me to approach other people, so I usually wait for them to make the first move.
- My ideas are often extremely complex, so I don't talk about them with other people.
- I much prefer to watch people doing things than to do them myself.

Fives in More Detail

What Motivates Fives

Believing that the world is full of danger, Fives seize on knowledge to prepare them for every eventuality. The belief that one can objectively analyze every situation and prepare for every possibility is an illusion, of course, but it goes to the core of how Fives perceive the world: read about it, study it, observe it, ruminate over it, in contrast with just wanting to jump in.

Private, sensitive, and smart, Fives hide their emotional vulnerabilities behind a mental facade. Pierce too close to their tender hearts and Fives are likely to respond with a witty put-down to regain control and mentally fend off an emotional attack.

Fives are often detail-oriented, scientists, and engineers, but their ability as a quick study enables them to see the big picture. This quality has catapulted many to the ranks of CEO in corporate America. They bring about exciting discoveries and excel in the fields of rocket science, computers, and medical research. Their ability to focus intently on a particular subject and have clear insight makes Fives the true inventors of the world.

261

Possible Messages Fives Got as Children

As sensitive individuals, Fives easily felt invaded by their parents or others as children and decided early on that the best protection was to detach themselves from their feelings and prepare to face the world by using their wits.

As children, fives probably felt that their own needs were not met by those around them, so they abandoned their own desires and began a lifelong quest to observe, rather than experience, the world. Creating a private sanctuary—as children, their room; as adults, perhaps an entire house— where they could carry out their cerebral pursuits becomes a life jacket for Fives.

Fives' Basic Fears

Nothing terrifies Fives more than having their "space" invaded by other people. They need to enter into relationships slowly and with care, keeping a comfortable distance as much as possible. Although Fives hope their intellectual preparation will protect them from life's dangers, on some level they know that it cannot. Fives also fear being caught off guard or being asked a question to which they don't know the answer (that's why they study so hard!). Fives also fear being needy or dependent on others. Individualists, often introverts, they view self-sufficiency as a crucial trait.

Fives' Possibilities for Personality Transformation

When Fives Live Unconsciously

❶ The details of what they learn are all that matters; practical application or relevance to their lives is not considered.

❷ They actively attempt to keep people away from them because they don't want real life interfering with their mental pursuits.

❸ Fearful of the dangers around them, they cling to learning in the false hope that knowledge will protect them.

❹ They create intricate theories but don't have the ability to judge their accuracy.

❺ They often feel cynical and despairing, and there are times when even they aren't inspired by their studies.

❻ Their emotions terrify them, causing them to retreat into intellect pursuits to avoid feeling and social interaction.

❼ Loners, they don't allow others into their world, and others consider them too eccentric to encourage friendliness.

❽ They retreat like hermits into their own little world and don't care about other people.

The Evolutionary Process for Fives of Average Awareness

❶ They focus on the details but may lose sight of the larger picture.

❷ They prefer a good book to an evening of conversation, but they'll suffer through a dinner party on occasion if they have to.

❸ They feel anxiety about things in the world they do not know about or can't control.

❹ Constructing elaborate hypotheses makes them feel important.

❺ They can become mired in studying obscure topics simply for the sake of learning something.

❻ Emotions make them nervous, hence their relationships are stormy and exhausting. They may think they want marriage, but their past partnerships haven't come close to such a commitment.

7 People enjoy an occasional intellectual conversation with them, knowing that personal life and emotion are off-limits for discussion.

8 They accept only what they know and can comprehend.

Evolved Fives with Heightened Inner Awareness

1 Visionaries, they easily perceive the truths of the world around them.

2 They love being with people because they can learn something from everyone.

3 They savor being part of the world and using their minds to comprehend their place in the grand scheme of things.

4 Their ability to see things in new ways leads to important innovations.

5 They can stay focused on an important subject for years without getting bored.

6 At one with their emotions, they feel contentment and at peace with themselves and the universe.

7 People love to be around them because they are so perceptive and because they have a terrific ironic sense of humor.

8 They are open-minded about people and things.

If You're a Five, What You Can Do to Become Your Best

1 Learn to be comfortable with your body. Take up sports or creative movement, or just jump and dance when no one is looking.

2 Find people you feel safe with, even a therapist to start, and begin opening yourself up beyond your head.

3 Make a decision to take action regarding a topic you know little about.

4 Resist the desire to learn everything there is about a given subject.

5 If you find yourself rambling on about subjects no one else cares about, redirect the conversation so that others can participate.

6 Stop yourself from feeling superior to others who aren't as "smart" as you. Recognize that intelligence takes many forms and that others may be ahead in other areas, for example, emotional intelligence, musical intelligence, etc.

7 Meditate or perform other centering exercises to be comfortable living in the present moment.

⑧ Go ahead and hug someone—it may take practice, but it will feel terrific!

⑨ Let others know what makes you uncomfortable. They will be less likely to unwittingly cross your boundaries.

⑩ When you feel the walls closing in, take deep breaths rather than running away.

⑪ Recognize that the world can be a wonderful place, filled with beauty and love, and need not be dark and frightening.

⑫ Find a charity or two where you can volunteer your time. You have a great sense of compassion if you can allow yourself to tap into it.

⑬ Avoid making mean-spirited, biting comments to others; be complimentary or say nothing at all.

⑭ Consider going on a group adventure (like Outward Bound or something similar) where you need to trust others to get through it. Then work on developing that trust in other areas of your life.

⑮ Learn to feel comfortable with your vulnerability.

264

Number Six: *Belonger*

OTHER NAMES THIS NUMBER GOES BY

Loyalist

Questioner

Facilitator

Traditionalist

Group Joiner

Likable Person

Faithful Skeptic

Doubter

Troubleshooter

Safety Seeker

MOTTO OF SIXES

Watch Your Back—and Your Front, Too

FAMOUS SIXES*

Spike Lee

Dabney Coleman

Joseph McCarthy

J. Edgar Hoover

Malcolm X

Marcia Clark

Richard M. Nixon

Ellen DeGeneres

*Excerpted from Don Riso, *Personality Types: Using the Enneagram for Self-Discovery* (Boston: Houghton Mifflin, 1996).

Duke Ellington
Loretta Lynn
George Carlin
Sid Caesar
David Letterman
Phil Donahue
Mel Gibson
Julia Roberts

Jack Lemmon
Mort Sahl
Jay Leno
Gene Wilder
Charles Grodin
Andy Rooney
Robert Redford
Marilyn Monroe

Sixes at a Glance

SIXES CAN BE GREAT IN RELATIONSHIPS BECAUSE THEY

▶ are loyal in the extreme
▶ are deeply compassionate
▶ often have a sense of humor
▶ are very empathic
▶ aren't pretentious
▶ are warm

▶ are reliable
▶ are honest
▶ are devoted to family
▶ come through in crises
▶ are hard workers
▶ stick to their commitments

SIXES CAN BE TROUBLE IN RELATIONSHIPS BECAUSE THEY

▶ worry so much
▶ are suspicious
▶ procrastinate
▶ have trouble relaxing
▶ obsess over decisions
▶ have little self-confidence

▶ sometimes withdraw
▶ can be paranoid
▶ can be sarcastic
▶ can be negative
▶ turn molehills into mountains
▶ are sometimes controlling

KEY TRAITS OF SIXES

▶ empathic
▶ compassionate
▶ loyal
▶ helpful
▶ giving
▶ loving
▶ practical
▶ responsible
▶ supportive
▶ trustworthy
▶ generous

▶ respectful
▶ steadfast
▶ likable
▶ sarcastic
▶ anxious
▶ suspicious
▶ cautious
▶ dependent
▶ helpless
▶ persecuted

BASIC ISSUES
- out of touch with their own thinking
- look to others for answers and for safety in what they perceive to be a dangerous world

PRIMAL NEED
- to feel secure

MOST AFRAID OF
- being helpless

TYPICAL PHYSICAL APPEARANCE
- the accepted "uniform" of the group
- wrinkled brow
- occasionally nonconformist

WHAT APPEALS TO SIXES
- careful analysis
- constant vigilance
- structured settings
- reassurance
- good causes
- danger

SIXES AT THE OFFICE
- questioning
- doubtful
- loyal
- prepared
- responsible
- fearful

HIGHEST ATTRIBUTE FOR A SIX TO AIM FOR
- bravery

MOST DESTRUCTIVE TRAIT TO WORK TO AVOID
- lack of self-worth

WHAT TEMPERS SIXES' TROUBLES
- their extreme loyalty to their relationships

WHAT DOESN'T APPEAL TO SIXES
- total relaxation
- making snap decisions
- trusting everyone
- laughing off mistakes
- throwing caution to the wind
- unpredictable situations

Is This You? Is This Him? Checklist for Sixes

▶ I am happy when I can feel protected by those around me.

▶ I am extremely reliable. Friends and romance partners know they can always count on me.

▶ I research my options extensively before making a major purchase. Even then, I wonder if I did the right thing.

▶ I can be a great worrier when I have a big decision to make.

▶ I love it when I am given a list of written organizational rules to follow.

▶ I frequently think about whether my boss or other authority figures like me.

▶ I unintentionally behave in passive-aggressive ways, for example, telling someone I'll do something and not following through.

▶ I enjoy laughing in the face of danger and occasionally doing something reckless.

▶ I am a hard worker and save most of what I earn.

▶ I am so concerned about doing the right thing that I procrastinate and sometimes do nothing at all.

▶ I have been told to "lighten up," but I just can't.

▶ I can appear calm and "together" to others, but inside I am often a bundle of nerves.

▶ After I've left the house, I frequently wonder whether I remembered to lock the door.

▶ I question other people's motives, especially when they say something nice about me.

▶ If I accomplish something significant, I wonder if it is going to unravel and disappear.

Sixes in More Detail

What Motivates Sixes

Plain and simple, Sixes enjoy worrying. Even if they have nothing to worry about, life is fine, and the world is rosy, they still search high and low until they uncover that potential tragedy that demands their attention. Sixes deduce, "All is right with the world; there's got to be something wrong." Sixes are desperate to feel secure in a world where they think danger lurks at every turn. Some may not appear anxious, but their easygoing style is merely a cover for their concern. "Life is hard and I must struggle to survive it," Sixes believe. "Things may come easily for other people, but they don't come easily for me."

Loyal to a fault and respectful of tradition, Sixes are steadfast and committed to their relationships. Their sense of compassion and insight allows for a great deal of intimacy. Sixes are often caring, warm, and endearing, if only their self-esteem would allow them to realize it.

Occasionally paranoid, like Richard Nixon, Sixes take one of two approaches in dealing with their anxiety. Either they retreat within themselves, appearing meek or guarded, or they draw courage by surrounding themselves with and receiving guidance from others. Sixes comprise a disproportionate share of membership in religious organizations, police forces, political parties, and other organizations. They decide to meet their enemies head-on and recklessly plunge into risky, even dangerous, situations. Many Sixes spend their lives vacillating between both of these responses.

268

Possible Messages Sixes Received as Children

Children need to trust their parents' ability to protect and comfort them. In the childhood of Sixes, such trust wasn't warranted. Perhaps the child was betrayed in some manner, or the parents were overbearing or nonexistent. (The children of alcoholics often show up in this personality number.)

Because they felt that their parents couldn't protect them from the dangers in life, Sixes learned to become the night (and day) watchmen themselves. Like security guards scanning a department store for trouble, Sixes remain ever on the lookout for impending disaster.

Sixes often feel overwhelmed by insecurity, retreating to the safety of groups and organized rules to help them feel comfortable. Ambivalent about their ability to successfully find their place in the world, Sixes frequently fluctuate in their reaction to it—one day being lovable, funny, and passive and the next, angry, mean-spirited, and aggressive. Ultimately, the best Sixes discover that they themselves are more trustworthy and reliable than other authority figures in their lives—a realization that allows them to temper their anxiety and live calmer, happier lives.

Sixes' Basic Fears

Sixes dream of a secure and enveloping world. A sense of being helpless in the presence of danger seems overwhelming. They worry endlessly that they will be unprepared for a catastrophe and, as a result, align themselves with others in supportive groups, focusing intently on discovering trouble spots before they erupt into crises.

Sixes fear being caught in situations where their own thinking and inner guidance systems will be called into play because they are doubtful of their own abilities, although many Sixes are quite smart and capable. Sixes are much more comfortable when the rules and regulations are spelled out in advance and they can tread carefully within those safe confines (however, Sixes will sometimes react in opposition to those rules, engaging in brazen and daredevil behaviors).

Sixes' Possibilities for Personality Transformation

When Sixes Live Unconsciously

❶ They are paralyzed when it comes to taking action in important matters and often procrastinate indefinitely.

❷ They constantly worry that friends and relationship partners are going to betray them.

❸ They carry with them a sense of doom and obsess over bad things that they believe are inevitable.

❹ They will blindly follow a guru or leader, feeling that person knows better than they do what is best.

❺ They are so dependent, no one would think of relying on them for help.

❻ They can be mean-spirited and lash out at others for no apparent reason.

❼ They are paralyzed by fear, and crises can overwhelm them, confirming their sense that the world is a terrifying place.

❽ They are too anxiety ridden to concentrate, and their work often suffers. They sabotage their own success, which furthers their anxiety.

The Evolutionary Process for Sixes of Average Awareness

❶ They consult others prior to taking action, but once they make a decision, they feel comfortable and satisfied with it.

269

2 They constantly test others to see if they are worthy of loyalty.

3 They focus on potential problems for themselves and others, even on those with a remote probability of occurring.

4 They feel most comfortable as a member of a group but have a tendency to divide the world into us versus them.

5 They sometimes behave in a passive-aggressive manner, promising help and then not delivering.

6 They recognize their tendency to be defensive and testy when they are insecure.

7 They can usually be counted on in a crisis but agonize over whether or not they are doing the right thing.

8 They criticize themselves for not living up to their own expectations and potential.

Evolved Sixes with Heightened Inner Awareness

1 They trust their inner self to do the right thing.

2 They easily form relationships with others.

3 They are great troubleshooters for others' problems as well as their own.

4 They are able to lead any group with foresight and ease.

5 Others can always count on them for help.

6 They recognize their insecurities and seek to strengthen their inner fortitude without inflicting stress on others.

7 They face major life crises with grace and confidence.

8 They are successful in work and life.

If You're a Six, What You Can Do to Be Your Best

1 When people say something nice about you, believe it!

2 When you come to a fork in the road, recognize that whatever path you choose is the right way for you.

3 Take one item about which you are procrastinating and act on it right now.

4 Know that fear is a healthy response to danger. Everyone is fearful at times. Try to make peace with your fear rather than seeing it as the enemy.

⑤ Meditate or engage in other stress-reduction activities when you feel anxious.

⑥ Congratulate yourself for every job well done.

⑦ Take action on something without asking anyone for his or her opinion.

⑧ Stop attending one group's meetings for a while to prove that you can survive without them.

⑨ Strive to see the world as good and loving rather than menacing and dangerous.

⑩ Stop blaming others for situations that you might be responsible for.

⑪ Try not to go back to your car to see if you turned off the lights. If you have to go back, be amused at yourself for doing so.

⑫ Remember that it is okay to refuse a request from someone.

⑬ If you say you are going to do something, do it.

⑭ On occasion, speak up against authority; even the most knowledgeable expert isn't always right.

⑮ Recognize that you are a great gift to the universe just by being who you are.

271

Number Seven: *Adventurer*

OTHER NAMES FOR THIS NUMBER

Doer	Dreamer
Enthusiast	Planner
Optimist	Experiencer
Generalist	Explorer
Visionary	Energizer

MOTTO OF A SEVEN

Last One In Is a Rotten Egg

FAMOUS SEVENS*

John F. Kennedy	Leonard Bernstein
Steven Spielberg	Malcolm Forbes

*Excerpted from Don Riso, *Personality Types: Using the Enneagram for Self-Discovery* (Boston: Houghton Mifflin, 1996).

Marianne Williamson
Wolfgang Amadeus Mozart
Federico Fellini
Timothy Leary
Jim Carrey
Elton John
Bruce Willis
Joan Collins
Larry King
Regis Philbin
Geraldo Rivera
Liberace
Auntie Mame

Elizabeth Taylor
Arthur Rubenstein
Dr. Richard Feynman
Robin Williams
Bette Midler
Liza Minnelli
Jack Nicholson
Noel Coward
Joan Rivers
Susan Lucci
Howard Stern
John Belushi
Martha in *Who's Afraid of Virginia Woolf?*

Sevens at a Glance

SEVENS CAN BE GREAT IN RELATIONSHIPS BECAUSE THEY

- love adventure
- have lots of energy
- know how to have fun
- are independent
- are spontaneous
- can achieve great things
- are generous
- genuinely like people
- are multitalented
- love to laugh
- have grand visions
- appreciate life

SEVENS CAN BE TROUBLE IN RELATIONSHIPS BECAUSE THEY

- can feel confined
- hog the spotlight
- can be inattentive
- try to run from problems
- don't always finish what they start
- can feel superior to others

KEY TRAITS OF SEVENS

- lively
- playful
- busy
- enthusiastic
- sensation seeking
- spontaneous
- extroverted
- generous
- joyful
- witty
- accomplished
- narcissistic
- materialistic
- undisciplined
- restless
- insensitive

272

- outrageous
- pleasure oriented
- spirited
- distracted
- demanding

BASIC ISSUES

- to avoid pain and fear, they focus on creating the next activity that will bring them pleasure, rather than thinking deeply about emotionally troubling or difficult issues.

PRIMAL NEED

- to be joyful

MOST AFRAID OF

- experiencing pain

TYPICAL PHYSICAL APPEARANCE

- brightly colored clothes
- dressed for adventure
- happy and upbeat

WHAT APPEALS TO SEVENS

- experiences
- travel
- variety
- having fun
- spontaneity
- independence

SEVENS AT THE OFFICE

- flexible
- creative
- visionaries
- experimenters
- motivators
- dabblers

HIGHEST ATTRIBUTE FOR A SEVEN TO AIM FOR

- thankfulness

MOST DESTRUCTIVE TRAIT TO WORK TO AVOID

- excess

WHAT TEMPERS SEVENS' TROUBLES

- Their ability really to enjoy life

WHAT DOESN'T APPEAL TO SEVENS

- routines
- clinginess
- staying home
- going where they've already been
- criticism
- dealing with problems

273

Is This You? Is This Him? Checklist for Sevens

▶ I prefer going out rather than staying home.

▶ If an exotic restaurant opens, I'm the first in line to try it.

▶ Something new always wins out over something I have done before.

▶ Others think I am pushy, but I feel that my ideas are better than theirs.

▶ I can be materialistic, and I see no reason to deny myself what I want.

▶ If one idea doesn't work out, I have plenty more to offer.

▶ I have many friends and acquaintances.

▶ I always see the glass as being half full.

▶ People always comment on my high energy level and charming manner.

▶ When romance partners are too clinging, I become edgy and anxious. I need my freedom.

▶ I love it when lots of people come to my parties.

▶ Sometimes I speak my mind even if what I say bothers other people.

▶ I appreciate all that I have in my life, even if I still want more.

▶ If an activity is risky, I am even more attracted to it.

▶ I get over painful experiences extremely quickly.

Sevens in More Detail

What Motivates Sevens

Sevens are energetic doers who act now and worry later. Sevens know that you only live once, and they want to make the most of it. "Life has so much to offer," Sevens typically feel. "I want to say 'yes' to everything." Sevens can be found on around-the-world cruises, or at least checking out the action all around town. They love to surround themselves with people and are social gadflies buzzing from one engagement to another.

Sevens seek to be happy and have fun in the world. They don't typically stop to acknowledge pain, their own or anyone else's, and fear the issues they'd have to confront if they stopped moving long enough to pay attention. Their impulsiveness and refusal to heed others' cautions can also bring them trouble.

At their best, Sevens are visionaries who see the big picture and let others worry about the mundane details. They inspire others with their wealth of energy and ideas. They are capable of juggling many activities simultaneously.

Possible Messages Sevens Received as Children

"Seize the day!" Sevens might have heard as children. "Don't deprive yourself of anything." Sevens were taught that one cannot be protected from the pain of life; it is preferable to ignore it. Staying busy, generating endless options, and acting as if all is right with the world will somehow keep any pain from surfacing. Sevens don't want problems to interfere with their fun in life. They tend to limit long-term relationships that can have the potential of bringing pain, even if it means sacrificing joy. They believe they are somehow smarter than the suffering masses and can avoid difficulties by being in perpetual motion.

Sevens' Basic Fears

Because their need to experience and take action is so intense, Sevens fear being stuck in restrictive situations. The idea that an activity, event, or fun excursion might happen without them fills them with dread. Sevens are desperate to be where the action is, and if there is no action, they will create some.

275

Experiencing pain terrifies Sevens. They fear slowing down and can't stop to smell the roses for fear of encountering a thorn. Any heartbreak that might accompany the loss of a loved one or cherished relationship keeps many Sevens from forming significant attachments. They often couch this in terms of wanting to "keep their options open."

Sevens' Possibilities for Personality Transformation

When Sevens Live Unconsciously

❶ They don't have nearly enough and are consumed by acquiring material possessions.

❷ They are gluttonous and find gratification in stuffing themselves with food and drink.

❸ They don't allow themselves to feel fear or pain and use continual activity as a way of insulating themselves.

❹ They tend to be manic with wild mood swings.

❺ They run from activities before they are finished so they won't have to live with the results.

6 They can be pushy, demanding that others do for them *now!*

7 They are too self-centered to care about others.

8 Every interaction with others must be exciting and distracting.

The Evolutionary Process for Sevens of Average Awareness

1 They appreciate what they have but need more to really be happy.

2 They eat and drink to excess and abhor self-deprivation.

3 They are uncomfortable with negative emotions, such as fear and pain, but are willing to acknowledge them.

4 They are prone to uninhibited gestures like dressing outrageously or being the center of attention.

5 They don't focus on any one area long enough to be proficient but dabble in many pursuits.

6 They use their "up" personality to hide pain or disappointment.

7 They can listen to others' problems, but only for a short while.

8 If they are idle or bored, they create a drama with those around them.

Evolved Sevens with Heightened Inner Awareness

1 They are grateful for the many blessings in their lives.

2 They eat and drink according to their bodys' needs.

3 They are accepting of all feelings, including fear and pain, as natural and human.

4 Their emotions are responsive to the situation at hand and remain on an even keel.

5 They use their many talents to spread goodness in the world.

6 They are genuinely enthusiastic about life's possibilities.

7 They enjoy helping other people.

8 Although they like to sustain a high energy level, they can also be comfortable with peace and calm.

If You're a Seven, What You Can Do to Become Your Best

1 Take stock of all the things you are grateful for and give a daily prayer of thanks.

2 Force yourself to "save for a rainy day."

❸ Reduce impulse buying.

❹ Avoid overeating.

❺ If you're sad, don't be afraid to cry.

❻ In difficult situations, trust that all things must pass.

❼ Enjoy quiet time, without TV or background noise.

❽ Really listen to another person. Resist the urge to talk about yourself.

❾ Make a detailed list of tasks, and discipline yourself to follow it carefully.

❿ Don't allow your fears to draw you into dangerous activities.

⓫ Go to a favorite place to experience the beauty in familiarity.

⓬ Give a favorite object to another person.

⓭ Live fully in the moment.

⓮ Remember that you are perfect just the way you are.

Number Eight: *Leader*

OTHER NAMES THIS NUMBER GOES BY

Boss	Top Dog
Chief	Ruler
Champion	Commander
Challenger	Captain
Asserter	Director

MOTTO OF AN EIGHT

Only the Strong Survive

FAMOUS EIGHTS*

Martin Luther King, Jr.	Franklin Delano Roosevelt
Lyndon Johnson	Mikhail Gorbachev
G. I. Gurdjieff	Pablo Picasso
Richard Wagner	Indira Gandhi
Kathleen Turner	Marlon Brando
John Wayne	Charlton Heston

*Excerpted from Don Riso, *Personality Types: Using the Enneagram for Self-Discovery* (Boston: Houghton Mifflin, 1996).

Sean Connery
Norman Mailer
Barbara Walters
Lee Iacocca
Frank Sinatra
Roseanne
Ross Perot
Saddam Hussein
Jim Jones

Ernest Hemingway
Mike Wallace
Ann Richards
Donald Trump
Bette Davis
Leona Helmsley
Fidel Castro
Napoleon
Don Vito Corleone from *The Godfather*

Eights at a Glance

EIGHTS CAN BE GREAT IN RELATIONSHIPS BECAUSE THEY

- are committed to family
- will go the extra mile for you
- are often financially successful
- make you feel protected
- easily make decisions
- are honest
- don't play games
- are energetic
- are resourceful
- enjoy life
- are independent
- have a tender side

EIGHTS CAN BE TROUBLE IN RELATIONSHIPS BECAUSE THEY

- don't easily compromise
- are easily angered
- need to be the boss
- want to win every fight
- enjoy getting revenge
- can steamroll others
- can be demanding
- aren't easily satisfied (with sex, food)
- are possessive
- pick at your faults
- can be vengeful
- can scare people away (especially a female Eight)

KEY TRAITS OF EIGHTS

- independent
- positive
- honest
- self-reliant
- confident
- nonconformist
- assertive
- strong
- courageous
- responsible
- caring
- controlling
- egocentric
- confrontational
- combative
- arrogant

- decisive
- energetic
- protective
- domineering
- angry

BASIC ISSUES
- try to deal with the "dangers" of the world by force of will and personal power

PRIMAL NEED
- to be in control

MOST AFRAID OF
- being weak

TYPICAL PHYSICAL APPEARANCE
- power suits
- take-charge expression
- occasionally nonconformist attire

WHAT APPEALS TO EIGHTS
- power
- high energy
- being assertive
- being confident
- having achievements recognized
- a willingness to take prudent risks

EIGHTS AT THE OFFICE
- straightforward
- unceremonious
- charming
- easily makes decisions
- intimidating
- protective of others

HIGHEST ATTRIBUTE FOR EIGHTS TO AIM FOR
- benevolence

MOST DESTRUCTIVE TRAIT TO WORK TO AVOID
- domination

WHAT TEMPERS EIGHTS' TROUBLES
- their ability to rely on their own strengths

WHAT DOESN'T APPEAL TO EIGHTS
- weakness
- other people's rules
- compromise
- beating around the bush
- being hypersensitive
- suppressing anger

Is This You? Is This Him? Checklist for Eights

▶ I have great confidence in my own abilities.

▶ I love it when other people respect me.

▶ I consider money to be a very important way of keeping score.

▶ When I go to a meeting, I immediately search out those with power.

▶ I could never be just a member of an organization; I want to run the show.

▶ Sometimes I don't listen to other people's perspectives because I know that mine is right.

▶ People who don't stand up for their point of view make me crazy.

▶ I know that my bark is often worse than my bite.

▶ I feel that powerful people have to protect those who give them their power.

▶ Sometimes my direct, honest comments get me into trouble with people.

▶ Compromise is a sign of weakness to me.

▶ It's advantageous if people are a little afraid of me.

▶ When I'm alone with my romantic partner, I can be surprisingly tender, even a little mushy.

▶ I believe in acting first and asking questions later.

▶ I need to have time alone.

Eights in More Detail

What Motivates Eights

Someone has to be the boss, the visionary, and the leader, and Eights believe that someone should be them. Take-charge initiators, Eights meet challenges head-on, setting the course for others to follow. Eights love to take responsibility and never worry about negative outcomes that their actions might produce. To Eights, the consequences of not taking action are much more forbidding.

Eights can use their power for good or for ill. They can use their courage to fight the bad guys and protect the meek, and to generously distribute all the spoils; or they can steamroll others into doing everything their way, depleting, exhausting, and sometimes even annihilating others in the process.

When Eights are without power, they quickly figure out how to influence those in charge or, better yet, how to take charge themselves. Having to follow someone else's agenda is extremely distasteful to Eights. They trust themselves to do the right thing more readily than they would trust someone else. Intense personalities, Eights do everything with gusto, which is why some Eights are overweight, oversexed, and chronically exhausted.

Possible Messages Eights Received as Children

Eights may have been bullied or abused as children. They may have felt put down or insignificant. According to Eights, the way to feel strong is to be strong and to eliminate weakness and vulnerability. It is better to be the one in power than subject to the whims of other rulers. Extremely self-confident, Eights trust themselves to make the correct decisions and do what's right.

To Eights' way of thinking, power is wonderful because it can be used not only to further one's own goals but also to champion causes. Evolved Eights will use their strength not solely to build organizations and acquire power but also to encourage the self-worth and confidence of those around them. Eights are indeed capable of using their might for less high-minded endeavors, ruthlessly bullying others to ensure that they get their way. Eights may think they need to take a tough, macho stance (women included), but beneath their gruff exterior, there often lurks a tender teddy bear who enjoys feeling close to others.

Eights' Basic Fears

Eights are terrified of being weak and vulnerable. If they relinquish the reins of power to someone else, who knows what will happen? Mindful of being victimized, perhaps as children, Eights are terrified of such a situation recurring. To ensure that it does not, Eights put on their suits of armor to shield and, to some extent, separate themselves from the world. Unlike those old-fashioned knights, however, Eights wear their armor permanently, making it difficult to get past their hardened shell to a soft interior.

Eights hate to be taken care of. Even when severely ill, they won't allow themselves to be patients. Being viewed by others as an invalid or needful of assistance is avoided at any cost.

281

Eights' Possibilities for Personality Transformation

When Eights Live Unconsciously

1 They dominate all who touch their lives.

2 They are terrified of being controlled and will do anything to convince themselves that rules don't apply to them.

3 They threaten or belittle others until they are supported in their endeavors.

4 Their relationships are adversarial.

5 They will do something dangerous because they want to feel like "outlaws."

6 They must win at all costs to further their fragile sense of self.

7 They come out "guns blazing" to intimidate others before being challenged by them.

8 They must preserve their sense of feeling powerful, no matter what it takes.

The Evolutionary Process of Eights of Average Awareness

1 They can be bossy, but they are caring and loving to a small circle of friends.

2 They want to keep all that they have created.

3 People follow them when offered something tangible (e.g., a job, money).

4 They don't care much about the welfare of those who are not part of their endeavors.

5 If it is profitable personally or financially, they will flirt with danger.

6 They believe they are special because they are powerful and successful.

7 They often "shoot from the hip" as a display of power.

8 They consider asking others for help a sign of weakness.

Evolved Eights with Heightened Inner Awareness

1 Their self-confidence and joy attract others to them.

2 They genuinely want to do good with their leadership talents.

❸ They are natural leaders in whom people believe and respect.

❹ They provide for and protect those who are less fortunate.

❺ They will risk danger, if necessary, to achieve something truly important.

❻ They recognize that their power is a gift from the universe.

❼ They choose to act, or not act, based on what is truly required.

❽ They can ask others for help when necessary.

If You're an Eight, What You Can Do to Be Your Best

❶ Thank others publicly for their assistance.

❷ Consider another person's point of view before making a decision.

❸ Recognize that not everyone likes a good fight.

❹ See compromise as an ideal, not a sign of failure.

❺ Criticize a person's actions, not his or her entire being.

❻ Avoid speaking harshly to others; try softening your voice.

❼ Make those around you equal members of the team.

❽ Get out of your business mode at home and around friends.

❾ Learn to relax and have fun.

❿ Stop throwing your money around as a way of being in control. Let others pay once in a while.

⓫ Knock before entering another person's room or office.

⓬ Be sympathetic to another person's pain. Be sharing and caring.

⓭ Surrender your will to the Higher Power who gives you all your blessings.

⓮ Empower others. Ultimately, that is the greatest use of anyone's prowess.

⓯ Recognize that you are perfect, even with your fears and vulnerability.

Number Nine: *Peacemaker*

OTHER NAMES THIS NUMBER GOES BY

Peacekeeper

Mediator

Natural

Negotiator

Preservationist

Harmonizer

Unifier

Pacifier

Conciliator

MOTTO OF A NINE

Give Peace a Chance

FAMOUS NINES*

Abraham Lincoln

Carl Jung

Gerald Ford

Princess Grace of Monaco

Walt Disney

Garrison Keillor

Kevin Costner

Woody Harrelson

Ringo Starr

Janet Jackson

Linda Evans

Perry Como

Marc Chagall

Jim Henson

Joseph Campbell

Ronald Reagan

Queen Elizabeth II

Walter Cronkite

George Lucas

Sophia Loren

Keanu Reeves

Ron Howard

Whoopi Goldberg

Nancy Kerrigan

Ingrid Bergman

Norman Rockwell

Edith Bunker on *All in the Family*

Marge Simpson on *The Simpsons*

Nines at a Glance

NINES CAN BE GREAT IN RELATIONSHIPS BECAUSE THEY

- are so accommodating
- rarely raise their voices
- don't judge others
- don't worry unnecessarily
- help calm others down
- are easygoing
- accept you as you are
- are very perceptive

*Excerpted from Don Riso, *Personality Types: Using the Enneagram for Self-Discovery* (Boston: Houghton Mifflin, 1996).

- are flexible
- exude peacefulness
- make others feel loved
- enjoy life

NINES CAN BE TROUBLE IN RELATIONSHIPS BECAUSE THEY

- can be passive-aggressive
- lack initiative
- don't know what they want
- can avoid taking action
- can be sluggish
- ignore problems
- won't argue back
- are indecisive
- wilt when criticized
- have trouble changing gears
- can be flighty
- are sometimes stubborn

KEY TRAITS OF NINES

- easygoing
- trusting
- consistent
- supportive
- good-natured
- peaceful
- empathic
- open
- loving
- collegial
- patient
- optimistic
- serene
- diplomatic
- passive-aggressive
- sluggish
- inactive
- distracted
- obscure
- inattentive
- stubborn

BASIC ISSUES

- out of touch with basic instincts due to an almost desperate desire to be accommodating to others

PRIMAL NEED

- to be "at one" with everything

MOST AFRAID OF

- conflict

TYPICAL PHYSICAL APPEARANCE

- comfortable clothes
- a look that "fits in"
- congenial smile

WHAT APPEALS TO NINES

- keeping the peace
- fairness
- harmony
- structure
- mutual support
- taking time to make decisions

285

NINES AT THE OFFICE
- collaborate
- team player
- procrastinator
- easily distracted
- diplomatic
- empowering

HIGHEST ATTRIBUTE FOR A NINE TO AIM FOR
- purposefulness

MOST DESTRUCTIVE TRAIT TO WORK TO AVOID
- inaction

WHAT TEMPERS NINES' TROUBLES
- their love of people

WHAT DOESN'T APPEAL TO NINES
- self-promotion
- on-the-spot decisions
- worrying
- arguing
- deadlines
- competition

Is This You? Is This Him? Checklist for Nines

- I love bringing other people together for a common goal.
- I feel we are all connected to one another and to the world.
- I trust most people to be who they say they are.
- Getting along with people is very important to me.
- My values are more Midwest than Manhattan.
- I get really upset when people yell.
- There's no sense in worrying about things that probably won't happen.
- Sometimes I find myself wishing for a magical solution to problems.
- I use food, TV, or other pleasures as a substitute for what I really desire.
- It takes me a long time to start something.
- Once I've started something, it is hard for me to change gears.
- Others think I'm so calm, but often I feel anxious underneath.
- I'm an empathetic listener, but I don't always focus specifically on what people say.

▶ To others, I can appear distracted.

▶ I like to have time each day to relax or meditate.

Nines in More Detail

What Motivates Nines

Many people lack the ability to hold two opposing points of view without needing to come down on one side or the other. For Nines, nothing is more joyous than bringing diverse people and opposing agendas together to resolve differences. Nines are such terrific mediators because they don't cling to a particular outcome or position. Instead, they comfortably identify with all viewpoints presented.

People often love being around Nines because they are calm, impartial, and nonjudgmental. They appear to be connected to the Oneness of the Universe and the links among all people on earth. Nines bring out the best in others, remaining neutral. What Nines give up in the process, however, is their ability to firmly take a stand. After many years of such disconnection, Nines often have no idea of what their own opinions are.

Nines make great listeners to other people's troubles, but their ability to easily disengage makes them appear distracted or unfocused (think Phoebe from *Friends*!). Their desire not to commit to anything can also make them sluggish and prone to procrastination. Once they get their motors going, however, just try to stop them!

Possible Messages Nines Received as Children

Nines often come from volatile households with warring parents, or from families with so many kids that individual desires couldn't possibly be accommodated or even considered. Nines could opt to fight for what they want but may feel it's not worth the price. Peace in the house is much more valuable. If that means eliminating the highs with the lows, so be it. Nines find contentment by walking the middle ground.

As a result, they come to feel that their opinions and wishes don't matter, so they stop trying to get in touch with them. Many Nines take this thought process even further, deciding that they themselves don't count much either.

Nines' Basic Fears

Nothing terrifies Nines more than being disconnected from others. Being united with those around them is critical to Nines. They are willing to sub-

287

jugate their desires to those of everyone else. Their sense of self is intricately linked to their affiliation with others. To Nines, breaking those bonds is equivalent to destroying self.

Because the ties that bind are frayed by conflict, Nines are terrified of having angry disagreements with others. Therefore, Nines are considered pushovers by strong-willed individuals, but to a Nine, always letting others have their way makes perfect sense.

Nines' Possibilities for Personality Transformation

When Nines Live Unconsciously

❶ They feel as though they are watching their lives unfold on a movie screen or are waiting for the picture to begin.

❷ They feel too detached and passive to connect with anyone.

❸ They are frequently depressed and out of touch with reality.

❹ Others become angry and frustrated by their neglect.

❺ They are detached from their own desires.

❻ They shut down their emotions, except for an occasional passive-aggressive response.

❼ They don't have the energy or interest to do anything for anybody.

❽ They passively wait to be rescued and have their problems solved magically by someone else.

The Evolutionary Process for Nines of Average Awareness

❶ They are present occasionally but often remain in a dreamlike fog.

❷ They idealize other people as a way of feeling more attached to them.

❸ Others see them as distracted and absentminded.

❹ Others feel they don't really care.

❺ They don't admit to what they want, deferring instead to society or other individuals.

❻ They fear abandonment if they express anger, so they keep their emotions suppressed.

❼ They don't focus much on people they don't care about.

❽ Committing to anything is difficult, so they perpetually mull over options, procrastinating for as long as possible.

Evolved Nines with Heightened Inner Awareness

1 They are able to be fully present and in the moment

2 They feel a true sense of connection to others and to their own beings.

3 They are serene and display the patience of a saint.

4 They bring out the best in those around them.

5 They are aware of their desires and can readily request them from others.

6 They feel comfortable with all their emotions, including anger.

7 They have a wonderful ability to ease discord and settle conflicts.

8 They can arrive at a decision and act on it.

If You're a Nine, What You Can Do to Be Your Best

1 Offer your opinion without waiting to be asked.

2 Think about what *you* most enjoy doing.

3 When faced with a problem, come up with a solution and act on it, within a deadline.

4 Talk to others about your feelings and fears.

5 If you are asked what *you* want to do, don't be afraid to speak up.

6 If you have a shocking or unusual opinion on a particular topic, don't hesitate to share it.

7 Recognize that it is sometimes healthy to react with anger or outrage.

8 Express your anger physically—throw a pillow or hit someone with a foam-rubber bat.

9 Treat yourself to something you greatly enjoy: take a long, relaxing bath, go on a leisurely outing, have some gourmet food or chocolate, go shopping or to a concert, do whatever makes you feel good.

10 Try to keep diligently focused during an entire conversation.

11 Take up a mind/body exercise to enhance movement and concentration.

12 Live each day as if it were your last.

13 If you are waiting for Prince Charming to rescue you from your life, stop waiting and start looking.

14 Spend an hour each day on your own.

15 Accept that others will love you for yourself.

Now That You've Got His Number, Are Your Personalities Complementary or Conflicting?

N ow that you've determined your number and had your partner take the PPP to learn his number, you can learn how your personalities complement or conflict with each other.

Keep in mind that **there isn't a perfect PPP pairing, because there are no perfect people.** We can only strive to understand ourselves while being tolerant and compassionate toward others. The PPP is simply a tool for furthering awareness and understanding to help you create a more intimate, fulfilling relationship with whomever you choose.

As you look at the pairings, you may realize that you are repeatedly attracted to men of the same number. For instance, you may have been attracted to calm, peaceful men who were great listeners as opposed to take-charge, leader types. Discovering the characteristics that attract you, as well as assessing the positive and negative qualities of that number, will assist you in creating harmonious relationships with that type of personality. Remember that every Smart Heart woman is different. A friend who has the same number you do may not be attracted to the same type of man at all.

You might be comfortable with a certain number combination, but it may not necessarily be the best one for you. Moving beyond your comfort zone expands your horizons and possibilities. If you are a Number Eight, for example, you might learn to temper your willfulness by spending time with a more easygoing Nine, rather than with an equally obstinate Eight. It may be hard at first for you to deal with someone who isn't as intense at you are. You may wonder why he is so relaxed and easygoing, but his peaceful disposition may help you learn to balance your own energies.

Using the PPP on Yourself and in Your Relationships

Your number or his number isn't what is important. It is the level of *awareness and the state of evolution* of your divergent personalities that matter. What are your attributes, and how well do your manage your negative qualities? It is more empowering to clean up your own act, change your own negative traits, and proceed on your own path of evolution than to try to correct your partner's faults or weaknesses. **The only person you can change, develop, and transform is yourself.**

According to Mona Coates, Ph.D., a noted expert on the PPP, "Understanding and accepting your and his personality numbers leads to a reduction in unrealistic expectations, hurt feelings, and communication breakdowns. This understanding frees energy that most people tie up in guilt, anger, and depression, resulting in better, more satisfying relationships and personally more complete self-acceptance."

By understanding their personality numbers and the traits attributed to them, Gina and Bruce were better able to resolve a problem that could have been a source of conflict. Every summer, Bruce's parents visited them for an entire month. Gina, a Five, cringed at the thought of having guests, even family, stay for such a long period of time, intruding on her privacy and quiet. Bruce, a One, felt his parents should stay for as long as they wanted. Due to his parents' advancing age, he feared he wouldn't have much time left with them. Through awareness of their personality types, and by understanding each other's needs, Bruce and Gina were able to come up with a compromise that pleased everyone. Bruce paid for his parents to stay at a nearby motel for the entire visit, while Gina agreed to have them over for dinner several times each week, encouraging Bruce to also take his parents out for dinner occasionally without her. This win-win situation not only pleased Bruce's parents, as well as Gina and Bruce, it also greatly enhanced their relationship because each partner respected those core traits that were important.

291

The sections that follow provide a list of the traits that a given PPP number may possess. In making conscious partnering selections, you can decide which numbers appeal most to you. Based on the advice of a number of personality experts, I suggest ways to best communicate and live harmoniously with a particular number, whether you're presently in a relationship or looking for a prospective partner. You can also look up the combination of your PPP number with his to determine the areas of discord requiring special attention in the relationship.

Warning: You can never force a man to learn about his number or work to improve those traits that *you* don't like or that you feel are limiting your relationship. Playing armchair psychologist by telling your number-one boyfriend that he is screwed up because he is so judgmental will undermine relationship happiness.

Some Important Reminders About All Combinations

- ▶ No specific pairings are inherently better than any others.
- ▶ Great possibilities exist within all PPP pairings.
- ▶ Seek someone who is more evolved and aware of his positive and problematic traits, regardless of his PPP number.
- ▶ Be aware of potential problem areas ("Not-so-Good News") within each pairing to encourage the long-term success of your relationship.

Number One: *Perfectionist*

You'll especially love being with a One if you:

- ▶ Feel that ethics and principles are highly important in your partner
- ▶ Want someone who hangs in there until things are done right
- ▶ Are attracted to people who can take a stand for right versus wrong
- ▶ Like having details attended to
- ▶ Enjoy having everything neat, orderly, and organized
- ▶ Admire a mate who strives to improve the world and himself, even under difficult circumstances
- ▶ Are attracted to conscientious hard workers
- ▶ Like a partner to be steadfast, reliable, and predictable

▶ Want a partner who has uncompromising standards and high ideals

▶ Don't mind having a partner who has very little time to relax and goof off

▶ Value someone who will help you be the best you can be

▶ Enjoy making things better and appreciate constructive criticism

▶ Want a partner who demonstrates affection through hard work and serious effort

▶ Appreciate someone who can forgo his own needs in order to meet high and rigorous standards

▶ Want a good and moral partner

How Best to Communicate with a One

▶ Take nit-picking in stride. Ones have an incredible need to make everyone better than they are. Try not to take negative comments personally.

▶ Admit your own faults and mistakes, including what you are doing to improve.

▶ If you must criticize, be gentle! Sandwich helpful suggestions between heaps of praise. Ones are extremely sensitive to others' pointing out their imperfections.

▶ Humor works well. Critiques made lightly or jokingly (but not mockingly) will be more palatable than straightforward suggestions.

▶ Resist the tendency toward absolutes. Instead of black or white, encourage shades of gray.

▶ Be logical and succinct, delineating things in order whenever possible. A One will be more receptive to your points.

▶ Gently encourage the One to be open about feelings and desires. Ones are notorious for keeping "messy" human traits to themselves.

▶ Frequently tell him how wonderful he is and what a great job he is doing.

Key Ways to Live Peacefully with a One

▶ Be neat! Even if you haven't made your bed since grammar school, if you want your man to feel comfortable at home, it's time to practice hospital sheet corners again.

▶ Don't suggest too many outrageous or new activities at once. Ones are most comfortable with what they know, but they will venture into exotic territory if led in one toe at a time.

▶ Ones like to be right all the time. You may be certain you are correct in your assessment of something, but be diplomatic in how you express it. Sometimes silence is golden.

▶ Do your fair share. Your partner may say he wants to pay the monthly bills, balance the checkbook, and plan all the meals, but that's only because he wants to do it his way. Ones value fairness, and he'll be thrilled if you tackle half the projects, as long as you are meticulous.

▶ Think before speaking. Decide whether or not your constructive criticism may ultimately be counterproductive.

▶ Encourage the One to express his anger before it has a chance to build inside and surface inappropriately.

▶ Always look your best. Ripped jeans and a T-shirt may have been good enough for a previous boyfriend, but Ones hate anything slovenly.

▶ Find solo projects you enjoy. Most Ones work a lot, and you will be more accepting of this if you're occupied with your own creative pursuits.

How the Combinations Fare

Ones and Ones

GOOD NEWS:

▶ Both strive for beautiful ideals, ranging from a great house to a more peaceful world, and are willing to act toward realizing them.

▶ Both are committed to the success of the relationship once they put their energy into it. Both are willing to share the chores along with the fruits of their labor.

▶ Their efforts are never halfhearted, and they are fully committed to excellence in their likes and in their relationships.

NOT-SO-GOOD NEWS:

▶ Each thinks things should be done his or her way.

▶ Each is hesitant to admit to errors, so corrections might never be made.

▶ If one person fails to meet his or her household responsibilities and obligations, resentment quickly surfaces.

Ones and Twos

GOOD NEWS:

▶ Ones can get attention without having to ask for it, whereas Twos are thrilled to figure out what Ones need and will readily fulfill it.

▶ Twos will initiate and plan social activities, while Ones make the events even better.

▶ Ones offer the stability and responsibility that Twos crave.

NOT-SO-GOOD NEWS:

▶ Ones happily spend a lot of time at the office, leaving Twos emotionally out of touch and physically wanting.

▶ Ones don't focus on tokens of affection, which Twos count on to be assured that their partner still loves them.

▶ Twos don't accept criticism well, but Ones love to dish it out.

Ones and Threes

GOOD NEWS:

▶ Both have lots of energy for activities, animated conversations, projects, and social climbing.

▶ Both are reliable and dependable and care about their families and friends.

▶ Both spend a lot of time at the office, and neither will notice if the other isn't home.

NOT-SO-GOOD NEWS:

▶ Ones hate it when Threes put up a false front; it just isn't right.

▶ Threes can't stand it when Ones are critical.

▶ Both can get a lot accomplished around the house, but sparks can fly over the quality of the work due to Ones' perfectionist streak.

Ones and Fours

GOOD NEWS:

▶ Fours help Ones feel comfortable with a wide range of emotions, including negative feelings, while Fours find comfort in a Ones' even temperament.

▶ Both maintain high ideals for themselves and society. They abhor mediocrity and halfhearted performances.

295

▶ Fours can frequently test a partner's commitment, but loyal Ones aren't easily deterred.

NOT-SO-GOOD NEWS:

▶ Fours' tendency toward melodrama and moodiness can be incomprehensible to self-disciplined Ones.

▶ They can depress each other over what's missing in life.

▶ Fours demand more time for processing feelings than emotionally controlled Ones ever want to provide.

Ones and Fives

GOOD NEWS:

▶ Both enjoy spending a lot of time alone with their own activities, work, and projects.

▶ Fives are basically nonjudgmental, a stance that delights Ones who hate to be criticized.

▶ Both place great emphasis on knowledge and constantly learning new things. They have lots of bookcases, and their library cards are active.

NOT-SO-GOOD NEWS:

▶ Because both fear expressing anger, issues may linger interminably beneath the surface prior to an emotional volcanic erruption.

▶ Fives prefer to stay home, while Ones attend many social activities, especially when it's considered the right thing to do.

▶ Controlled and reserved, this pairing can be dry and emotionless if both parties aren't careful.

Ones and Sixes

GOOD NEWS:

▶ Frequently united by a desire to make the world better, this pairing can be beautifully defined by its high ideals and the ability to accomplish them.

▶ In trying times, they are a united front against obstacles, creating a stronger, enduring relationship.

▶ Both are willing to work hard to support the relationship in whatever way is required.

NOT-SO-GOOD NEWS:

▶ Extreme worriers, each might reinforce the other's anxiety.

▶ Each has a tendency to procrastinate, so important household or relationship matters may go unattended.

▶ Both hate to get angry, so trouble is often suppressed until an unexpected outburst, often in the form of a snide remark or sarcastic comment.

Ones and Sevens

GOOD NEWS:

▶ Ones enjoy the energy, enthusiasm, and fun of a Seven, while Sevens feel more grounded by the planning and principles of a One.

▶ Both are idealists who want to make the world a better place.

▶ Both will run the household and their lives in a way that produces high-quality, fun results.

NOT-SO-GOOD NEWS:

▶ Both can get so involved in their own activities that they spend little time bonding with each other.

▶ While Ones value rules and regulations, Sevens hate to feel constricted, and conflicts can easily develop.

▶ Sevens don't like to analyze themselves or worry about what ails them. They'd rather have a good time, while Ones feel that self-reflection and improvement are what life is all about.

Ones and Eights

GOOD NEWS:

▶ Ones' methodical planning and Eights' energy and power can be joined together to create great success.

▶ Eights encourage Ones to express their anger (after all, Eights express theirs all the time). This clears the air and prevents problems from escalating.

▶ Great sex can result from a mutual need to release anger and excess energy.

NOT-SO-GOOD NEWS:

▶ Both know they are always right, so compromise is out of the question.

▶ Eights don't worry if they say or do things to hurt others. Ones are mortified by such abominable behavior.

▶ The conflict between Eights' excesses and Ones' inhibitions can cause frequent fighting. Those screaming neighbors are probably Eights and Ones.

Ones and Nines

GOOD NEWS:

▶ This pair easily creates a serene, peaceful household, which both participants blissfully enjoy.

▶ Nines are very accepting, enabling Ones to accept themselves.

▶ Nines encourage Ones to relax and occasionally let themselves go long enough to have a good time.

NOT-SO-GOOD NEWS:

▶ Because both suppress their anger, resentment is often left to fester until it can't be ignored.

▶ Nines can be unfocused and distracted when forced into action, leaving Ones frustrated and resentful.

▶ Both are prone to procrastination, and important things don't get accomplished.

Number Two: *Helper*

You'll especially love being with a Two if you:

▶ Value the exchange of love and feelings above all else

▶ Enjoy consistent closeness and togetherness

▶ Want your partner to be warm and gracious

▶ Enjoy open, emotional sharing and baring your soul

▶ Prefer a mate who is demonstrative and highly expressive

▶ Are attracted to someone who is a "natural helper"

▶ Like a partner who gives compliments and feedback freely

▶ Want a partner who is extremely sensitive to your needs

▶ Like the sense of being needed by your partner

▶ Want your partner to be a real "giver" who is somewhat possessive of your love

▶ Feel loved when your partner can seemingly read your mind without explanation and respond quickly

▶ Want a partner who enjoys serving others and assisting those in need

▶ Want a partner who makes friends easily and feels comfortable approaching strangers

▶ Feel good when your partner wants to be indispensable in your life

▶ Appreciate a partner who is self-sacrificing and makes a deep emotional investment in others

How Best to Communicate with a Two

▶ Praise, praise, praise! Although Twos detest false flattery, they live to hear the words "Thank you" and "You are wonderful."

▶ Acknowledge a Two's help or good ideas. Letting him know his importance to you is a surefire path to his loving heart.

▶ Be honest about your desires. No need to play games to get what you want; a Two is happy to please.

▶ Don't embarrass him. Twos can be hypersensitive to criticism.

▶ Encourage him to explore and communicate his needs directly. The alternative is anger and frustration.

▶ Don't accept "Nothing is bothering me," when something is clearly amiss. Keep pressing until the truth comes out.

▶ Phrase things in terms of what you want rather than what "should" be.

▶ Start as many sentences as possible with "I love you."

Key Ways to Live Peacefully with a Two

▶ Be prepared to spend a lot of time with him. Twos need quantity in addition to quality time.

▶ Be sure he knows you value him. Flowers and gestures of affection go a long way.

▶ Plan lots of romantic dinners and intimate moments together.

▶ Touch and hug him often.

▶ Be aware that a Two fears rejection. He needs constant reassurance of your love, otherwise he'll start imagining that he means absolutely nothing to you.

▶ Recognize that those sudden bursts of anger are a release mechanism for unexpressed, unmet needs. Encourage a Two to express his needs more directly to avoid unanticipated emotional explosions.

▶ Don't be resentful when a Two jumps in to help even when you don't require it. Twos can't stop themselves! Appreciate his efforts and surrender your desire to do it yourself.

▶ Accept the fact that Twos have many acquaintances and friends whose needs may supersede yours.

How the Combinations Fare

Twos and Ones

See "Ones and Twos."

Twos and Twos

GOOD NEWS:

▶ Both are physically expressive, so there's never a shortage of hugs and kisses!

▶ Both love spending lots of time together and with groups of other people.

▶ They share common interests, especially other people and charity work.

NOT-SO-GOOD NEWS:

▶ Both are servers, and neither admits to needing assistance him- or herself.

▶ Neither can express his or her own wants directly, so guilt and manipulation often result.

▶ Both may look outside the relationship for people who need them more than their partner does.

Twos and Threes

GOOD NEWS:

▶ Threes live for work and strive for material success, while Twos are happy to assist them in acquiring it. Everyone can win with this arrangement.

▶ Threes tend to seek financial success, while Twos happily attend to hearth and home, even if the Two also has a career.

▶ Both care about what others think and will work to keep positive public profiles.

NOT-SO-GOOD NEWS:

▶ Threes love to work all the time, leaving Twos feeling neglected and alone.

▶ Threes are out of touch with their feelings, while Twos require romance and emotional responsiveness.

▶ Threes can be so self-absorbed that they are oblivious to the hidden needs of Twos.

Twos and Fours

301

GOOD NEWS:

▶ Both can express flowery sentiment and lavish emotion without holding back, generating a rich emotional interaction.

▶ Fours help Twos learn to express feelings and desires as vociferously as they do, while Fours awaken to the value of focusing on the needs of others.

▶ Fours appreciate a good relationship and will effusively let Twos know how valuable they are to them. This is music to a Two's ears.

NOT-SO-GOOD NEWS:

▶ Both have the tendency to withdraw from intimacy and will subsequently advance when their partner retreats.

▶ Fours easily find flaws in others, while Twos reel under criticism.

▶ Twos need to be around a lot of people, which most Fours avoid, especially when experiencing one of their mood swings or depressions.

Twos and Fives

GOOD NEWS:

▶ This couple can balance each other beautifully, the Two drawing the Five into participation in the world, while the Five encourages the Two to focus internally rather than externally.

▶ Fives offer Twos stability within their dramatic lives, while Twos teach Fives that they can survive by opening their hearts.

▶ Twos are highly social, frequently leaving Fives alone (which the independent, cerebral Five doesn't mind at all).

NOT-SO-GOOD NEWS:

▶ Fives and Twos are emotional opposites, and tensions can erupt. Whereas Fives tightly restrict their undesirable feelings, Twos let them flow like Niagara Falls.

▶ Twos love to meet new people at parties and attend grand events, activities that are anathema to a Five.

▶ Fives consider hugging or giving thoughtful gifts foolish, while Twos live for these tokens of affection.

Twos and Sixes

GOOD NEWS:

▶ Sixes' constant worries are eagerly soothed by Twos.

▶ Sixes' loyalty and dedication are helpful in Twos feeling loved and secure.

▶ Sixes often work for needy causes, projects that Twos approach with gusto.

NOT-SO-GOOD NEWS:

▶ Sixes are doubtful of Twos' motives in offers of assistance.

▶ Sixes' obsessive pessimism can drive Twos to distraction.

▶ A Two can help a Six become a shining star professionally, but Sixes are ambivalent about achieving lofty goals.

Twos and Sevens

GOOD NEWS:

▶ Optimism abounds in this partnership, and both share dreams of future success.

302

▶ Twos help Sevens learn to confront their hidden pain, while Sevens give Twos permission to relax and enjoy themselves instead of helping others all the time.

▶ Good times, lots of people, great events, and plenty of freedom—this couple knows how to have fun!

NOT-SO-GOOD NEWS:

▶ Both have intimacy issues. Sevens worry that a close partnership will tie them down, while Twos doubt that their partner will still love them once they reveal themselves.

▶ A Seven's desire to be constantly in motion may unnerve a Two's sense that he or she is the utmost priority.

▶ Sevens don't want to focus overtly on the relationship, while Twos want to talk about it incessantly.

Twos and Eights

GOOD NEWS:

▶ Eights are demanding, and Twos are happy to oblige.

▶ Their sex lives will be great! Physical expression is vital to an Eight, while Twos experience sex as a sign that they are wanted.

▶ Beneath the Eight's harsh exterior beats a tender heart, offering a Two all the warmth he or she requires.

NOT-SO-GOOD NEWS:

▶ Eights focus their considerable energy on trying to be of service, while Twos are uncomfortable with receiving rather than giving.

▶ A powerful Eight can overwhelm an inhibited Two.

▶ Twos want to improve them, but Eights think they are perfect just the way they are.

Twos and Nines

GOOD NEWS:

▶ Nines' perceptiveness allows them to detect the hidden desires of Twos, who have difficulty with forthright expression.

▶ Both need to be with other people, a motivation for persistence in a relationship others might give up on.

▶ Twos can help ignite passion in Nines, while Nines can help Twos discover who they really are.

303

NOT-SO-GOOD NEWS:

▶ Nines can be distracted in their interactions, leaving Twos feeling they are no longer important.

▶ An unmotivated Nine can greatly frustrate a Two, who wants someone he or she can guide to the top.

▶ Nines can detect Twos' desire to subtly push their own agendas, and they resent it.

Number Three: *Striver*

You'll especially love being with a Three if you:

▶ Are attracted to high achievers and "go-getters"

▶ Want a partner who is a self-starter and naturally leads the team

▶ Value your partner's appearance and encourage him to look sharp and attractive

▶ Are willing to sacrifice some quality time together in order to accomplish mutual goals

▶ Value competence and productivity

▶ Enjoy giving praise and acknowledgment for your partner's high achievements

▶ Prefer the kind of partner who is socially adept, interacts well with others, and makes a good first impression

▶ Value the importance of work at the expense of leisure

▶ Like a partner who completes the job and does what it takes to "get to the finish line"

▶ Enjoy a partner who is competitive and a real winner

▶ Like your man to exercise and be concerned about looking his best physically

▶ Value industriousness and financial security more than you value self-disclosure and sensitivity

▶ Appreciate the prestige of titles, degrees, and credentials

▶ Want a mate who will produce positive results, regardless of the circumstances

▶ Prefer an energetic, charming man who can be a role model for others

How Best to Communicate with a Three

▶ Acknowledge his achievements. The way to a Three's heart is through honoring his successes.

▶ Reveal your negative feelings or pain, on occasion, so he can eventually get in touch with his darker emotions.

▶ Be exceptionally gentle if you need to rebuke him. Threes interpret even a slight criticism as an indication of failure.

▶ Don't expect lots of discussion about feelings. Be grateful if your Three acknowledges having any emotions at all.

▶ Allow him to boast of his successes, but let him know he's great even if he didn't achieve anything.

▶ Let him know scripted lines of affection are insufficient. Encourage him to speak from the heart.

▶ Demand complete truthfulness. Threes are notorious for shading the facts if it helps their image.

▶ Set specific goals for your relationship and speak in terms of what can be accomplished. Action, rather than feelings, resonates with a Three.

305

Key Ways to Live Peacefully with a Three

▶ Recognize that work will often take precedence over the relationship. Professional stature and financial success, crucial goals for a Three, require time and attention.

▶ Get involved with satisfying solo projects so you're less resentful when your partner leaves you for the office.

▶ Strive to keep your home life peaceful. Threes burn a lot of energy working hard and promoting an image of success and need to recharge in a calm environment.

▶ Pay attention to your appearance and strive to be your best. Threes care a lot about image and believe their partner's appearance reflects on them personally.

▶ Accept that Threes always compare themselves to others. If his attention is on another couple, it isn't a sign that he would rather be with another woman instead of you.

▶ Be wary of inauthentic feelings that merely reflect how a Three *thinks* he should react. Encourage him to explore his genuine emotions.

▶ Plan on participating in dinner parties or social activities that are useful to a Three's successful career. If he says a client is coming over for dinner, start cooking.

▶ Let your partner know your love him regardless of his achievements. Eventually, he might start to believe it.

How the Combinations Fare

Threes and Ones
See "Ones and Threes."

Threes and Twos
See "Twos and Threes."

Threes and Threes
GOOD NEWS:

▶ Both enjoy moving in high-society circles and associating with powerful people.

▶ They share energetic, positive attitudes toward life and feel they can accomplish anything.

▶ A Three needn't worry while working late at the office; his or her partner probably isn't home either.

NOT-SO-GOOD NEWS:

▶ With a full work schedule, it can be hard to devote time to the relationship.

▶ Both minimize the importance of emotion, often substituting an overly active life for a truly meaningful one.

▶ Rather than completing each other, they are often competitors.

Threes and Fours
GOOD NEWS:

▶ Threes can uplift brooding Fours, while Fours teach Threes how to look inward and explore their emotions.

▶ A Four can spend a Three's money with refined and unique tastefulness.

▶ This couple will look spectacular, fit, dapper, and unique, as they both give credence to the world's opinion of them.

NOT-SO-GOOD NEWS:

▶ Fours want attention, time, and intimacy—things most Threes are short on.

▶ Fours seek sympathy for their inner pain, but Threes often want to slap a bandage on problems and move onward.

▶ A Four's moodiness and tendency toward depression can put a major crimp in the active lifestyle of a Three.

Threes and Fives

GOOD NEWS:

▶ Both numbers can keep themselves occupied for days, allowing their partners time to joyously focus on their own projects.

▶ Threes help Fives get out in the world, while Fives can assist Threes in discovering the joys of calm reflection.

▶ Neither partner is fond of mushy sentiment; both happily communicate commitment in drier, more nonverbal ways.

NOT-SO-GOOD NEWS:

▶ Threes go where the action is, while Fives detest anything outside of a book or their own minds.

▶ Fives revere privacy, while Threes broadcast everything that makes them appear successful.

▶ Threes worry about others' opinions, something Fives can't comprehend at all.

Threes and Sixes

GOOD NEWS:

▶ Threes can assist Sixes in feeling comfortable with their successes, while Sixes can aid Threes in recognizing that image isn't everything.

▶ With a Three, a Six will engage in new activities, while a Six can encourage a Three to slow down a bit.

▶ Threes don't dwell on potential disasters, while Sixes plan for every contingency. This can be a useful combination when trouble does occur.

NOT-SO-GOOD NEWS:

- ▶ Threes are natural optimists, while Sixes are extreme pessimists. This clash can drive them both crazy.

- ▶ Sixes diffuse their worries by expressing their concerns of impending doom, while Threes don't want to hear such negative nonsense.

- ▶ Watching a Three shine can foster insecurity in a Six who is doubtful of his or her own success.

Threes and Sevens

GOOD NEWS:

- ▶ With this pairing, energy abounds. Neither partner is likely to turn down an adventurous activity.

- ▶ Threes help Sevens focus on being productive and achieving their goals, while Sevens assist Threes in learning to have more fun.

- ▶ Upbeat and optimistic, each can be a joy for the other to be around.

NOT-SO-GOOD NEWS:

- ▶ Both are on the move, but they sometimes head in different directions. With ceaseless activity, it's a challenge to ensure that they spend enough time together to develop the relationship.

- ▶ Both prefer to ignore minor problems, but, left unattended, those seemingly small troubles turn molehills into mountains.

- ▶ Each is easily sidetracked from family responsibilities, dropping the ball into the other's lap.

Threes and Eights

GOOD NEWS:

- ▶ Both are generally financially successful, so they are not lacking money.

- ▶ Both focus on work, so neither shows concern if no one's home for dinner.

- ▶ Both want to go full steam ahead until a project is completed.

NOT-SO-GOOD NEWS:

- ▶ Each has emotional issues, preferring to "do" rather than to "feel."

- ▶ Each may want to run the relationship his or her own way.

- ▶ Both are used to being applauded for their actions, but they stint on mutual recognition of each other.

Threes and Nines

GOOD NEWS:

- ▶ A Nine is energized by a Three's busy itinerary, while a Nine's peaceful presence has a calming effect on a Three.

- ▶ Both diligently avoid confrontation.

- ▶ Threes are content knowing that Nines understand and accept them for who they are, not for their achievements.

NOT-SO-GOOD NEWS:

- ▶ A Nine is easily swayed by a Three's desires, even if they are not what a Nine really wants.

- ▶ A Three can be frustrated by a Nine's slow, deliberate pace.

- ▶ Threes may be so busy and self-absorbed that they don't notice Nines' unhappiness or dissatisfaction.

Number Four: *Individualist*

You'll especially love being with a Four if you:

- ▶ Feel attracted to a partner who is "different"

- ▶ Seek a profound sense of compassion and sensitivity in your mate

- ▶ Enjoy high levels of originality and creativity

- ▶ Need a lot of space and permission to be unusual and nontraditional

- ▶ Don't mind your partner's eccentricities and not following the crowd

- ▶ Love the arts and have refined tastes

- ▶ Treasure a mate who needs you emotionally and understands your losses and sorrow

- ▶ Want someone who is not interested in a boring, mundane, or traditional lifestyle

- ▶ Benefit from a mate who is not afraid to admit his deepest feelings and faults

- ▶ Feel good knowing that your partner is available to offer sustained emotional support through intense crises

- ▶ Don't mind being immersed in intensely dramatic, romantic, sometimes tragic aspects of life

▶ Appreciate rich imagination, wit, and innovation

▶ Enjoy flare and intensity

▶ Understand natural longing and can empathize with deep melancholy

▶ Enjoy an original, one-of-a-kind partner

How Best to Communicate with a Four

▶ Be authentic. Fours hate phoniness and posturing with a passion.

▶ Praise him frequently, especially what is unique and special about him.

▶ Speak in terms of emotion, not cold, hard facts. Tell the whole, elaborate story rather than racing to the punch line.

▶ Be delicate with criticism. Even a slightly harsh word can make a Four miserable for days!

▶ Their intellect can be strong, but their intuition is stronger. Ask "How do you feel about that?" rather than "What do you think?"

▶ If you need a quick answer, phrase your question comparatively (e.g., "Which restaurant do you prefer, this one or that one?").

▶ Listen, listen, listen. Fours need to express their inner tumult without being judged.

▶ Be empathic to the feelings a Four genuinely experiences, even if you think the reaction is completely overblown.

Key Ways to Live Peacefully with a Four

▶ Honor his intuition. Fours make most of their decisions based on what feels right to them.

▶ Learn to feel comfortable with their emotional range, their despair and ecstasy. Joy is fleeting, but darkness too shall pass.

▶ Expect him to want what he can't have. To him, the grass is always greener on the other side, although even if he had those things, he wouldn't be happy.

▶ Be comfortable in revealing your feelings. Fours are terrific listeners who allow you to share what's in your heart.

▶ Repeatedly tell a Four how valuable he is simply being himself. The message won't be received, so tell him again.

▶ Let the Four be the creative spirit of the household. His taste may be unusual, but it is generally good.

▶ Don't be taken aback by a Four's penchant for high drama and intense emotion. They try to stir up excitement when things have grown complacent.

▶ Be romantic! Gifts and romantic gestures are welcome. Thoughtfulness is important to a Four.

How the Combinations Fare

Fours and Ones
See "Ones and Fours."

Fours and Twos
See "Twos and Fours."

Fours and Threes
See "Threes and Fours."

Fours and Fours
GOOD NEWS:

▶ They experience a mutual understanding of their heightened emotions, and they revel in it.

▶ Both will work hard to create a special, unique, deeply felt relationship.

▶ Although commitment is difficult for them, once they do commit, Fours will stay together, passionately, forever.

NOT-SO-GOOD NEWS:

▶ When they are simultaneously melancholic or depressive, the household may come to a standstill for hours, days, or even weeks.

▶ Both are prone to frequently finding fault with their partner.

▶ Both are quick to blame their partner for their own unhappiness.

Fours and Fives
GOOD NEWS:

▶ Fives can learn to be more expressive of their emotions, while Fours can benefit from reining theirs in a bit.

▶ Both have great insight, and they share a desire to discover meaning in the world around them.

▶ Both can be passionate about art, music, philosophical ideas, and other common interests.

NOT-SO-GOOD NEWS:

▶ Both are prone to spending lots of time alone in their own worlds, and the relationship may suffer from neglect.

▶ Fives rarely display or discuss their emotions, while Fours seek constant disclosure.

▶ Fives may appear apathetic about the relationship, and Fours perceive even slight neglect as complete rejection.

Fours and Sixes

GOOD NEWS:

▶ Once they commit, Sixes' loyalty to relationships allow Fours to feel safe and secure.

▶ Fours feel comfortable revealing their dark emotions to Sixes, who are likely to understand and empathize.

▶ Both perceive themselves as swimming against the tide.

NOT-SO-GOOD NEWS:

▶ Both can be pessimistic about the future.

▶ Both can blame or attack their partners due to their own insecurities.

▶ A Six's worries can further burden an easily depressed Four.

Fours and Sevens

GOOD NEWS:

▶ Fours help Sevens face their emotional depths, while Sevens can bring joy, activity, and fun into Fours' lives.

▶ Sevens can avoid immersion in Fours' emotional dramas.

▶ Sevens are energetic and passionate about things they love, as are Fours.

NOT-SO-GOOD NEWS:

▶ Sevens don't want to deal with negative emotions, an area of tremendous focus for most Fours.

▶ When serious issues arise, Fours will experience and discuss them for hours, while Sevens think two minutes is sufficient.

▶ Sevens just want to have fun, which is difficult when Fours aren't in the mood.

Fours and Eights

GOOD NEWS:

▶ To hell with rules or social convention; each does things his or her own way.

▶ Eights avoid getting pulled into Fours' emotional dramas.

▶ Fours seek straightforward emotion and intensity, and Eights provide that by being themselves.

NOT-SO-GOOD NEWS:

▶ When Fours get depressed, Eights will stay away, leaving Fours feeling rejected.

▶ Eights' powerful way of expressing opinions can overpower Fours, causing them to feel crushed or defeated.

▶ Eights can be crude and blunt in front of others, easily embarrassing emotional Fours.

Fours and Nines

313

GOOD NEWS:

▶ Nines can make Fours feel truly accepted exactly as they are.

▶ Nines can learn to intensify their own emotions, while Fours value Nines' serenity and balance.

▶ Both are good listeners who empathize with what their partners are experiencing.

NOT-SO-GOOD NEWS:

▶ A Four's preference for emotional intensity isn't satisfied by the even temperament of a Nine.

▶ Both are quick to blame, but neither accepts criticism very well.

▶ Nines can be spacey, absentminded, and immersed in their own world, leaving Fours feeling abandoned and unloved.

Number Five: *Observer*

You'll especially love being with a Five if you:

- Are attracted to an independent, unpretentious mate

- Want a partner who doesn't try to control you or your decisions

- Prefer a mate who is self-reliant and doesn't drain your energy

- Appreciate thought-provoking ideas from your partner

- Enjoy a mate who may not be overly concerned with appearance or how others view him

- Like a partner who can entertain himself and doesn't expect constant communication

- Admire a partner who thinks before he speaks or acts

- Feel comfortable with a man who listens and observes rather than wanting to be the life of the party

- Are easily bored with small talk and seek substantive conversation with your mate

- Appreciate simplicity and the ability to keep a confidence

- Want a mate who respects your boundaries and doesn't intrude upon your privacy

- Prefer a partner who is cautious, reasonable, and retains emotional control

- Prefer a partner with a sense of humor and a sharp wit

- Feel comfortable with a mate who is resourceful and thrifty

- Want a mate with mental agility and acute vision

How Best to Communicate with a Five

- Don't demand decisions or information. Fives are extremely private people who hate having their "space" invaded. Express your desires and allow him to respond when he is ready.

- Expect pauses and reflection during conversations. Fives aren't quick with a superficial retort or offhand comment.

▶ Be prepared to offer an opinion first. Fives don't risk rejection by going out on a limb.

▶ Give him the details. Not content with knowing the ultimate solution, they evaluate the logical progression of thought that went into your decision.

▶ In discussions of a sensitive nature, give him plenty of warning. Fives hate to be surprised or ambushed.

▶ Don't be concerned if all that you tell him doesn't register. His listening ability may be impaired by his overly active mind.

▶ Save long, flowery exposition for your girlfriends. Fives appreciate efficient and succinct expression.

▶ Engage him in what specifically interests him. Your usually quiet partner can expound on a subject for hours.

Key Ways to Live Peacefully with a Five

▶ Respect his privacy. It's a serious issue for him, and a closed door means "Do Not Disturb!" If your Five feels invaded, he'll find a more accommodating place to spend his time.

▶ If possible, give him a separate room for reading and working.

▶ Keep dinner parties and group social activities to a minimum. To a Five, the best time is contemplative.

▶ Develop outside interests, and allow your Five plenty of time for his own pursuits.

▶ Don't expect him to whisper sweet nothings in your ear or constantly declare his love for you. A Five's way of displaying affection is primarily nonverbal.

▶ Be prepared to handle the details of your social life and vacations. It's tough enough for the Five just to show up!

▶ Make him feel secure and comfortable releasing his emotions. Don't push or pressure, but let him come around when he is ready.

▶ Don't check up on him. Fives need to know they can go out for a while without having to explain where they have been.

How the Combinations Fare

Fives and Ones
See "Ones and Fives."

Fives and Twos
See "Twos and Fives."

Fives and Threes
See "Threes and Fives."

Fives and Fours
See "Fours and Fives."

Fives and Fives

GOOD NEWS:

▶ They respect each other's privacy and introverted inclinations. Superficial small talk, house guests, and social activities can happily be kept to a minimum.

▶ Both value doing their own thing, even if it means they are apart a great deal of the time.

▶ Shared interests can spark intense intellectual conversations.

NOT-SO-GOOD NEWS:

▶ Even Fives can feel ignored by partners who distance themselves emotionally.

▶ Noncommunication about vital issues can sometimes cause small problems to escalate.

▶ Furthering the relationship can be difficult with each focused on separate activities.

Fives and Sixes

GOOD NEWS:

▶ Both can be content with a low-key relationship, sharing quiet time at home.

▶ Once a mutual commitment is made, each will try to ensure that the relationship succeeds.

▶ Both are intellectually curious with a strong mental facility.

NOT-SO-GOOD NEWS:

▶ Sixes can feel paranoid when Fives are emotionally withdrawn or even physically disappear for a while.

▶ Sixes are annoyed by Fives' constant need for reassurance.

▶ Both tend to procrastinate when faced with important decisions.

Fives and Sevens

GOOD NEWS:

▶ Both allow their partners time for individual pursuits.

▶ A Five can become more receptive to people and group activities with a Seven, while a Seven can learn to slow down and enjoy intellectual pursuits.

▶ Sevens love to initiate and plan social activities, while Fives are happy to follow along.

NOT-SO-GOOD NEWS:

▶ Both can easily detach from the relationship, thus weakening their commitment and preventing the relationship from blossoming.

▶ Both tend to hide their true emotions.

▶ A Seven's need to be the center of attention can be exhausting for a Five, while a Five's single-minded, narrow focus can bore and frustrate a Seven.

Fives and Eights

GOOD NEWS:

▶ Eights encourage assertiveness and emotional expression in Fives, while Fives assist Eights in reflection before revelation.

▶ If Eights work late, Fives are thrilled to have the house to themselves.

▶ Both feel comfortable being honest and direct with each other.

NOT-SO-GOOD NEWS:

▶ Each steers clear of emotional trouble, rather than dealing with a situation.

▶ Eights frequently want to engage in battle and can be frustrated when Fives withdraw.

▶ Eights like loud, lively discussions, which can overwhelm Fives.

317

Fives and Nines

GOOD NEWS:

- Both enjoy engaging in activities together as a way of expressing affection.

- Both give each other a lot of emotional space and plenty of time to assimilate their feelings.

- Fives solidify Nines' commitment to other people, as well as the relationship, while Nines facilitate Fives' emotional expression.

NOT-SO-GOOD NEWS:

- Nines often rely on their partners to define their lives, a burden most Fives don't want.

- Both will retreat into their own worlds, offering little support to a developing relationship.

- Fives withdraw emotionally from relationships, leaving needy Nines feeling abandoned.

Number Six: *Belonger*

318

You'll especially love being with a Six if you:

- Value loyalty and commitment above all else

- Prefer to be with a team player who expects no special treatment

- Enjoy a partner with a strong sense of belonging in romantic and family life

- Appreciate a partner who is cautious and looks before he leaps

- Like the feeling of togetherness when the two of you are fighting for a common cause

- Dislike pretense and/or grandstanding in a mate

- Especially value conscientiousness, diligence, and responsibility in a mate

- Want a mate who prefers the status quo over the new and adventurous

- Like a partner who greatly contributes to the relationship and values working as a team

- Prefer a partner who respects authority and tradition but can take a strong stand and be a rebel on occasion

▶ Admire a mate who will champion the underdog and fight for a cause he believes in

▶ Rely on your partner to follow rules, meeting expectations with no sudden surprises

▶ Like a man who is quick to uncover fraud, scams, and hidden agendas

▶ Seek a partner who is committed and steadfast and has fortitude when the road is rocky

▶ Value the unconditional support and safety of a close family bond

How Best to Communicate with a Six

▶ Sixes love to know what you expect from them, so be direct.

▶ Acknowledge his concerns; don't downplay them. His fears are tangible, even if you think they are needless.

▶ Be forthright in your opinions so that he doesn't have to hunt for hidden motives.

▶ Flattery will get you nowhere, and manipulation is useless. If you want something, ask for it.

▶ When he gets angry, calm down before responding. Your rage will only amplify his.

▶ Be pragmatic and realistic. Sixes don't want you to accentuate the positive and eliminate the negative.

▶ If you reasonably explain why you want him to do something, rather than insisting on it, he will be more amenable to your wishes.

▶ Be aware that even gentle criticism feels like a sledgehammer to him.

Key Ways to Live Peacefully with a Six

▶ Constantly reassure him that you love and value him.

▶ Help him counter his imagined anxieties with "just the facts"; for example, if he's worried about a vehicle's safety record, read him *Consumer Reports*.

▶ Encourage exercise and physical activity. Sixes need positive ways to release their anxiety.

319

- Don't threaten or embarrass him into trying something new. Lead him gradually into uncharted territory.

- Treat your obligations as seriously as he does. If you say you will do something, fulfill your commitment.

- Find a charitable cause you can volunteer for together.

- Encourage his career, but don't push him. Sixes can be successful at work, but most are uncomfortable in the spotlight.

- Have a neat and organized home. Routines make him feel more comfortable and secure.

How the Combinations Fare

Sixes and Ones
See "Ones and Sixes."

Sixes and Twos
See "Twos and Sixes."

Sixes and Threes
See "Threes and Sixes."

Sixes and Fours
See "Fours and Sixes."

Sixes and Fives
See "Fives and Sixes."

Sixes and Sixes

GOOD NEWS:

- Both value their partners' willingness to anticipate potential problems rather than leaping blindly into danger.

- Both love structure and implementing order in daily routines.

- Once they commit to a relationship, they remain loyal.

NOT-SO-GOOD NEWS:

- With both envisioning a worst-case scenario, they paralyze each other.

- When quick decisions need to be made, no one can make them. They are interminably indecisive.

- They become paranoid about their partners' motivations.

Sixes and Sevens

GOOD NEWS:

▶ Sixes can be greatly supportive during tough times and teach Sevens not to fear their pain, while Sevens can help Sixes to be more joyful.

▶ Sixes don't have an opportunity to worry when Sevens keep them so busy.

▶ Loyal Sixes can help flighty Sevens understand the value of commitment.

NOT-SO-GOOD NEWS:

▶ Carefree Sevens are impatient with Sixes' proclivity toward pessimism, rendering Sixes even more anxious.

▶ Sevens often don't feel bound by absolute honesty, while Sixes hate deception of any kind.

▶ Sixes prefer routine, while Sevens feel restricted by anything that curtails their sense of freedom.

Sixes and Eights

GOOD NEWS:

▶ Both value directness and will be straightforward.

▶ Eights are comfortable making decisions about which Sixes are ambivalent.

▶ A nervous Six finds comfort in the protective nature of an Eight.

NOT-SO-GOOD NEWS:

▶ Eights can bully their partners, and Sixes particularly hate to be pushed around.

▶ Sixes' anxiety appears as weakness to Eights, who are contemptuous of vulnerability.

▶ Sixes need constant reassurance of their partners' love, but Eights see such token displays of affection as puerile.

Sixes and Nines

GOOD NEWS:

▶ Nines are a calming influence for anxiety-ridden Sixes.

▶ Both abhor conflict, so their relationship can be peaceful and serene.

▶ When both feel happy and secure, they're a fun-loving, active couple.

NOT-SO-GOOD NEWS:

▶ Nines aren't often direct with their feelings, leaving Sixes suspicious of their motives and intentions.

▶ Both find it difficult to initiate action, leaving things at a standstill.

▶ Nines' inclination to space out can cause concern in Sixes about their partners' commitment to the relationship.

Number Seven: *Adventurer*

You'll especially love being with a Seven if you:

▶ Enjoy adventurous, fun-filled activity

▶ Prefer a mate who is upbeat and optimistic

▶ Like to spend time with a partner who is eclectic, flexible, and thinks that variety is the spice of life.

▶ Prefer a partner who refuses to dwell on the past

▶ Prefer a partner who isn't dependent, needy, or inaccessible

▶ Prefer a partner who actively enjoys life's pleasures and wants to share creature comforts

▶ Want to be entertained and never bored

▶ Want a mate who is outgoing, friendly, charming, and sometimes impulsive

▶ Desire a partner who knows how to live the good life and can make it happen

▶ Prefer a partner who enjoys planning events and activities

▶ Seek a wide range of social experiences, friends, and travel adventures

▶ Enjoy a mate who is periodically self-indulgent and goes to extremes to have a great time

▶ Prefer a person who doesn't whine, complain, or dwell on negativity

▶ Love spontaneity and serendipity

▶ Desire a playful, sensual mate who views life as an unlimited smorgasbord

How Best to Communicate with a Seven

▶ Be upbeat. You'll hold his attention longer if you're enthusiastic and energetic.

▶ Try not to say no. Sevens detest limits or obstacles. Be diplomatic in standing your ground and suggest good alternatives.

▶ Criticize gingerly, as Sevens have difficulty dealing with negativity.

▶ Expect the conversation to center on him. A Seven loves to be in the spotlight.

▶ Don't expect him to be aware of or be able to express what's bothering him. Sevens don't readily focus on pain. Help him feel secure in experiencing a full range of emotions and assure him that, ultimately, your lives will be enriched.

▶ Appreciate his great ideas.

▶ Expect to repeat things several times. Sevens will overlook your requests as their minds race ahead to further possibilities.

▶ Don't order him around; sevens hate to be told what to do

Key Ways to Live Peacefully with a Seven

▶ Be accepting when a Seven has a change of plans. With so many possibilities in life, Sevens have a hard time committing to anything.

▶ Go out and do things a Seven loves. Otherwise, he will be out doing them without you.

▶ Let him do most of the social planning.

▶ Recognize that many of his suggestions are just possible ideas or options. Most of what he throws against the wall doesn't stick.

▶ Delicately help him face his problems, rather than avoiding them through activity.

▶ Focus more on shared activity, less on shared feelings.

▶ Help him to feel free, even in a committed relationship. A Seven hates to feel that his options are limited.

▶ Be open to experiencing diverse things and appreciate your Seven for introducing them to you.

How the Combinations Fare

Sevens and Ones
See "Ones and Sevens."

Sevens and Twos
See "Twos and Sevens."

Sevens and Threes
See "Threes and Sevens."

Sevens and Fours
See "Fours and Sevens."

Sevens and Fives
See "Fives and Sevens."

Sevens and Sixes
See "Sixes and Sevens."

Sevens and Sevens
GOOD NEWS:
- ▶ Both love to plan grand adventures, so their activities will always be spectacular.
- ▶ Both have high energy levels; when one wants to dance late into the night, the other is happy to keep up the tempo.
- ▶ Both are extremely optimistic, so the future will always look bright.

NOT-SO-GOOD NEWS:
- ▶ Both attempt to avoid pain and deep feelings, so the relationship may remain superficial and emotionally dissatisfying.
- ▶ Neither wants to restrict his or her freedom, so their time together might be limited and the relationship will suffer.
- ▶ Both talk about themselves incessantly, so nobody's listening.

Sevens and Eights
GOOD NEWS:
- ▶ They share a high energy level and they both love to go out and have fun.
- ▶ Equally independent, they grant each other the time and space to pursue individual activities.

▶ Neither is overly concerned about what they *should* do; they focus instead on what they desire in this moment.

NOT-SO-GOOD NEWS:

▶ When Eights make plans, they expect Sevens to be there, while Sevens have difficulty adhering to a schedule.

▶ Eights may be given to angry outbursts, which Sevens don't want to deal with.

▶ With both wanting to be heard, each can feel resentful if he or she is overlooked or ignored.

Sevens and Nines

GOOD NEWS:

▶ Sevens introduce Nines to diverse activities they wouldn't discover on their own, while Nines help Sevens learn to slow down and relax.

▶ Both happily refuse to look at areas of discomfort.

▶ Sevens are self-absorbed, and Nines are happy to be absorbed by them.

NOT-SO-GOOD NEWS:

▶ Both see such an array of possibilities that making decisions can be next to impossible.

▶ Neither likes conflict, and dealing with difficult situations may mean ignoring them altogether.

▶ With Sevens taking all the credit, Nines can feel underappreciated.

▶ Nines' addiction to routines can make free-spirited Sevens go crazy.

325

Number Eight: *Leader*

You'll especially love being with an Eight if you:

▶ Enjoy feeling protected and defended by a courageous mate

▶ Like a strong, decisive partner who is a natural leader

▶ Need to lean on a partner who is unafraid to fight life's battles

▶ Want to know exactly where your man stands on all important issues

▶ Are more attracted by strength and drive than sensitivity and caring

▶ Appreciate a partner who is powerful and passionate and is capable of giving to others

▶ Feel good about a partner who puts himself on the front lines and faces problems directly

▶ Desire a man who will intensely pursue conflict resolution and dig deep to solve problems

▶ Are attracted to someone who is self-reliant, brave, and inwardly confident

▶ Want a mate who does not count the cost of his personal efforts or contributions

▶ Like your partner to take the initiative and render decisions without requiring your approval

▶ Admire a mate who will go to any lengths to protect his loved ones

▶ Respect a partner who forcefully speaks out on issues of justice and fair play

▶ Enjoy a man who is extremely supportive of the weak, young, or disadvantaged

▶ Prefer a mate with a "can-do" attitude and an authoritative presence

How Best to Communicate with an Eight

▶ Be direct. Eights want to take a straight line to the hard facts.

▶ Include him in early planning stages so he can weigh in with his own opinion.

▶ Don't tell him what he *should* do. He's the boss.

▶ Be honest. Eights truly want to know what you think because they'll certainly keep you apprised of their opinions.

▶ Don't whine to get what you want.

▶ If something is bothering you, let it out. Eights would rather hear problems directly so they can attempt to solve them.

▶ Don't address his anger with your own. It is more prudent to retreat temporarily to allow tempers to cool before responding.

▶ Remember that behind that gruff exterior is a sweet teddy bear who will do anything for the woman he loves.

Key Ways to Live Peacefully with an Eight

▶ Be wholehearted in your actions. Eights don't do anything halfway. Sex, social activism, spirited discussion, enjoyment, and argument will take place at full throttle.

▶ Recognize that his bark is much worse than his bite. What appears to be an order or ultimatum may actually be a suggestion.

▶ Work out, eat right, and get enough sleep so you'll have the stamina to meet his high energy level.

▶ Respect his desire to work hard and to have time alone.

▶ Be the voice of moderation and balance, because your Eight won't be.

▶ Uphold your commitments. Eights will honor their promises, and they want you to do so as well.

▶ Don't expect much privacy. An Eight typically views a closed door as a barrier to be crossed.

▶ When you are an appreciative recipient, your Eight will shower you with everything you desire (time, money, sex, affection).

327

How the Combinations Fare

Eights and Ones
See "Ones and Eights."

Eights and Twos
See "Twos and Eights."

Eights and Threes
See "Threes and Eights."

Eights and Fours
See "Fours and Eights."

Eights and Fives
See "Fives and Eights."

Eights and Sixes
See "Sixes and Eights."

Eights and Sevens

See "Sevens and Eights."

Eights and Eights

GOOD NEWS:

► Eights live with gusto and are thrilled when their partners can match their energy level and appetite for life.

► Both value directness and honesty.

► Both enjoy arguing and, after the fight, neither is the worse for wear.

not-so-good news:

► Both want to be in control, and constant clashes are the result.

► Shouting matches can be common, and while either Eight might not actually mind this, their children, friends, and neighbors can certainly be affected by their discord.

► They withdraw when feeling vulnerable emotionally, and neither wants to initiate reconciliation.

Eights and Nines

GOOD NEWS:

► Eights help Nines learn to move their will and energy into action, while Nines can teach Eights to consider another person's viewpoint.

► Both can be generous and loving toward their partners and close friends.

► Eights demand a lot of attention, and Nines aim to please.

NOT-SO-GOOD NEWS:

► Eights seek action and excitement, and Nines don't generate it on their own.

► Nines' true desires need to be drawn from them, but Eights are so busy pushing their own agendas that they might lose patience in trying.

► Passionate argument can be stimulating to Eights, whereas Nines have no interest in engaging in conflict.

Number Nine: *Peacemaker*

You'll especially love being with a Nine if you:

▶ Enjoy harmony, peace, and tranquillity

▶ Want to feel at one with your mate and emotionally united

▶ Appreciate a partner who can see all sides of an issue and doesn't insist on one way of thinking or doing things

▶ Want a partner who's flexible, adaptable, and goes with the flow

▶ Prefer a partner who will remain calm and serene even in the face of major conflicts

▶ Appreciate a mate who dislikes conflict and never knowingly attempts to cause trouble

▶ Want a mate who does not rush important or final decisions

▶ Prefer a nonjudgmental and unpretentious partner

▶ Enjoy a mate who can listen without needing to exhort his own opinion

▶ Appreciate diplomacy and mediation

▶ Value your mate's ability to hold you in great esteem as well as to respect others

▶ Seek a tranquil haven where your partner will not inflict harsh opinions or criticism upon you

▶ Value modesty, gentleness, and approachability in a mate

▶ Place high value on your partner's empathy and validation of your feelings

▶ Appreciate a mate who can relax and be comfortable and undemanding

How Best to Communicate with a Nine

▶ Offer lots of encouragement and the opportunity to state what he really wants. Otherwise, his wishes will remain a reflection of yours.

329

▶ Provide definitive choices rather than open-ended options, or a Nine will never make up his mind.

▶ Never ask for a quick decision. Nines ponder endless possibilities, and opportunities flabbergast them.

▶ Nagging will prompt him to tune out your requests.

▶ Sometimes saying "yes" really means "I don't have the heart to tell you 'no' right now."

▶ Be tactful with criticism; Nines love harmony and hate dissonance.

▶ Suggest, rather than demand; harshness upsets his equilibrium.

▶ Frequently tell him how much you care about and appreciate him.

Key Ways to Live Peacefully with a Nine

▶ Take charge of the details of running the household yourself rather than waiting for the Nine to eventually get around to it.

▶ Create routines that are comfortable for both of you.

▶ Watch out for passive-aggressive responses. Encourage the Nine to express what he wants and be assertive about getting it.

▶ Take up meditation or other techniques that can promote a sense of calm and balance.

▶ Suggest activities that he really enjoys rather than letting him always be amenable to your desires.

▶ Actively listen to what he has to say rather than allowing him to continually focus on your needs.

▶ Encourage him to take some active responsibility for the relationship. Nines are the perpetual followers at the dance, but then they'll blame you if you miss a step.

▶ Set short-term goals for things that need to be accomplished; Nines are notorious for being unable to complete tasks that don't have deadlines attached to them.

How the Combinations Fare

Nines and Ones
See "Ones and Nines."

Nines and Twos

See "Two and Nines."

Nines and Threes

See "Threes and Nines."

Nines and Fours

See "Fours and Nines."

Nines and Fives

See "Fives and Nines."

Nines and Sixes

See "Sixes and Nines."

Nines and Sevens

See "Sevens and Nines."

Nines and Eights

See "Eights and Nines."

Nines and Nines

GOOD NEWS:

331

- ▶ Both joyfully accept their partners just the way they are.

- ▶ Both strive for a peaceful, serene home life, an environment that offers each of them contentment.

- ▶ Their easygoing attitudes comfortably accommodate their partners' needs.

NOT-SO-GOOD NEWS:

- ▶ Even minor decisions aren't arrived at because they're stuck in a quagmire of indecisiveness.

- ▶ Neither wants to create conflict, so problems get sidestepped rather than dealt with directly.

- ▶ This low-energy pair is in danger of trudging through life as if they were walking through molasses, rather than going for the brass ring with gusto.

Delving Deeper, Knowing More: Discovering Values, Beliefs, and Interests

B efore you can determine the compatibility of you and your partner, you need to assess your thoughts and feelings on a variety
of issues, including lifestyle, education, family, and personal
habits. You then need to discern your partner's thoughts and
feelings. You can learn a lot by observation. Many of the more esoteric subjects require direct conversation with him. If you've never really thought
about these issues yourself or attempted a mutual discussion of this nature,
anticipating that present or potential problems will magically work themselves out or won't be of future consequence, this chapter will give you a
method for discovering your own beliefs, values, and interests and will help
you to discover his.

To build a strong and lasting foundation for a long-term relationship,
you must consider more than romantic impulses. If ignored, certain differences can cause damage to even the most loving relationship. In this chapter, you will learn the critical topics every Smart Heart woman should
discuss with her present partner, if she's currently involved in a serious relationship, or her prospective partner, if she is seeking a long-term involvement.

Many women in my practice futilely hoped that significant differences
with their partners would simply disappear. "Who cares if we're from

different ethnic backgrounds or have different religious beliefs?" they ask as they become more entrenched in a challenging partnership. "*West Side Story* was thirty years ago. Things like that don't matter in this day and age."

Tragically, those same women tell a different tale one, five, or even fifteen years into their partnership. Strain on a relationship accumulates as they face the stares and glares of strangers for the hundredth time. Even the reactions of neighbors or friends can cause strain due to different racial, economic, religious, or cultural backgrounds. It can be a struggle for families to arrange vacations around religious holidays. The strain of continually honoring and respecting differences that "didn't matter" before can cause friction and even break up relationships that were previously rock solid.

A Smart Heart woman can't afford to delude herself into thinking that love and commitment alone are enough to overcome *every* obstacle. Reality has a way of impinging on our idealism, especially over time. You may be convinced you both can surmount the barriers existing between you, but if they are major, you probably cannot. The world is not yet a color-blind heaven or economic utopia. A Smart Heart woman does not subvert her cherished lifestyle, goals, and values for those of her partner, otherwise resentment is inevitable.

When it comes to compatibility, a Smart Heart Woman:

- Understands that the best relationships are built on commonality
- Discovers what is relevant to the relationship, i.e., values, goals, and background, rather than hoping and praying that things will magically work out
- Expands her world by incorporating her partner's thoughts and perspectives
- Accepts her partner as he is, not as what she hopes he will become
- Acknowledges and accepts the differences between her and her partner
- Doesn't dismiss or minimize the differences and is willing to compromise to develop a clear, mutual understanding

333

Good and Lasting Relationships Are Based on Similarities, Not Differences

The most successful relationships are relatively like-minded. There is validity in your parents' and grandparents' dictum to marry within your race or religion. It's not as archaic a thought as you would imagine. While intolerance may have been a factor in that mode of thinking, consider the idea that it is easier to form a lasting union with someone of similar traditions, values, and objectives than with a person of disparate beliefs.

The odds of a successful relationship are greater if you share a common foundation. This may not be apparent in the early stages when both parties happily accommodate each other. If he needs to celebrate Easter at his church and your Buddhist festival occurs at the same time, you might be willing to overlook your own celebration during your first year together. Easter is an annual event, however, and his desire to worship is not going to disappear. The strength of his convictions may have been part of his initial attraction for you. If religion is important to you, your willingness to compromise your spirituality or neglect your own rituals will weaken. A relationship is potentially much more harmonious if you both observe the same holidays and don't require compromise in such a significant area.

Occasional compromise is fine, but habitually relinquishing things of great importance is not. For instance, I'm not a sports fan, but I gladly went to baseball games with my partner Johnny because it meant so much to him. Similarly, he accompanied me to the theater, which I dearly love. Compromise in these areas was acceptable to us (although I admit to taking a good book to the game to avoid boredom) because we loved being in each other's company *and because* most *of the time we were engaged in activities that we enjoyed equally.* If we hadn't had common interests, however, our divergent activities might have been more difficult to endure.

Although you may be soul mates with great chemistry, affection, and synchronicity between you, if you are different personality types with little in common, there will be difficulty. If there are only slight differences, with each of you open to change and compromise, the relationship may even be stimulated, revealing fresh, diverse avenues to explore, allowing one to see what the other has experienced in life. In welcoming another person's interests and perspectives, we grow as individuals and the relationship is well served. You needn't surrender what gives you pleasure or defines you personally in order to please another. If you do, it will be a cause for distress and resentment. Differences are inevitable. No two people are exactly alike, and it's the differences that keep life interesting.

Minor differences can create a harmonious balance and an opportunity to learn new skills and abilities. For example, if you are disorganized with money, his methodical approach may assist you in keeping track of the bills. When his skills *enhance* your own, or vice versa, your productivity as a couple expands.

Major Differences Are Dangerous, Not Deadly

In a short-term fling or affair, similarities and differences aren't of much consequence. A long-term relationship, however, involves a great deal of work and endurance under the best of circumstances, so why place more hurdles in your path than necessary? Your energy is better used in creating pleasure and fun. There are no hard-and-fast rules saying how many differences are too many, but constant compromise and accommodation rob you of energy and could tip the scales if you are vacillating or if the relationship is already tenuous.

335

Warning: Values Are Hardest to Compromise

With focus and commitment, differences in background and lifestyle are relatively easy to overcome. Fundamental differences in values and philosophy are another matter. In addition to loving someone, you need to respect him. It is difficult, sometimes impossible, to respect someone who violates your core sense of self. Your values define your innermost being and comprise your essence. Compromise is not advisable in the area of dearly held values. It can be destructive to your spirit as well as to your relationship. If charitable contribution is meaningful to you, you won't be happy with a partner who is stingy and won't tithe a cent. If you take pride in your trustworthiness, you won't respect an undependable partner.

To Angela, a client of mine, truth was paramount. In her regard for honesty, shading of the truth was deception. When asked out on a date, she never said she was busy if she was not. She forthrightly stated her availability, or lack thereof.

Bradley attracted Angela's attention immediately. They went to places they mutually enjoyed, from the symphony to the seashore. Although they hadn't been acquainted as children, it turned out that they had grown up in neighboring towns and had gone to the same schools. Their families had even attended the same church years earlier. They had compatible histories and life experiences.

Angela was excited to find someone whose background was so similar to her own. There was never any tension between them concerning where they were going or where they had been. One day, she was at his house when the phone rang.

"Could you answer that?" Bradley asked. "If it's a guy named Rodney, tell him I'm not home."

"What do you mean you're not home?" Angela replied. "You're standing right here."

"You know what I mean," he told her as the phone rang a second time. "I'm here, but I'm just not here for Rodney."

Angela answered the phone, telling Rodney that Bradley was not there, but that she would be happy to take a message. Afterward, Angela felt awful about lying, even though Bradley later passed it off as a "little white lie, no big deal." This was only the first in a string of "little white lies" that Bradley requested of Angela. He never asked her to blatantly lie on a dramatic scale, but Angela's respect and love for Bradley began to waver as she became resentful of having to compromise her most important value. Moreover, she asked herself, If he could lie so easily to business colleagues, family, and friends, what would prevent him from lying to her someday, if he hadn't already done so?

Never surrender your values in the name of love. It could cost you everything, and, in the end, no one gains. You'll have contempt for yourself and distrust for your partner. Because Bradley was so right for her in so many ways, she sensibly brought him into couples' therapy to address this issue. Eventually, Angela was able to disengage herself from participating in Bradley's "white lies" and, after realizing how vital honesty was to her, he was able to compromise by not enlisting her collusion.

Know What Your Deal Breakers Are

Honesty issues might have been a deal breaker for Angela had Bradley not been willing to work through the issue. Every person has certain issues with which his or her partner must be in alignment, aware that violation of certain principles could terminate the relationship. A Smart Heart woman must know what her deal breakers are, then be willing to spell them out explicitly for her partner.

For me, physical violence, or even the threat of it, is a cause to end a relationship. He may seem to be Mr. Right in every other respect, but one angry shove, hit, or punch, and he's history! Conversely, I can forgive infidelity, if it's a single occurrence and there's a promise that it won't happen again. For other women, the reverse may be true, contingent on their beliefs, values, experience, or background. Your deal breakers are based on your values and past experiences. For example, a woman whose first husband died a lingering death from cancer might feel that she could not again be with a man with a serious illness. Someone who grew up with a history of family depression may not be able to tolerate such a condition in a husband. A deal breaker can be a belief, rather than a condition or action—for example, a man from a different religion not agreeing to raise your children in your chosen faith.

As a Smart Heart woman, apprise your partner of your deal breakers from the outset so you don't ambush him later. Determine what you will or will not tolerate and articulate that to your partner. Other deal breakers may include:

337

▶ Physical or emotional abuse

▶ Alcoholism or substance abuse

▶ Family health history (e.g., genetic conditions or premature death due to heart attack)

▶ Infidelity

▶ Religious conversion or intolerance

▶ Not wanting children

▶ Apathetic or casual attitudes toward divorce

▶ No affinity for animals

▶ Lack of honesty, ethics, or morality

Take a few moments to compile your own list of unacceptable behavior, beliefs, or values in a relationship. The list might be just a single item or it might be quite lengthy. (If it is too long, you may be using these obstacles to prevent involvement at all, something an evolving Smart Heart woman needs to confront honestly.) Once you have your list, tell your partner so that you can discuss it, along with his deal breakers. If Angela had initially told Bradley her strong feelings about "white lies," they might have avoided awkwardness and difficulty earlier in the relationship. She caught him by surprise when she suddenly expressed her resentment and anger several months into the relationship, rather than in the beginning. Bradley valued Angela and the relationship, however, and he was grateful to have the opportunity to rectify their mistakes and accommodate her feelings by making an effort to change.

How to Get the Information and Answers You Need

How do you know what your goals, values, and interests are? What do you and your partner individually bring to the relationship? First, be honest with yourself about what it is that you enjoy, value, believe, and desire. You can then start the mutual-discovery process from the first date onward. You need to be willing to be proactive in this process, rather than just accepting any crumb of information he tosses your way. Observe, listen, and probe until you are comfortable that you have enough information to make a wise and intelligent choice. What does he say and do? Don't accept vague generalities as answers, but gently ask for more specifics. Be inquisitive. Ask friends and family what their perceptions of your partner are. Over time, if he is resistant to revealing himself, discuss this with him. If he continues to withhold from you, move on to someone more honest and open.

Assessing Your Compatibility with Your Partner

I have provided a series of questions to help you discover areas of similarity between you and your partner, along with the differences. This is not a quiz. You won't get a score at the end. These completion statements are simply one way to bring a greater degree of awareness to your relationship.

Even if you do not now have a serious relationship partner, it will be helpful to read these statements so that you can become more conscious of your own values and interests. You can also use this knowledge to determine what a man is passionate about. If you are in a relationship with a potentially serious partner, you may already know where he stands on many of these issues. You do not have to present him with these statements and run down the list line for line, but over time, you can subtly and tactfully obtain the answers you're looking for. They are in the form of "I" statements, so if you are gathering his opinions on these issues, you can change them to "My partner" or "He." Before a Smart Heart woman makes the conscious choice to be with someone long term, she should know the answers to these questions, along with the "touchy" topics presented in the following chapter.

Write down your answers, if you prefer. Be honest with yourself. Pay special attention to the categories that you consider to be deal breakers, those issues on which you are inflexible. If the man you are currently dating has somehow violated your beliefs or disrespects your values, you need to address that with him. If he is not willing to do so, let him go.

Take careful note of the larger discrepancies, as well as the smaller differences between you. It is tempting to avoid the differences, hoping they'll be outweighed by the similarities, but even one major disparity decreases your chances for long-term success. Even if some answers change over time, if you are making a conscious choice about a particular man right now, use the current answers for both of you *right now.* Included after each sentence are sample responses to get you going. The sentences can be answered in many ways. Trust your first impulse, write it down, and let your consciousness flow.

339

Values

1 I believe that honesty _____.
[must be honored at all times, no matter what; is generally a relative concept but is critical in a relationship; is a meaningless word]

2 I believe that reliability _____.
[is the most important attribute in a partner; is pretty important, but no one can always do what he says he will; may be admirable, but the real world constantly gets in the way]

3 I give to charity _____.
[regularly; occasionally; never—I don't believe in it]

4 To me, community means _____.
[knowing those around you and helping them out regularly; waving to your neighbors and helping in an occasional crisis; nothing—I'm completely self-sufficient and only help those in my immediate world]

5 I believe that trust _____.

[is such an important concept that I prefer to trust everyone; is something a person has to earn before receiving; is a self-righteous idea]

6 Fidelity is _____.
[absolutely essential in a trusting relationship; an unrealistic ideal—everyone strays now and then; something to strive for]

7 Loyalty is _____.
[something I demand of others; isn't really important to me; isn't an obligation to be expected of anyone]

8 Open communication with my partner _____.
[is the foundation of all relationships; is a nice ideal, but I don't believe in sharing every single thought or feeling; is an impossible goal—if I want to talk, I call my friends]

9 I believe that physical violence _____.
[is intolerable under any circumstances; is understandable if a person is pushed to it; is a legitimate response when someone is threatened or wronged]

10 My political orientation is _____.
[left; right; nothing, because politics are meaningless outside of Washington]

11 Important values to me are _____.
[home and family; community; religious affiliation and spiritual beliefs; education]

Lifestyle and Interests

1 My idea of a great time is _____.
[staying home, reading and having hot chocolate by the fireplace; going out for dinner and an occasional movie; frequenting nightclubs and staying out late socializing]

2 On the weekends, I wake up _____.
[at dawn; at a reasonably early hour, but not in a rush; by afternoon]

3 Drinking and/or drugs _____.
[are completely acceptable, and I freely indulge in them; are fun and I use them recreationally; are not for me, but I understand why others might use them; are something I cannot tolerate]

4 My approach to eating is: _____.

[I eat only healthful foods. All things in moderation. I don't care what I eat. I love eating anything and all of it.]

5 My approach to exercise is: _____.
[I go to the gym several times a week. I exercise a little. I hate exercising—life is too short.]

6 When it comes to restaurants, _____.
[I love to eat out every night of the week at new and exotic places; I like to eat out occasionally but stick to simple things—fancy is not my style; I prefer home-cooked meals]

7 I love to travel _____.
[to expensive resorts; and camp out in exotic or obscure places; only to visit relatives; not at all, I'm afraid to travel]

8 I participate in or watch sports activities _____.
[all the time—I'm a major fan; on occasion; never, it's torture for me—there are a million other things I would rather do]

9 The hobbies I have _____.
[are solitary activities and occupy a lot of my time; take a moderate amount of time but can be shared with my partner; are none— I work and see friends.]

10 The kind of music I like is _____.
[light jazz or pop; country; classical; rock, alternative, or Top 40]

11 The books I most enjoy are _____.
[the classics; romance novels; mysteries or thrillers; nonfiction; none— I prefer magazines and newspapers]

12 The most adventurous activities I participate in are _____.
(skydiving, scuba diving, bungee jumping, mountain or rock climbing; skiing, boating, and other moderate activities; walking or hiking; none— I'm not really adventurous)

13 I would prefer to live _____.
[in a big city, preferably in an apartment in a downtown area; in a suburban condo or house, perhaps near a city but where I would have privacy and space; in a rural area—perhaps an old farmhouse]

14 I prefer the part of the country that _____.
[is always warm and sunny; has four seasons; is cold; is near mountains; is near the ocean]

⓯ When/if I have children, I'd prefer to _____.
[hire a nanny and return to work immediately; take a few years off and later return to my career; be a stay-at-home mother full-time]

⓰ If my career or my partner's career required us to be in different locations, _____.
[one of us would need to give up his/her career so we could be together; it would be okay to live in separate cities and see each other on weekends; it would be time to talk about splitting up]

⓱ In terms of pets, I prefer to have _____.
[lots of different kinds of animals; a dog or a cat; none—animals are too much responsibility]

⓲ I would prefer a household _____.
[with an "open-door policy," i.e., lots of neighbors, friends, and relatives tromping through; with occasional visitors; that is quiet and private—I want a lot of time without my partner around]

Work Habits and Goals

❶ I view my work as _____.
[something that gives pleasure and meaning to my life; somewhat enjoyable; a necessary evil if I want to eat]

❷ Working long hours or traveling for business _____.
[are things I enjoy doing—I love the fast-paced work life; are things I do on occasion when I have to; are nonissues for me—at five o'clock, I'm on my way home, regardless of what's still on my desk]

❸ Being in business with my relationship partner or working from home
_____.
[would be great—we'd be together all the time; are options we'd have to evaluate carefully; would drive me nuts—I couldn't tolerate so much togetherness—it's important to have separate lives]

❹ My monetary goals when it comes to work are_____.
[to make a lot of money quickly; to earn a decent living, but money isn't everything to me; to have enough so I can pay the rent and buy food]

❺ I hope I can retire _____,
[early—there are so many other things I want to do; at the average age of sixty; never—I want to work forever]

Family Background and Education

1 I come from a background that is best described as _____.
[upper class; middle class; below the poverty line]

2 My family's race is _____.
[one race, never been blended in all the generations; racially mixed; I
don't know much about my ancestry]

3 The household I grew up in was _____.
[quiet—I was an only child with no nearby relatives; bustling with a few
siblings and relatives; so crawling with people we could barely remember one another's names]

4 My childhood was _____.
[extremely happy; typically dysfunctional; miserable and abusive]

5 My education level is _____.
[an advanced degree; college; high school; I never had a change to finish high school]

6 I would like to _____ _____.
[continue my education by taking some training courses; do nothing
further educationally—I'm happy as I am; keep learning]

343

Marriage and Divorce

1 My plans for marriage are _____.
[to tie the knot right away; to eventually marry, but I'm in no great rush;
none—it's just a meaningless institution and I don't believe in marriage.]

2 My view of marriage and divorce is: _____.
[if the marriage doesn't work out, divorce is a viable alternative; I will
work very hard to make it succeed; when I say, "Till death do us part,"
I mean it]

3 My relationship with my mother is _____.
[very close—she's my best friend; okay—we get together for holidays,
but we're not very close; estranged]

4 My relationship with my father is _____.
[very close—I want to marry a man just like him; fairly close—I'll always be "Daddy's little girl"; we never talk or see each other]

⑤ When I think about marriage _____.
[I'm a hopeless romantic—I believe in "happily ever after"; I realize it'll be hard work, but the commitment is worth it; I see it as a business partnership between two individuals; I don't think about it at all—I have other priorities; I don't believe in it]

⑥ If I were married and discovered that my partner had cheated on me

_____.

[I would bear in mind that no one's perfect and I could forgive him; it would indicate a problem in the relationship that we need to solve; I'd divorce the creep immediately; it wouldn't matter at all—I believe in an open relationship and no one person can fulfill all of our needs]

⑦ (If applicable) I have been married before, and that relationship failed because _____.
[my partner was entirely at fault; of me—I blame myself because I didn't try hard enough; we both contributed to its demise, but I've dealt with those mistakes and won't repeat them; it wasn't mean to be]

⑧ (If applicable) I have been married before, and my ex-spouse is some-one whom _____.
[I never see or talk to because it is too painful; I see or talk to occasionally, but only with appropriate boundaries; I see often, and we're still friends]

Children

❶ I want my own children _____.
[more than anything in the world, but if it doesn't work out, I'll survive; not at all]

❷ The number of children I want is _____.
[one; maybe two or three, the average American family; as many as possible]

❸ I'm hoping my partner and I have children _____.
[as soon as we get married; in a few years; the later the better—there is so much more I want to do first]

❹ My parenting style _____.
[is very strict; is fairly lenient, but I believe in discipline and rules; is that the kids should be free and decide for themselves]

5 (If applicable) I have children already, and I feel that my partner

_____.

[loves them as his own; tolerates them, but I'm not sure he loves them; would prefer that I didn't have kids at all]

6 (If applicable) I have children already, and in relation to my partner they

_____.

[love him like a true parent; have some reservations, but we all are working on it; hate my partner]

7 (If applicable) We both have children and they get along _____.
[really well, like natural siblings; pretty well—like most kids, they have their moments when they do and don't get along; badly—they can't stand each other, there's a lot of anger and resentment]

For a Smart Heart woman, when it comes to compatibility:

▶ The best relationships are based on a variety of shared interests, values, viewpoints, and preferences.

▶ Small differences can expand and enhance your life.

▶ A large number of differences (even one or two major ones) can signify trouble and must be consciously addressed before you make a major commitment.

▶ Differences in values are the hardest to overcome.

▶ If the differences are insurmountable, this may not be the right partner for you.

▶ Even one difference you consider a deal breaker may warrant ending the relationship.

▶ With commitment, communication, and perhaps outside coaching, you may be able to resolve many, if not all, of your problem areas and have a happy, long-lasting partnership.

15

Touchy Topics

B efore you can know if you and your partner are truly compatible, you must evaluate your thoughts and beliefs on five potentially touchy topics: sex, money, spirituality/religion, health, and family/in-laws. These are tough topics to talk about. If you want to make the most carefully considered partnering choices, you must broach these touchy subjects with your potential partner as early in the relationship as possible. As a Smart Heart woman, you need not completely agree with your partner on all these topics, but you should understand where he stands on them to determine if his beliefs, values, and ideas are reconcilable with yours.

Assuming you have been dating a man for a while and have been consciously assessing his appropriateness for you, some of these issues may have come out in the natural course of conversation and spending time with him. You will probably need to delve deeper to discover the subtle variations on these key questions. For instance, you wouldn't ask "Do you like sex?" but "In what positions?" "How often? More in the morning or evening?" You wouldn't just ask "Do you go to church?" but rather "Would you want our child to be baptized?" You wouldn't ask "How much do you earn a year?" but rather "How do you manage your money? Is it important to save for the future, or would you rather spend it as you make it?" You wouldn't ask "Will we be seeing your parents at Thanksgiving?" but "Will your mother move in with us if your elderly, ill father passes away?"

These are not issues you want him to spring on you months or years after you have been involved in a committed relationship with him. It is important for you to address these issues with your partner early on before they erupt nine months or nine years later to cause serious conflict and possibly irreversible damage.

Differences in These Areas Need Not Be Deal Breakers

As with the values and lifestyle questions detailed in the previous chapter, differences in these areas need not derail a Smart Heart woman's relationship. You may not like the idea of your mother-in-law moving in with you someday, or that he owes $10,000 to the IRS, but by asking pointed questions, you will be better informed and able to decide if you can live with these realities before you commit to the relationship. The question then becomes: Can you live with these differences? Do they conflict with or complement your beliefs and needs? By discussing them, you can start to find out how you really feel. Knowing sooner, rather than later, if your differences are too great to overcome will enable you to release your man from the relationship and move onto someone more suitable for you.

347

If you ignore the differences, they will not go away. Differences in beliefs require honest discussion and commitment to understanding and compromise. You become a Smart Heart woman by working through these touchy topics with your potential partner. Then, you can mutually design a path leading to a satisfying and fulfilling long-lasting relationship.

Be prepared for some of his answers to surprise you. You might assume that if he had salient or relevant comments to make, he would have made them a long time ago, but many men don't reveal personal or emotional issues without coaxing. One client of mine, Jodi, told me that her fiancé, Richard, didn't reveal a family history of suicide until a month before their wedding. His father committed suicide, as did his older brother and uncle. She felt as if he had been hiding something or was keeping secrets from her. Most men, including Richard, can't figure out how to say something so difficult unless someone or something forces the issue.

How can you get your partner to open up about his thoughts, feelings, and opinions on these touchy topics without making him feel pressured or uncomfortable? Below are important questions in each category based upon discussions with numerous women, in both relationships that have worked and those that did not. Use them to guide your conversations with your partner, and add your own questions to the list. If it will help you clarify your thoughts before you undertake such a discussion, feel free to write in the blank spaces provided at the end of each list.

Important Tips for Discussing Touchy Topics with Your Partner

1 Don't force him to respond to every single question.

2 Bring up each topic one at a time, or at various moments when you are comfortable, have privacy, and have time to talk without interruption.

3 Open up conversations by talking about yourself first, using "I" statements, as discussed in earlier chapters; for example, explain how you feel about wealth, and then ask him how he feels about it.

4 Venture deeply into any topics that are particularly troublesome or important to you; for example, "Do you like to use sex toys in bed? Do you like to do that all the time or just occasionally?"

5 Tell him how you feel about his answers; for example, "Occasionally I like to experiment with somebody I trust, but I would prefer to let things just happen naturally. Maybe we could talk about specific things you enjoy and figure out what we would both like." Then see how he responds.

6 Be sure to have detailed discussions about each of these sensitive topics.

If you are not comfortable with the answers to these questions, you need to keep talking with him about them. If you can't find a middle ground, seek professional help. If you still can't reach a resolution, you need to let him go and find someone who shares your views.

If, however, in incorporating the Smart Heart Partnering Process into your relationship you've determined that you are in sync on most of these touchy topics, you just may have found a man who is right for you. If that is the case, you can feel confident that you have made a conscious, wise, and aware partner selection.

Touchy Topic #1: Sex

Without a doubt, a frank discussion of sex is as difficult for most of us to have with our partner as it was for our parents to have with us! It's a topic men feel extremely vulnerable about.

A caveman's worth may have been determined by how many saber-toothed tigers he could kill, but a modern male's sexual exploits serve as a primary way to gauge his masculinity. Let a man know you want to discuss his sex life and he is liable to run for cover, fearing that you might judge him or his personal prowess. Because a man can be quite vulnerable and sensitive, an insensitive woman can easily emasculate him. Offering a hint of disappointment with a man's anatomy or performance is enough to deflate his sense of sexual power, even to the degree that arousal or potency becomes difficult.

Why risk misunderstanding? Discussion is important, because making fully conscious choices in your relationships has to include being sure you are sexually compatible. Sex is vital to a romantic, long-term relationship. Research studies on sex and marriage verify that a robust sex life is an indicator of a healthy marriage, whereas couples with dissonant beliefs on sexual practices or timetables are known to have a higher divorce rate.

When one partner has a constant craving for sex and the other couldn't care less, or if a man can't find his way to the bedroom where his mate languidly lounges in lacy lingerie, tension and misunderstanding result. This is especially true when a woman loves sex more than her partner does (the stereotype notwithstanding, this frequently happens!). Women tend to let men be the initiators, so a woman who wants to make love all the time but who waits for her man to make a move will feel frustrated and unhappy.

If sex with your partner is not satisfying, you need to share your feelings with him—not in an accusatory fashion but in a calm, delicate manner. Often, men don't understand that women need more than a little quick foreplay to enjoy sex fully. They need tender words, lots of romance, and attention to the rest of the relationship. The following questions can reveal some important answers. Feel free to add any questions that pertain to your interests and sexual preferences and be honest.

Sexual Matters

▸ How often do you like to have sex, and how long do you like a typical lovemaking session to last?

▸ What are your favorite ways to have sex?

▸ What words would you use to describe your typical lovemaking session (e.g., *tender, rough, energetic, slow,* etc.)?

▸ What are some of your sexual fantasies? Would you enjoy acting out any of those fantasies?

▸ What is the most "on the edge" behavior you would ever participate in?

▸ What would you absolutely, positively, never, ever do with your partner?

▸ How do you feel about sex toys and other aids?

▸ How do you feel about sex with more than one person or with someone other than your relationship partner?

▸ How much do you want to know about your partner's sexual history?

▸ Are you aroused by your partner's looks, smells, tastes, touch, and kisses?

Touchy Topic #2: Money

Money is the other topic, along with sex, about which men are extremely uncomfortable. When they aren't judging themselves by their lovemaking abilities, men measure their accomplishments by the kind of car they drive or the amount of money in their investment portfolios. Never ask a man directly "How much are you worth?" He will either decide that you are a gold digger out for his money or fear that he compares unfavorably to someone else (this is true whether he makes $30,000 a year or $30,000,000!).

After a significant time spent dating a man, you can cleverly ask how much money the two of you might have if you combine your finances. One way to do this is to volunteer your side of the financial equation first, by revealing information about business investments or financial worth.

If your financial situation is more solid or promising than your potential partner's, be sensitive in exploring this frontier. Many men feel threatened or inadequate when their wives are more financially successful than they are. Financial disparity can lessen the odds for marital success.

One of my clients, Kathryn, found that her relationship partner was so threatened by her successful business that she closed its doors to stay with him. Kathryn was used to wearing $1,000 designer suits and getting $100 haircuts, a lifestyle she was hesitant to give up when she ended her business for Zack. He was a gorgeous hunk whom she loved, and she thought that, magically, his construction business, which hadn't fared well, would be able to support her in the same style. Zack wanted to provide her with the things she was used to, but for all his love and intentions, he could not. Monetary tensions soon started to tear the relationship apart. Kathryn came crying to my office.

She began to use the Smart Heart Partnering Process and realized that she had not consciously thought through her decision to close down her business for the sake of the relationship. Her heartbreak and resentment might have been avoided had she been more aware of his inability to support her financially in the style to which she was accustomed. If both of them had been able to communicate their needs and discern how each could contribute to meeting those needs, she might still be with Zack. By not utilizing her usual business acumen, Kathryn sacrificed her entire enterprise without discussing the situation in a rational, adult manner. It cost her not only her business but her relationship as well.

In order to become a Smart Heart woman, you must consciously think through the implications of your partner's financial position and his future prospects. Make your relationship decisions with the knowledge of whether or not you can be happy with the reality of his situation, or if you must compromise and/or adjust your needs.

Money Matters

▶ Who in the relationship should be the primary moneymaker? How would you feel if the other person earned more?

▶ Do you want or need your spouse to work?

▶ Would you co-mingle funds and pay all bills out of one joint account or maintain separate accounts?

▶ What is your present financial worth?

▶ Where do you see your financial situation in five or ten years? Could you be happy living on a moderate income if it worked out that way?

▶ Who would be in charge of the finances, you or your partner?

▶ What are your major financial obligations? Do you owe anyone—e.g., the IRS, a relative, a credit card company—a substantial amount of money?

▶ Are you comfortable taking on debt?

▶ How do you like to invest your money—in a risky offshore venture, the stock market, a savings account or IRA?

▶ Do you live according to your income? Are you frugal or do you over-spend? Do you presume you'll always be solvent? What if unforeseen events alter your present situation?

My father thought money was _____.

My mother thought money was _____.

My partner thinks money is _____.

I think money is _____.

Touchy Topic #3: Spirituality and Religion

Religious convictions are generally formed by dragging children to a house of worship; they subsequently rebel as teenagers, then rediscover their faith as adults. After having children of their own, parents drag them to church, and the pattern repeats itself through the generations.

Creating a family causes many people to rethink their approach to re-ligion. With a Jewish husband and children, Friday nights formerly reserved for movies and pizza suddenly may become dedicated to sacred Shabbat rit-uals. With a Catholic or Protestant mate, Sunday mornings may no longer be for sleeping in but for going to an early mass or church service.

Just because your relationship partner might not be presently practic-ing a religious or spiritual ritual doesn't mean that he doesn't have thoughts or convictions about the role he wants religion and spirituality to play in his future family life. You must question your partner and search beyond his habits and current actions to discover the core of his beliefs.

Religious or Spiritual Preferences

▶ What are your and your partner's religious and spiritual preferences, and how will they affect your relationship and your children? How ob-servant are you?

► Would you want to be married in a religious ceremony? Which denomination?

► Which holidays and rituals would you want your family to observe, and how do you want to observe them?

► Do you want to be actively involved in a church, synagogue, or other organized religion?

► What religious or spiritual experiences do you want to provide for your children?

► In which religious ceremonies or rituals would you want your children to participate—e.g., baptism, circumcision, communion, bar mitzvah?

► What kind of religious education would you desire for your children?

► If you aren't religious, do you consider yourself spiritual? How does that manifest itself?

► (If relevant) Would you feel comfortable if your children attended your partner's place of worship, assuming it's different from your own?

► (If relevant) Would you feel comfortable having symbols from your partner's religion in your house—a Christmas tree if you are Jewish, say, or a statue of Buddha if you are Catholic?

353

Touchy Topic #4: Health

A Smart Heart woman involved with a man with health problems must be clear that those problems will probably not go away and may, in fact, worsen as your man ages. One always hopes for a miracle, but don't engage in any kind of unrealistic, wishful thinking when planning your life. To a certain extent, you need to be prepared for a life as a caretaker. If you aren't ready to do that, you should lovingly release your man so he can find someone who is willing to take on that obligation. If your partner has a severe or life-threatening illness, you may still choose to be his partner; just be clear about the implications of that decision and how it will affect your life.

Health issues aren't static. Health is an ongoing state of mind and body. Major health problems can unexpectedly arise at any time. You can't know what the future holds for your or your partner's health. Still, a man with a family history of stroke or heart attack is a more likely candidate for one than someone whose family tree rivals the ancient redwoods in longevity. If you don't think you can handle the role of caretaker (perhaps you grew up in a house where a parent had a disabling illness), it is better to be clear about that before you get involved with a man with a high risk of serious health concerns. On the other hand, you may consciously decide that you are ready, willing, and able to handle such a situation should it arise or that you can be of loving service to your partner in existing circumstances.

Genetic makeup is another consideration if you are planning to have children. If your partner's gene pool contains a possibility of schizophrenia, dwarfism, Down's syndrome, or any other serious condition, it could turn up in your own children. This isn't necessarily something to run away from, but a Smart Heart woman making clear and conscious partnership choices needs such information to make an informed decision.

Health Watch

- ▶ Do you have AIDS or another life-threatening illness?
- ▶ Do you have any medical conditions that require special care now or later?
- ▶ Does your family history include debilitating diseases, such as stroke, cancer, diabetes, etc.?
- ▶ Do you have any conditions that might cause infertility?
- ▶ Do you have a family history of alcoholism, substance abuse, or eating disorders?
- ▶ Are you or any family members prone to severe depression or mental illness?
- ▶ Has anyone in your family committed suicide?
- ▶ Is there a familial genetic condition that you could pass on to your children?
- ▶ Is there a family history of long life?
- ▶ If they're deceased, what did your grandparents or parents die from?
- ▶ If I developed a serious health condition, do you think you would be able to take care of me?

Touchy Topic #5: Future In-Laws

Mother-in-law jokes abound, but for the couple who has to deal with intrusive or controlling in-laws or parents, it isn't a laughing matter. When you marry a man, you marry his family, and problematic parents become problematic in-laws.

Before you run for cover, *remember* that there is no difficulty that can't be overcome if both partners are willing to work on it. If his parents want to control his life, don't respect you, are overbearing or excessively needy, harmony can be reached as long as your mate is willing to set boundaries. If he is unable or unwilling to do this, a Smart Heart woman must clearly relay the message that his parents are going to be a major problem in the relationship. You must decide if that is acceptable in your life, and your partner must decide how to deal with it.

His parents may keep an appropriate distance until children arrive, at which point they may want to race over every ten minutes to tell you how best to raise your kids. A Smart Heart woman should observe how her partner's parents behave around siblings who have children and make the assumption that they will act the same way with her children.

Life spans are increasing, and if his parents are elderly or ill they might require your care. What is the status of your own parents' health? If his parents are deceased or not a part of his life, you need to consider that your children won't have grandparents if your own parents are no longer alive. None of these issues is necessarily a deal breaker, but a woman making conscious partnering choices needs to consider the answers to these questions carefully.

Family Affairs

▶ Do his parents send him money, call him several times a day, or make major decisions about his life? Will that continue after you get married or move in together?

▶ Is he willing to set appropriate boundaries for his parents' involvement in your lives? If he cannot (some people can't until their parents die), a variety of problems may arise.

▶ Do both his and your parents respect your privacy?

▶ Are his parents overbearing with other siblings and their children?

▶ Are his parents truly happy about his relationship with you, or are they jealous that you are "stealing" their son away?

▶ Have you spent enough time with his parents (and he with yours) to assess the family you're entering?

355

▶ Does he come from a large family, and, if so, can you feel comfortable spending holidays and other times with such a brood? If he comes from a small family where holiday gatherings will be sparse and quiet, how does this compare or conflict with your vision of holidays?

▶ Do you plan on taking one or both of your parents into your home or paying for their nursing care if they become infirm? How does he feel about that?

▶ Does he envision taking one or both of his parents into your home or paying for their nursing care if they become infirm? How do you feel about that?

▶ Are his parents alive? If so, does he maintain regular contact with them? (This will affect whether or not you can count on in-laws or grandparents as a resource in your lives.)

By asking these questions, you open up the lines of communication between the two of you—forming the basis for a stronger relationship. Also, by asking these questions early in the relationship you allow yourself to make a commitment with your eyes wide open and won't be taken by surprise down the road.

Conclusion:
Using the Power of
Your Choices Wisely:
Stop, Look, and Listen

Your relationship choices profoundly affect the lives of you and your children (if you have any). You can be fulfilled at work and happy with your friends and family, but if you have made a poor relationship choice, you can count on being miserable. I cannot stress too emphatically the importance of awareness and conscious intent in taking responsibility for your partner selections, not to mention the power and peace you will discover when you stop being a martyr, quit manipulating men to try to get your needs met, and stop using seduction as a way to control your partner. There is no white knight coming to rescue you! **You, and you alone, are responsible for protecting yourself from further heartache, disappointment, or relationship disaster.** Getting smart with your heart requires that you expand your awareness and understanding so that you can choose more wisely. As you engage your head, you will begin to develop a deeper understanding of your own motivations, desires, and needs. By being aware of what you want, and consciously defining and designing your relationship objectives, you will save precious time, money, and energy and be able to circumvent costly relationship mistakes.

By reading this book and doing the exercises, you have planted within your own consciousness seeds to make love and proactive partnerships grow. My prayer for you is that, starting today, you:

- ▶ Stop indulging in magical thinking and rid yourself of sexual impulsiveness and unrealistic romantic expectations.

- ▶ Start using your head, along with your heart, to make more rewarding, responsible, and fulfilling partnership choices.

- ▶ Begin to design your relationship objectives and start implementing them today.

If you are currently in a long-term relationship, you've probably already discovered how the Smart Heart Partnering Process has deepened your present understanding of your mate and helped increase your capacity for compassion and tolerance for both yourself and your partner. If you're looking for a prospective mate or date, the more you use the process, the better you will become at recognizing problematic partnerships before you leap into them. You will be more adept at initiating conversations that further your evaluation and understanding of the man you are dating, and you will be able to look with clarity while consciously listening and observing his responses.

If, during this process, you've discovered you've made a bad bet—uncovered issues and habits that you know now will adversely affect your ability to manifest a loving relationship—I strongly recommend that you seek professional help or coaching to assist you in changing your negative and destructive relationship patterns so that you can release him quickly. If you insist on continually dragging mistakes from the past into your present relationship, you can create only a negatively recurring future. Remember that you deserve the best, and in order to have it, you must commit to freeing yourself from demoralizing habits, images, and ideas that inhibit your ability to create positive, proactive relationships.

There are no guarantees, but you can greatly increase your odds of success.

No matter how aware, awake, or diligent you are, there are no guarantees that things are going to work out the way you want when you want them to. The Smart Heart Partnering Process will help you learn to lay the groundwork for success. You need to commit to it and put it into practice. If it doesn't work out the way you want this time, don't quit. Keep trying, and keep in mind that it is progress, not perfection, you are seeking.

Although life, by definition, is difficult, we can overcome most obstacles if we persevere. I tell clients that rejection is God's protection and redirection. Relationships are no exception. To reap the rewards of a satisfying, intimate partnership, you must be willing to take risks and a leap of faith. Knowledge is power. The more you use the Smart Heart information and process, the greater the odds of your ultimate relationship success.

You can utilize the Smart Heart Partnering Process over the course of your lifetime. Your lifestyle preferences, economic circumstances, and objectives will change as you mature. What we long for at the age of twenty will be vastly different from what seek at thirty, forty, or fifty. Even if we start out in the best of relationships, we often grow apart because of our personal evolution. This is not a failing; it is a process. It can never be wrong to share our love with each other, to learn and grow. We may have learned and experienced all we could from a particular relationship. When you end long-term relationships, it's important that you don't beat yourself up about it or feel as if you've failed, particularly if you have tried your best. Sometimes what you have come together for is done, the gift has been given, the lesson learned. When the relationship is finished, we need to be able to recognize when it's time to let go and to move on.

One of my clients, Nancy, was an executive in her thirties who married an equally driven career man who didn't want children. Nancy agreed that they would never have kids, but eleven years into the marriage she changed her mind. She was a successful vice president at Disney and now felt she wanted a child. Her husband was furious.

"How dare she change her mind after we both agreed on this!" Barry adamantly shouted in my office. "If she wanted children, she should have said so up front and not ambushed me so many years into our relationship!"

From her viewpoint, Nancy hadn't "ambushed" him at all. When she had agreed not to have children, she thought it was what she truly wanted. Over time, however, she developed a deep desire for a family. Nonetheless, Barry felt completely betrayed. After coming to couples therapy, he became aware that Nancy wasn't trying to trap or trick him but that her feelings had changed as she matured. Although Barry didn't want their lives to change with the addition of a child, he didn't want to lose Nancy, either. He made a concession to support her decision even though it wasn't his first choice. He decided he could lovingly and generously give his wife the child she wanted. Eventually Barry grew to love their child in ways he could not have imagined possible.

As you become a Smart Heart woman like Nancy, and while you do ongoing footwork, you will recognize that your and your partner's present needs and wants (physical, mental, spiritual, and emotional) will likely change as time passes. It is important for you to be conscious of the lifestyle you are currently creating but to remain open to change if your life takes an unexpected turn. You can expand your thinking without necessarily altering your core beliefs or morals. The Smart Heart Partnering Process will allow you to continually reevaluate yourself, your man, and your relationship so that you both can be engaged in ongoing growth and development.

You can count on having to take more than one risk before creating the kind of relationship that you want. In a study of successful men and women whose businesses had earned more than a million dollars per annum, a common thread was revealed. It was not their level of education, energy level, family background, or personality types, but two major things:

1. They experienced an average of 3.5 failures and/or bankruptcies before they created their million-dollar company.

2. They were willing to embrace risk and be comfortable with it.

Even a prepared, awake, and aware Smart Heart woman knows, in the final analysis, that it's the willingness to take the risk and to make the first step that gets you where you're going.

The following is a handy reference guide for reminding yourself of the key Smart Heart components.

Now that you are a Smart Heart woman, each time you are approached by a new man, you will always:

1. Decide (know what you want)

2. Design (have a plan of action to move toward your goal)

3. Declare (tell him what you want)

4. Act (take action to get what you want)

5. Risk (be willing to take a leap of faith)

6. Practice (practice, practice, practice—you can never fail if you never quit)

7. Start over (if you aren't satisfied, begin again—you haven't failed, you're in transition, experiencing a delay in reaching your destination)

These tools and techniques are valuable only if you use them. Remember, the more you practice, the better you become. As you continue on your path of relationship evolution, keep in mind:

1. It's your job this lifetime to be the best you can be, whether you are in a relationship or not.

Celebrate your own magnificence daily. You are a unique, desirable woman who doesn't *need* a man for financial support or even to have children. Create your own fulfilling life so that you can find your own happiness. The person who benefits most from an expansive, expressive life is you. If your life is fascinating to you, it will be fascinating to a prospective date or partner. Dating different men can help you learn a tremendous amount about yourself. Use the process of dating to find not only a lifetime partner but also something infinitely more valuable—a greater sense of self.

2. If it's "no," let him go.

Don't aimlessly wander from one man to another. Don't stay in any relationship for the wrong reasons or let him determine the course of the relationship. Take charge of your romantic life. If a man is a bad bet, let him go. If he doesn't want to be married or in a long-term relationship and you do, let him go. If you feel pressured, anxious, or pushed into commitment, slow down and take another look at your needs in the relationship.

3. Practice getting out of relationships.

Women are great at getting into relationships and terrible at getting out of them. Take the initiative to end a bad relationship instead of staying in one you know isn't right. *Practice* so you can strengthen your resolve. If you can't get out on your own, be willing to get professional help.

4. Don't settle for anything less than your relationship objective.

A wonderful man who shares your goals, values, and interests is out there waiting for you and wants to give you the happiness that you deserve. Going after a guy simply because you want to be married or are afraid of being alone is selling your soul short. You are too important for that. *Love only those who are capable of loving you,* those who can accept and return your love in the way you need and want to be loved.

5. Men are visually oriented.

Before a man will open his heart, he needs to be visually and physically attracted to you. What usually attracts a man sexually is a healthy, fit, and vibrant physical body. Some women believe that after they are secure in a

361

relationship, they don't need to maintain their appearance or health because their partner should love them for who they are inside, not for their bodies. Men need to be physically desirous of you in order to remain interested over the long haul. Not only will you benefit by maintaining your health and physical fitness, but you will also be able to keep his interest, excitement, and the sexual vibrations strong for a more energetic connection with your partner.

6. Determine if he is a Knight, Prince, or King (and if you are a Maiden, Princess, or Queen).

Your own developmental stage in life greatly affects your expectations of what you want and need from your partner. Where a man is, developmentally, significantly influences what he is capable of giving and where his life focus will be. By evaluating whether he is a Knight, a Prince, or a King, you'll discover if he can really give you what you want.

7. Understand the distinct roles of the three forces of love and how they impact your ability to see clearly.

Feeling sexually and erotically attracted to a man is wonderful, but mature, adult love is a conscious decision. When we love consciously, we choose to act in loving ways toward our romantic partners even if we don't *feel* like it. If you don't use will and intellect, the erotic force and great sex will quickly fade. With love as the catalyst, you can keep the flame alive for a thousand lifetimes.

8. Be conscious about what distorted images, ideas, and beliefs you may have acquired from your family of origin and/or primary caretakers.

We all carry unconscious expectations from childhood about men and relationships. When we choose to bring submerged images into conscious awareness, we are able to make our own choices and not be unconsciously victimized by our parents' mistakes.

9. If you are looking for a long-term relationship, don't jump in the sack.

Stop falling in love and then into bed on the first or second date. Continue to enjoy great sex and feel the pleasure of this God-given gift, but don't allow your physical needs to ruin your ability to evaluate clearly who your man really is.

10. Stay away from Bad Boys and Bad Bets.

There are plenty of Bad Boys in the world, and even the smartest, most

362

sophisticated women have been seduced by them. Don't dismiss signs that your man may be a Bad Bet. Heed your intuition. If you can't hear your inner voice, pay attention to the warnings of friends and family. In extreme cases, find a good personal investigator to double-check those gut instincts. You can't change him, and you will end up only hurting yourself, if he doesn't beat you to it.

11. Become more knowledgeable about your own personality type, both the good and the not-so-good qualities.

The ways you see and react to the world have tremendous bearing on how you manage relationships. Use the Personal/Partner Profiler to learn how you relate to the world. Take the steps necessary to help you further evolve and mature within your personality type to be the best that you can be.

12. Get his number, and get it quickly!

Obtain a clearer understanding of his personality type so that you can understand and head off conflicts your two styles might create. Remember, knowledge is power. The more you know why your partner behaves in a certain way, the less likely you are to take things personally or become resentful or upset.

13. Search for the common ground between you.

Remember, the greater the similarities, interests, values, and goals you share, the better the odds for a successful relationship. It's not old-fashioned for you to look for someone whose lifestyle and background are like yours. Doing so will make living with him easier than having to overcome major barriers in order just to be with each other. Life is easier when you have to work hard only *outside* the home.

14. Be willing to talk about touchy topics.

It can be tough to talk about money, sex, health, spirituality, and in-laws, but it is mandatory. These issues will never go away. If you wait to discover your differences haphazardly or negotiate them only after getting seriously involved or married, your relationship may not survive.

15. Know what your deal breakers are.

Make the distinction between deal breakers and differences. Minor differences usually can be worked out by being flexible and loving, through compromise or therapy. Deal breakers are beliefs, ideas, actions, or attitudes that are non-negotiable. A deal breaker will take you past your point of no return. Know what you will and will not tolerate, and be willing to tell your partner your limits. Resolve not to stay with a man who violates your principles.

16. Risk, risk, risk, and practice, practice, practice.

If you make a mistake, keep moving forward. You are looking for **progress, not perfection.** Be gentle, forgiving, and compassionate with yourself, and be willing to try again. Persistence and fortitude are valuable assets for reaching your relationship objectives.

17. HAVE FUN!

The most important thing for you to remember is that it's the journey, not the destination, that counts. Set your course and enjoy the ride! God bless, and *go for it!*

Bibliography

Resources on Relationships and Love

Anand, Margo. *The Art of Sexual Ecstasy.* Los Angeles: Jeremy Tarcher, 1989.

Arrien, Angeles. "Power and Love in Relationships" (audiotape). Sounds True Catalog, 735 Walnut St., Boulder, CO 80302; 1-800-333-9185.

Bloomfield, Harold. *Lifemates.* New York: Plume, 1989.

———. *Love Secrets for a Lasting Relationship.* New York: Bantam, 1992.

Branden, Nathaniel. *If You Could Hear What I Cannot Say.* New York: Bantam, 1983.

———. *The Six Pillars of Self-Esteem.* New York: Bantam, 1994.

Corn, Laura. *237 Intimate Questions Every Woman Should Ask a Man.* Oklahoma City: Park Avenue Publishers, 1993.

Crenshaw, Theresa L. *The Alchemy of Love and Lust.* New York: Putnam, 1996.

Dym, Barry, Ph.D., and Michael L. Glenn, M.D. *Couples.* New York: HarperCollins, 1993.

Estes, Clarissa Pinkola, Ph.D. "How to Love a Woman: On Intimacy and the Erotic Life of Women" (audiotape). Sounds True Catalogue, 735 Walnut St., Boulder, CO 80302; 1-800-333-9185.

Fishman, Barbara, Ph.D., and Laurie Ashner. *Resonance.* San Francisco: HarperSanFrancisco, 1994.

Fossum, Mavis, and Merle Fossum. *The More We Find in Each Other.* New York: HarperCollins, 1992.

Godek, Gregory. *1001 Ways to Be Romantic.* Boston: Casablanca Press, 1993.

Gordon, Lori H., and Jon Frandsen. *Passage to Intimacy.* New York: Simon & Schuster, 1993.

Gray, John, Ph.D. *Men Are from Mars, Women Are from Venus*. New York: HarperCollins, 1992.

Hazelden Foundation. *Seasons of the Heart*. San Francisco: HarperSanFrancisco, 1993.

Hendrix, Harville. *Getting the Love You Want: A Guide for Couples*. New York: Pocket, 1988.

———. *Keeping the Love You Find: A Guide for Singles*. New York: Pocket, 1992.

———. "Marriage as a Path to Wholeness" (audiotape). Sounds True Catalog, 735 Walnut St., Boulder, CO 80302; 1-800-333-9185.

Houghton, Alanson R. *Partners in Love*. New York: Walker, 1988.

Jampolsky, Gerald, M.D., and Diane Cirincione. "Holy Relationship: Healing Together" (audiotape). New Dimensions Radio, P.O. Box 410510, San Francisco, CA 94141-0510; 415-563-8899.

Johnson, Catherine. *Lucky in Love: The Secrets of Happy Couples and How Their Marriages Survived*. New York: Pocket, 1992.

Johnson, Robert. *We*. San Francisco: Harper & Row, 1983.

Keith, Staci. *Drive Your Woman Wild in Bed*. New York: Warner, 1994.

Kingma, Daphne Rose. *The Men We Never Knew*. Berkeley: Conari Press, 1993.

———. *True Love: How to Make Your Relationship Sweeter, Deeper, and More Passionate*. Berkeley: Conari Press, 1991.

Lerner, Harriet. *Dance of Intimacy*. New York: HarperCollins, 1988.

Lugaila, Terry. "Marital Status and Living Arrangements." U. S. Bureau of the Census report, March 1997.

Mayer, Anne. *How to Stay Lovers While Still Raising Your Children*. Los Angeles: Price Stern Sloan, 1990.

Moore, Thomas. *Care of the Soul*. New York: HarperCollins, 1992.

———. *Soul Mates: Honoring the Mysteries of Love and Relationship*. New York: Harper Perrenial, 1994.

Osherson, Samuel, Ph.D. *Wrestling with Love: How Men Struggle with Intimacy with Women, Children, Parents, and Each Other*. New York: Fawcett, 1992.

Pearson, Judy C. *Lasting Love*. Dubuque, IA: W. C. Brown, 1992.

Person, Ethel S. *Dreams of Love and Fateful Encounters*. New York: Penguin, 1988.

Pintar, Judith. *The Halved Soul*. London: HarperCollins, 1992.

Powell, John. *The Secret of Staying in Love*. Valencia, CA: Tabor, 1974.

————. *Unconditional Love.* Allen, TX: Argus Communications, 1978.

Prather, Hugh, and Gayle Prather. *A Book for Couples.* New York: Doubleday, 1988.

Rich, Penny. *Pamper Your Partner.* New York: Simon & Schuster, 1990.

Ross, William Ashoka. *The Wonderful Little Sex Book.* Berkeley: Conari Press, 1991.

Simring, Sue Klavans, D.S.W., and Steven S. Simring, M.D., with William Proctor. *The Compatibility Quotient.* New York: Fawcett Columbine, 1990.

Stanway, Dr. Andrew. *The Art of Sensual Loving.* New York: Carroll & Graf, 1989.

U.S. Bureau of the Census. *Marital Status and Living Arrangements.* March 1997 (update) and June 30, 1998.

Welwood, John, Ph.D. *Journey of the Heart.* New York: HarperCollins. 1990.

Wolf, Sharyn. *Guerrilla Dating Tactics: Strategies, Tips, and Secrets for Finding Romance.* New York: Plume, 1993.

Resources on the Enneagram

Baron, Renee, and Elizabeth Wagele. *Are You My Type, Am I Yours?: Relationships Made Easy Through the Enneagram.* San Francisco: HarperSanFrancisco, 1995.

————. *The Enneagram Made Easy: Discover the 9 Types of People.* San Francisco: HarperSanFrancisco, 1994.

Brady, Loretta. *Beginning Your Enneagram Journey.* Allen, TX: Tabor Publishing, 1994.

Coates, Mona, Ph.D., and Ed Jacobs, M.Ed. "Battle Between the Sexes" (audiotape). Coates-Jacobs Personality Services, Intl.

————. "Discover Your Personality Type: Coates-Jacob Enneagram Survey." Coates-Jacobs Personality Services, Intl., 1995.

Elbert, Andreas, ed. *Experiencing the Enneagram.* New York: Crossroad, 1992.

Hurley, Kathleen V., and Theodore Dobson. *My Best Self: Using the Enneagram to Free the Soul.* San Francisco: HarperSanFrancisco, 1993.

————. *What's My Type?* San Francisco: HarperSanFrancisco, 1992.

Keyes, Margaret Frings. *The Enneagram Relationship Workbook.* Muir Beach, CA: Molysdatur Publications, 1992.

Naranjo, Claudio. *Character and Neurosis.* Nevada City, CA: Gateways, 1994.

————. *Ennea-Type Structures.* Nevada City, CA: Gateways, 1990.

————. *Enneatypes in Psychotherapy.* Prescott, AZ: Hohm Press, 1995.

Palmer, Helen. *The Enneagram.* San Francisco: HarperSanFrancisco, 1991.

————. *The Enneagram in Love & Work.* San Francisco: HarperSanFrancisco, 1995.

Richards, John. *The Illustrated Enneagram* Huntington Beach, CA: Horizon Nine Keys Publishing, 1994.

Riso, Don Richard. *Discovering Your Personality Type.* Boston: Houghton Mifflin, 1995.

————. *Enneagram Transformations.* Boston: Houghton Mifflin, 1993.

————. *Understanding the Enneagram.* Boston: Houghton Mifflin, 1987.

————. *The Wisdom of the Enneagram.* New York: Bantam, 1999.

————. *Working with the Enneagram.* New York: McGraw-Hill, 1999.

————. "The Power of the Enneagram" (audiotape). Nightingale Conant, Simon & Schuster.

Riso, Don Richard, with Russ Hudson. *Personality Types: Using the Enneagram for Self-Discovery.* Boston: Houghton Mifflin, 1996.

Rohr, Richard, and Andreas Ebert. *Discovering the Enneagram.* New York: Crossroad Publishing, 1990.

Resources on Personal Growth and Transformation

Baldwin, Christina. *Life's Companion: Journal Writing as a Spiritual Quest.* New York: Bantam, 1990.

Blatner, Adam, and Allee Blatner. *The Art of Play.* New York: Human Science Press, 1988.

Burt, Bernard. *Healthy Escapes.* New York: Fodor, 1993.

Hagan, Kay Leigh. *Prayers to the Moon.* San Francisco: HarperSanFrancisco, 1991.

Peck, M. Scott. *The Road Less Traveled.* New York: Simon and Schuster, 1985.

Pierrakos, Eva. *The Pathwork of Self-Transformation.* New York: Bantam, 1990.

Pierrakos, John. *Eros, Love, and Sexuality: The Forces that Unify Man and Woman.* Mendocino, CA: Life Rhythm Books, Samuel Weiser, Inc., 1998.

Roman, Sanaya. *Living with Joy.* Tiburon, CA: H. J. Kramer, Inc., 1986.

Steinem, Gloria. *Revolution from Within: A Book of Self-Esteem.* Boston: Little Brown, 1991.

Other Resources, Seminars, Workshops

To find out about Suzanne's upcoming workshops and seminars, contact:

No Limitz Productions
1-888-LIMIT99 (1-888-546-4899)
E-mail: nolimitzlove@earthlink.net

Core Energetics Institutes
115 E. 92nd St. #2A
New York, NY 10128
(212) 505-6767

Coates-Jacobs Personality Services, International
9121 Atlanta Avenue #327
Huntington Beach, CA 92646
(714) 963-5441

Enneagram Institute
222 Riverside Drive, Suite 10
New York, NY 10025
(212) 932-3306

Joan McClain
Partnership Adoration Xtasy Workshops
Celebrating Men, Satisfying Women
P.O. Box 4112
Culver City, CA 90231-4112
(310) 839-4223

A Final Note

....

Ten percent of the author's profits from this book will go to Angels in Action, a nonprofit organization that funds orphanages and schools for little girls.

Nothing works like word of mouth. If you enjoyed reading this book, please tell a friend about it.

If you found some of the ideas in this book useful, please share them with a friend.

If this book touched your life in some way, please write us at nolimitzlove@earthlink.net and tell me about it. I would love to hear from you.

Index

About the Author

....

SUZANNE LOPEZ is a licensed psychotherapist and certified Core Energetics therapist who has been in private practice in Los Angeles for almost two decades. She has successfully coached hundreds of individuals, couples, and families. She conducts group intensives and workshops, has been a national seminar speaker, and has taught at the graduate level. She is a regularly sought-after media expert, having made hundreds of appearances on major talk, magazine news, and morning shows. Committed to changing consciousness through the media, Suzanne is currently developing a nationally syndicated television show.

Suzanne is a second-generation Latina, the oldest of ten children, and a single mom with an adopted daughter. Energetic, dynamic, and articulate, she gets to the truth of the matter with great compassion and insight, without humiliating or hurting. She has been widowed, divorced, and is using the Smart Heart Partnering Process to find her next partner. Suzanne resides in the Hollywood Hills with her daughter, Angelica.